INTELLECTUAL FREEDOM MANUAL

FIFTH EDITION

OIF ALA

Compiled by the

Office for Intellectual Freedom

of the

American Library Association

AMERICAN LIBRARY ASSOCIATION
Chicago and London
1996

A revision of "Intellectual Freedom and Librarianship" by Judith F.
Krug and James A. Harvey from *Encyclopedia of Library and Information Sciences*, vol. 12, appears on page xv.

Composed by Publishing Services, Inc. in Bodoni and Palatino on
Xyvision/L330.

Printed on 50-pound Glatfelter, a pH-neutral stock, and bound in
10-point C1S cover stock by Braun-Brumfield, Inc.

The paper used in this publication meets the minimum requirements
of American National Standard for Information Sciences—Permanence
of Paper for Printed Library Materials, ANSI Z39.48-1992. ∞

Library of Congress Cataloging-in-Publicati on Data

Intellectual freedom manual / compiled by the Office for Intellectual
    Freedom of the American Library Association. — 5th ed.
        p.   cm.
    Includes bibliographical references and index.
    ISBN 0-8389-0677-X (alk. paper)
    1. Libraries—Censorship—United States—Handbooks, manuals,
etc.   2. Freedom of information—United States—Handbooks,
manuals, etc.   I. American Library Association. Office for
Intellectual Freedom.
Z711.4.I57   1996
025.2′13—dc20   95-47636

Printed in the United States of America.

04   03   02   01   00   7   6   5   4   3

Contents

Contents

Contents

Contents

Contents

Preface

This manual is designed to answer practical questions that confront librarians in applying the principles of intellectual freedom to library service. It is our hope that every librarian will keep this volume close at hand as a convenient reference work. If, for example, a librarian wants to know what the American Library Association can do to help resist censorship of library materials, how to handle complaints, or how to write an appropriate letter to legislators, help can be found in this volume. If the problem is complex—for example, the development of a materials-selection program—practical guidelines on how to tackle the problem are offered.

The introductory section of the manual explains the meaning of intellectual freedom in library service and how today's broad concept of intellectual freedom evolved from opposition to book censorship. Part I, *Library Bill of Rights,* and part II, Protecting the Freedom to Read, present the texts and historical development of ALA's intellectual freedom policies and guidelines (the Interpretations of the *Library Bill of Rights* are now arranged in alphabetical rather than chronological order, for convenient reference), and give concrete examples of problems librarians can expect to encounter or should anticipate in formulating policy for their own institutions.

Applying the principles and guidelines in this manual cannot ensure that the rights of librarians and users will never be challenged or that difficulties will not arise. But adhering to these principles in every library is absolutely essential if librarians and users are to enjoy the full benefit of freedom of expression under the First Amendment.

Special thanks and appreciation are due Anne Levinson Penway, assistant director of the Office for Intellectual Freedom, for her detailed, thorough, and meticulous work on this edition.

JUDITH F. KRUG, *Director*
Office for Intellectual Freedom

Introduction

Intellectual freedom can exist only where two essential conditions are met: first, that all individuals have the right to hold any belief on any subject and to convey their ideas in any form they deem appropriate; and second, that society makes an equal commitment to the right of unrestricted access to information and ideas regardless of the communication medium used, the content of the work, and the viewpoints of both the author and receiver of information. Freedom to express oneself through a chosen mode of communication becomes virtually meaningless if access to that information is not protected. Intellectual freedom implies a circle, and that circle is broken if either freedom of expression or access to ideas is stifled.

Intellectual freedom is freedom of the mind, and as such, it is both a personal liberty and a prerequisite for all freedoms leading to action. Moreover, intellectual freedom, protected by the guarantees of freedoms of speech and press in the First Amendment, forms the bulwark of our constitutional republic. It is an essential part of government by the people. The right to vote is alone not sufficient to give citizens effective control of official actions and policies. They must also be able to take part in the formation of public opinion by engaging in vigorous and wide-ranging debate on controversial matters. Censorship can only stifle this debate, thus weakening government by the people. In the words of Thomas Paine:

> He that would make his own liberty secure must guard even his enemy from opposition; for if he violates this duty he establishes a precedent that will reach to himself.[1]

Intellectual freedom is not only the bulwark of our constitutional republic but also the rallying cry of those who struggle for democracy worldwide. The metaphorical circle of intellectual freedom has expanded to global proportions over the past two decades with the advent of potent new communications technologies and the growing international recognition of the Universal Declaration of Human Rights, Article 19 of which declares the right of all people to freedom of expression. As the free flow of information transcends national boundaries, it becomes increasingly clear that prohibitions on freedom of expression in one country will inhibit the freedom of those in many other countries around the world. In an age of multinational media corporations, international computer links, and global telecommunications, we can no longer think simply in local terms. Promoting and defending intellectual freedom requires "thinking globally, and acting locally."

The ALA has recognized the importance of global thinking in an Interpretation of the *Library Bill of Rights*, titled "The Universal Right to Free Expression." Recognizing the crucial role that free access to information plays in the international arena, and the international effects of restrictions imposed on the creation, distribution, and receipt of information and expression, this Interpretation acknowledges free expression as a basic human right. The ALA also has recognized for many years the right of individuals to be free from governmental intimidation in the exercise of their right to free expression. The "Policy on Government Intimidation" was adopted February 2, 1973, and amended July 1, 1981.

Since that time, a multitude of new challenges to intellectual freedom have arisen in the United States. Significant changes in political, social, and economic conditions in the 1980s and 1990s are having a powerful effect on librarians' ability to defend intellectual freedom.

Intellectual freedom is challenged by groups across the political spectrum—from conservatives to liberals—and both old-fashioned political organizing and newer, nontraditional methods are being used to silence critics or suppress materials deemed objectionable for a variety of reasons. In the politically conservative climate that prevailed following the November 1994 congressional elections, free expression came under intensified attack—conservative religious organizations made headway in their demands for restrictions on the availability of information their members find offensive, often using the excuse of "protecting the children" to advance a broader social agenda of a "return" to more conservative times when all adhered to one view of "family values" and one type of fundamentalist Christian belief. Although such organized groups—including the Christian Coalition, Focus on the Family, Citizens for Excellence in Education/National Association of Christian Educators, Concerned Women for America, and local, ad hoc groups that often spring up around specific controversies—have been around for some time, through careful planning and dogged grassroots organizing, their political clout has grown substantially. Through their efforts and influences, virtually every session of Congress, as well as state legislatures, now features the introduction of sweeping antipornography, antigay or parental rights legislation designed to limit the availability of constitutionally protected information in schools, libraries, and bookstores.

Conservative religious organizations have alleged that schools and libraries are "promoting" occult or satanic religions in violation of the Establishment Clause of the First Amendment by making available materials on witchcraft, mythology, or fantasy. Other approaches to censorship used by individuals and groups across the political spectrum include labeling campaigns—voluntary or not— to "warn" consumers about the content of books, videos, television programs, or musical lyrics; "political correctness" campaigns to purge library collections of works deemed offensive because of racist, sexist, homophobic, ethnic, or religious stereotyping or themes; the proposal of legislation to force providers of Internet access to label or screen material posted or accessible; "protect the children" campaigns designed to stifle the availability for adults of sexually explicit information, using potential access by children as the mechanism; attempts by law-enforcement officials and others to gain access to confidential patron records; the use of the federal Racketeer Influenced and Corrupt Organizations (RICO) Act and state statutes on "harmful material" to prosecute booksellers, newspaper editors, and others for selling allegedly obscene materials (sometimes resulting in confiscation of inventories composed largely of nonobscene, constitutionally protected material); the use of Strategic Lawsuits Against Public Participation (SLAPPs) by developers, businesses, or public officials to intimidate critics and quell locally organized opposition to their projects or public policies; the use of zoning laws to restrict booksellers or movie theaters that allegedly sell obscene materials or show obscene films; and perhaps the most insidious and difficult to combat, the trend toward self-censorship to avoid legal battles, emotional duress, or any number of other deleterious consequences that may befall the purveyor of a controversial work.

Computer and communications technologies have revolutionized global information flow—making information on breaking events instantly accessible worldwide. The Internet has opened new avenues for communication about a virtually unlimited array of subjects on a scale never before heard of between people of differing backgrounds and means. This has inevitably created tensions—over the equitable allocation of costly computer services to library patrons and over access to an amazing breadth of electronic information, much of which some people consider inappropriate, especially for minors. The ALA Intellectual Freedom Committee has addressed these tensions in a new Interpretation of the *Library Bill of Rights* titled "Access to Electronic Information, Services, and Networks," which explains how long-standing principles of intellectual freedom apply in the arena of electronic-information access. Also relevant to the discussion of intellectual freedom and electronic information is the Interpretation "Economic Barriers to Information Access." Providing information via electronic means is costly—libraries must find strategies for providing access without discriminating against patrons of limited economic means.

At the same time the Internet and other computer networks have expanded global information access, a shrinking economy has given rise to greater social tensions among different racial, ethnic, religious, and class-based groups. These tensions have engendered calls for restrictions on speech in a misguided effort to curb the harassment or violence that often erupts as a result of real or perceived inequities and unaddressed frustrations. Unstable economic conditions also lead to budget cuts for libraries, schools, and academic institutions, making it easier to eliminate controversial materials and limit the diversity of collections under the guise of economic necessity, thus further limiting access to information for those who are least able to afford it.

Now more than ever, librarians need to be mindful of the special role libraries play as centers for uninhibited intellectual inquiry. Librarians have taken upon themselves the responsibility to provide, through their institutions, all points of view on all questions and issues of our times, and to make these ideas and opinions available to anyone who needs or wants them, regardless of age, background, or views. These statements should sound familiar; they are basic principles outlined in the *Library Bill of Rights,* which serves as the library profession's interpretation of the First Amendment to the United States Constitution.

The freedom of expression guaranteed by the First Amendment and Article 19, and the corollary to that freedom, the freedom to read, are uniquely fulfilled by the library. Any person, regardless of station, can have access to materials and information. Although libraries are widely recognized as the repositories of civilization, in order to guarantee that the freedom to read has substance, libraries must also acquire and provide information without prejudice or restriction. It is this latter point that gives the *Library Bill of Rights* and its guidance for professional librarianship special importance.

Intellectual freedom cannot bring itself into existence. Librarians must apply the principles of intellectual freedom to activities undertaken daily—materials selection, reference service, reevaluation, protection of confidential patron information, and most important, collection building. It is in acquisition and its product, the collection, that intellectual freedom must be reflected.

The role of the library as governed by the *Library Bill of Rights* cannot be filled by any other societal institution. Newspapers provide information, but it is perforce abridged and can reflect the prejudices of an editor or publisher. Schools educate but according to a program designed to fit the many; one attends school under conditions devised and imposed by administrators and educators. It is in the library, and in the library alone, that self-directed learning, to the limits of one's abilities and to the limits of what is known, can take place.

No one—least of all the librarian—should underestimate the importance of this role. If its significance has been overlooked by many, including librarians, perhaps it is because some librarians have been neither vigorous in the application of these principles nor imaginative in the provision of library services. With the application of the principles of intellectual freedom, with vision and imagination, librarians can—and do—measure up to their unique task.

NOTE

1. Thomas Paine, *Dissertation on First Principles of Government.*

ALA and Intellectual Freedom: A Historical Overview

Judith F. Krug and James A. Harvey

At the outset, two myths can be dispelled; namely, that intellectual freedom in libraries is a tradition and that intellectual freedom has always been a major, if not the major, part of the foundation of library service in the United States. Both myths, assumed by many librarians, are grounded in the belief that librarians support a static concept of intellectual freedom. Nothing, however, could be further from the truth.

The attitude of librarians toward intellectual freedom has undergone continual change since the late 1800s when, through the American Library Association (ALA), the profession first began to approach such issues with the semblance of a unified voice. ALA, however, has never endorsed a uniform definition of "intellectual freedom." Instead, through the Council, ALA's governing body, the Intellectual Freedom Committee (IFC), and the Office for Intellectual Freedom (OIF), ALA has promoted a variety of principles aimed at fostering a favorable climate for intellectual freedom—but without the limits imposed by a rigid definition. In effect, this approach has permitted a broad definition capable of meeting the needs of librarians as they arise.

The seeds of the general definition of intellectual freedom were sown in the movement against censorship of published materials and grew into a strong, central trunk from which many branches have continued to spring. One branch concerns the library user's access to all the materials in a library collection. Another pertains to the librarian's professional practice, particularly selecting and making available all published materials to all library users, and protecting the confidentiality of patron records to ensure that every individual may use the library freely and without fear of reprisal. At stake also is the librarian's personal intellectual freedom: participation in the democratic process, the right to free expression and to the right to pursue a chosen lifestyle without fear of negative professional repercussions. Yet another aspect of intellectual freedom encompasses the library as an institution and its role in social change and education. Of particular importance is the question of "advocacy" versus "neutrality." Can a library committed to intellectual freedom and to providing materials that represent all points of view also support one point of view?

Each of these branches in turn has sprouted a plethora of twigs, and viewed in its entirety the tree makes anything other than an issue-oriented approach nearly impossible. Consequently, the profession's stance on intellectual freedom has sometimes lagged behind that of society at large; most often it has paralleled public opinion; and, occasionally, it has anticipated changes in taste, mores, and social issues, and has taken positions in advance of the rest of the citizenry.

Censorship of Published Materials

The catalyst spurring librarians to take initial steps toward supporting intellectual freedom was the censorship of specific publications. "Censorship" in this context means not only deletion or excision of parts of published materials but also efforts to ban, prohibit, suppress, proscribe, remove, label, or restrict materials. Opposition to these activities emanated from the belief that freedom of the mind is basic to the functioning and maintenance of democracy as practiced in the United States. Such democracy assumes that educated, free individuals possess powers of discrimination and are to be trusted to determine their own actions. It assumes further that the best guarantee of effective and continuing self-government is a thoroughly informed electorate capable of making real choices. Denying the opportunity of choice, for fear it may be used unwisely, destroys freedom itself. Opposition to censorship derives naturally from the library's historical role as an educational institution providing materials that develop individuals' abilities, interests, and knowledge. Censorship denies the opportunity to choose from all possible alternatives and thereby violates intellectual freedom. The library profession has aimed to ensure every individual's freedom of the mind so that society as a whole benefits. Even in this central area, however, the professional position has fluctuated, being influenced by such factors as taste, quality, responsibility, morality, legality, and purpose.

One early incident concerning censorship, involving a substantial number of librarians, occurred in 1924 when the Librarians' Union of the American Federation of Labor reported that Carnegie Libraries fostered "a system under which only books approved in a certain manner may be placed on Carnegie Library shelves and that amounts to censorship and is so intended."[1] The ALA Executive Board considered the union's charges and offered to enlist volunteers to investigate the claims. Apparently, however, the union did not act upon the offer, and the matter was not considered further by the Executive Board.

In 1929, the Association indicated its future approach to censorship when the ALA Executive Board studied a proposed federal tariff bill and opposed prohibition of importing materials "advocating or urging treason, insurrection, or forcible resistance to any law of the U.S. . . . or any obscene book, paper, etc."

The board's opposition was based

> on the grounds that this clause creates an effective censorship over foreign literature, will ban many of the classics on modern economics, will keep out material relating to revolution in foreign countries, will indirectly stop the reprinting of such books by our own publishers, and is a reflection upon the intelligence of the American people by implying that they are so stupid and untrustworthy that they cannot read about revolutions without immediately becoming traitors and revolutionaries themselves; and because the question of social policy is withdrawn from the ordinary courts and placed in the hands of officials primarily chosen for their special qualifications in dealing with the administrative details of tariff laws.[2]

Ironically, just four years later, when the Executive Board received a letter requesting that the Association "take some action in regard to the burning of books in Germany by the Hitler regime," the matter was "considered briefly but it was the sense of the meeting that no action should be taken."[3]

In 1934, the Association recorded its first protest against the banning of a specific publication, *You and Machines,* a pamphlet by William Ogburn. Prepared for use in Civilian Conservation Corps camps under a grant from the American Council on Education, the pamphlet was denied circulation by the camps' director, who believed it would induce a philosophy of despair and a desire to destroy existing economic and political structures. Initially, the ALA president and executive secretary wrote a joint letter to President Franklin D. Roosevelt, stating that "[governmental] censorship on a publication of this character written by a man of recognized authority is unthinkable."[4]

Later the board discussed the banning further and appointed a committee to draft another letter for approval by the ALA Council. The result was a formal request that President Roosevelt "make it possible for the U.S. Commissioner of Education and the Education Director of the Civilian Conservation Corps to direct the educational policies to be operative in these camps and to make available the reading matter essential in a modern program of education."[5]

These examples illustrate the Association's wavering position and reflect the ambivalent attitude of the profession as a whole regarding censorship. A review of library literature reveals relatively few articles on intellectual freedom prior to the 1930s, and many of the articles that did appear supported censorship and only quibbled over the degree and nature of it. Typical was the opinion of ALA President Arthur E. Bostwick, whose inaugural address at the 1908 Annual Conference included these remarks:

> "Some are born great; some achieve greatness; some have greatness thrust upon them." It is in this way that the librarian has become a censor of literature. . . . Books that distinctly commend what is wrong, that teach how to sin and how pleasant sin is, sometimes with and sometimes without the added sauce of impropriety, are increasingly popular, tempting the author to imitate them, the publishers to produce, the bookseller to exploit. Thank Heaven they do not tempt the librarian.[6]

Given the multiplicity of professional attitudes toward censorship of print materials, it is not surprising that censorship of nonprint media was once viewed as completely outside the concerns of the profession. For example, as late as 1938, the ALA Executive Board believed it was inappropriate to protest when the Federal Communications Commission forced a radio station to defend its broadcast of Eugene O'Neill's *Beyond the Horizon*.[7]

The Association's basic position in opposition to censorship finally emerged in the late 1930s, when John Steinbeck's *The Grapes of Wrath* became the target of censorship pressures around the country. It was banned from libraries in East St. Louis, Illinois; Camden, New Jersey; Bakersfield, California; and other localities. While some objected to the "immorality" of the work, most opposed the social views advanced by the author.

ALA's initial response to the pressures against *The Grapes of Wrath* was the adoption in 1939 of the *Library's Bill of Rights*, the precursor of the present *Library Bill of Rights*, the profession's basic policy statement on intellectual freedom involving library materials. (See *Library Bill of Rights*, in part I.)

In 1940, one year after adoption of the *Library's Bill of Rights*, the Association established the Intellectual Freedom Committee. (Originally called the Committee on Intellectual Freedom to Safeguard the Rights of Library Users to Freedom of Inquiry, the Committee's name was shortened by Council action in 1948 to Committee on Intellectual Freedom and inverted through usage to Intellectual Freedom Committee.) The 1940 charge to the IFC was "to recommend such steps as may be necessary to safeguard the rights of library users in accordance with the Bill of Rights and the *Library's Bill of Rights*, as adopted by Council."[8] Although the IFC's role has varied, its main function has been to recommend policies concerning intellectual freedom, especially—but not limited to—matters involving violations of the *Library Bill of Rights*. Although its original statement of authority referred only to library users, in reality the IFC became active in promoting intellectual freedom for librarians and patrons as well. Its diversified role was recognized and formalized in 1970 when the Council approved a revised statement of authority:

> To recommend such steps as may be necessary to safeguard the rights of library users, libraries, and librarians, in accordance

with the First Amendment to the United States Constitution and the *Library Bill of Rights* as adopted by the ALA Council. To work closely with the Office for Intellectual Freedom and with other units and officers of the Association in matters touching intellectual freedom and censorship.[9]

The original *Library's Bill of Rights* focused on unbiased book selection, a balanced collection, and open meeting rooms. It did not mention censorship or removal of materials at the behest of groups or individuals. Over the years, however, the document has been revised, amended, and interpreted, often in response to specific situations with general implications. The first change, a 1944 amendment against banning materials considered "factually correct," was occasioned by attacks on *Under Cover,* an exposé of Nazi organizations in the United States, and *Strange Fruit,* a novel about interracial love. Reference to "factually correct" was later dropped, but the directive against removal of materials remained. Opposition to censorship of nonprint media was amended to the document in 1951 because of attacks on films alleged to promote communism. To combat suppression of communist materials or other allegedly "subversive" publications, the Association issued its "Statement on Labeling" (see part I, section 2.15), which stated that designating materials "subversive" is subtle censorship, because such a label predisposes readers against the materials. Responding to pressures against materials about civil rights activities, a 1967 amendment to the *Library Bill of Rights* warned against excluding materials because of the social views of the authors. In its 1971 "Resolution on Challenged Materials," the Association counseled libraries not to remove challenged materials unless, after an adversary hearing in a court of law, the materials were judged to be outside the protection of the First Amendment. (See "Challenged Materials," part I, section 2.5.)

The present *Library Bill of Rights* was last revised in 1980. Its interpretive documents were systematically reviewed and updated in 1980, 1981, 1982, and again in a process that began in 1989 and was completed in 1991. New Interpretations were adopted in 1993, and as of this writing the Intellectual Freedom Committee is working on another Interpretation to address access to electronic networks and services. New Interpretations will continue to be developed as necessary. Taken together, these documents recognize and explain that censorship of any materials, in any guise, eventually affects the library. The *Library Bill of Rights*, therefore, provides principles upon which libraries may stand to oppose censorship and promote intellectual freedom. Referring directly to censorship practices, the *Library Bill of Rights* states that no library materials should be "excluded because of the origin, background, or views of those contributing to their creation," and that materials should not be "proscribed or removed because of partisan or doctrinal disapproval" (also in part I).

On its face, the profession's view of intellectual freedom is a pure one, based on a strict reading of the First Amendment to the U.S. Constitution, which states, "Congress shall make no law . . . abridging freedom of speech, or of the press." Within the limits defined by the United States Supreme Court (for example, the legal doctrines governing obscenity, defamation, or "fighting words") the position relies on the extension of First Amendment principles via the Fourteenth Amendment to the states and their agencies, including publicly supported libraries. (Some state constitutions actually provide greater protection for free speech than does the First Amendment as interpreted by the United States Supreme Court—but no state is permitted to provide *less* protection for these fundamental rights.) In actual practice, the purist position sometimes gives way to compromises by individual librarians, resulting in removal, labeling, or covert nonselection of certain materials. Changing circumstances necessitate constant review of the *Library Bill of Rights* and often result in position statements to clarify the document's application. (See "*Library Bill of Rights:* Interpretations" in part I, section 2.)

If followed by librarians and governing bodies, however, the Association's policy statements provide an effective means of helping to prevent library censorship. Ideally, application of these policies to materials selection, circulation practices, and complaint handling establishes the library as an indispensable information source for individuals exercising their freedom of inquiry.

Free Access to Library Materials

Access to library collections and services is another concern of the profession. For intellectual freedom to flourish, opposition to censorship of materials is not enough. Free access to materials for every member of the community must also be ensured. ALA first recognized this in the 1939 *Library's Bill of Rights,* which included a proviso that library meeting rooms be available on equal terms to all groups in the community regardless of the beliefs and affiliations of their members.

Another policy on free access emerged from a study of segregation made by the Association's Special Committee on Civil Liberties during the late 1950s. One result of the study was a 1961 amendment to the *Library Bill of Rights,* stating that "the rights of an individual to the use of a library should not be denied or abridged because of his race, religion, national origins, or political views." This amendment was broadened in 1967, when "social views" and "age" were incorporated to emphasize other areas of potential discrimination. "Age" was included to resolve a long-standing debate on the right of minors to have access to libraries on the same basis as adults. It should be noted that the addition of "age" illustrates one instance in which the library profession acted well in advance of public opinion.

In 1971, at the urging of the Task Force on Gay Liberation of the Social Responsibilities Round Table, the Association recommended that libraries and ALA members strenuously combat discrimination in serving any individual from a minority, whether it be an ethnic, a sexual, a religious, or any other kind of minority. In 1980 the *Library Bill of Rights* was revised to encompass all discrimination based on "origin, age, background, or views." Interpretations of the *Library Bill of Rights* addressing specific issues that fall under these deliberately broad categories include "Access for Children and Young People to Videotapes and Other Nonprint Formats," "Access to Resources and Services in the School Library Media Program," "Free Access to Libraries for Minors," "Economic Barriers to Information Access," and "Access to Library Resources and Services Regardless of Gender or Sexual Orientation." (See part I, section 2.)

Another aspect of the library patron's access to materials was broached in 1970 when the Internal Revenue Service requested permission from several libraries to examine circulation records to determine the names of persons reading materials about explosives and guerilla warfare. The Association responded by developing its

"Policy on Confidentiality of Library Records," urging libraries to designate such records as confidential and accessible only "pursuant to such process, order, or subpoena as may be authorized under the authority of, and pursuant to, federal, state, or local law relating to civil, criminal, or administrative discovery procedures or legislative investigatory power." (See part II.) The rationale of the policy was that circulation records are purely circumstantial evidence that a patron has read a book and that fear of persecution or prosecution may restrain users from borrowing any conceivably controversial materials, for whatever purpose.

The question of library records and the confidentiality of relationships between librarians and library users arose again in 1971 regarding the "use of grand jury procedure to intimidate anti–Vietnam War activists and people seeking justice for minority communities." In response, the Association asserted "the confidentiality of the professional relationships of librarians to the people they serve, that these relationships be respected in the same manner as medical doctors to their patients, lawyers to their clients, priests to the people they serve," and that "no librarian would lend himself to a role as informant, whether of voluntarily revealing circulation records or identifying patrons and their reading habits." (See part II.)

In late 1987 it was disclosed that FBI agents were visiting libraries in what are best described as "fishing expeditions." Agents generally first approached library clerks and solicited information on the use of various library services (e.g., interlibrary loan, database searches) by "suspicious looking foreigners" and, in some instances, asked to see the library's circulation records.

A public confrontation between the IFC and the FBI eventually ensued. The IFC stressed the inextricability of First Amendment and privacy rights, as well as the fact that the Bureau was requesting that librarians violate not only a professional ethic but also the law in thirty-eight states and the District of Columbia. (As of this writing, there are confidentiality laws in forty-five states and attorney general opinions supporting confidentiality in two states.) The Bureau refused to back away from what it characterized as a program to alert librarians to the possibility that libraries were being used by foreign agents as a place to recruit operatives, that librarians themselves were sometimes targeted for approach by foreign agents, and that valuable material was being stolen by these agents and their operatives. The IFC emphasized, in congressional testimony and in the media, the principle of open access to publicly available information and the central role of libraries in this society as providers of that access.

In the fall of 1989, through a Freedom of Information Act (FOIA) request, the ALA obtained documents from the FBI in which 266 individuals, all of whom had in some way criticized the Library Awareness Program (LAP), were identified as subjects of FBI "index checks." These documents also suggested that the Library Awareness Program covered parts of the country other than solely New York City, as previously claimed by the FBI.

Early in 1990, the ALA wrote to President George Bush, then director of the FBI William Sessions, and the relevant House and Senate committees, urging that the LAP be discontinued and that the files of the 266 individuals be released to them and expunged from FBI records. Director Sessions responded in March 1990 defending the program and denying that any investigation of the 266 had taken place, claiming that "index checks" were administrative and not investigative in nature. Subsequently, individuals were urged to make their own FOIA requests, but only one person who filed such a request later reported receiving any information from the FBI.

In addition, the ALA filed yet another FOIA request, which was denied, as was the appeal of that denial, on the grounds that the FBI was in litigation with the National Security Archive (NSA) over the same issue. The FBI promised to give the ALA any information released to the NSA and eventually did so. Nevertheless, the ALA reserved the right to bring suit against the FBI for denying its right of appeal and obstructing a legitimate attempt to gain information under the Freedom of Information Act.

The FBI has never publicly abandoned the Library Awareness Program, and may still be conducting it.

Federal agencies are not alone in attempting to make use of library patron records. Local law-enforcement officials, journalists, students, parents, fund raisers, marketing professionals, civil litigants and politicians have been known to seek borrowing records, registration data, mailing lists, and other information about library patrons. In 1990 a library director in Decatur, Texas, challenged one such attempt in court and won an important victory for library confidentiality policies. In *Decatur Public Library* v. *The District Attorney's Office of Wise County,*[10] the district attorney, investigating a child-abandonment case, subpoenaed the records of all libraries in Wise County, requesting the names, addresses, and telephone numbers of all individuals who had checked out books on childbirth within the previous nine months, the titles they borrowed, and the dates the materials were checked out and returned. The police had no evidence indicating that the person who abandoned the child might have borrowed library books or otherwise used the library. They were simply conducting a "fishing expedition."

The director of the Decatur Public Library refused to comply with the subpoena and, with the help of the city attorney, filed a motion to quash it on behalf of the library's patrons. On May 9, 1990, Judge John R. Lindsey ruled in favor of the library and quashed the subpoena. His decision recognized the library's standing to assert a constitutional privilege on behalf of its unnamed patrons and clients, affirmed a constitutional right of privacy available to patrons, and held that the State was unable to demonstrate a compelling governmental objective under its police powers or other legitimate function of government to warrant intrusion of those rights.

In 1995, the issue of library user confidentiality again reached the courts in connection with a lawsuit brought by a tobacco company, Brown and Williamson, against the University of California. The company alleged that the University of California at San Francisco library possessed in its collection documents stolen from the company that purportedly showed that the tobacco industry had known of a link between smoking and cancer for many years and had failed to disclose it. The documents had previously been leaked to the press and discussed in congressional hearings at the time the lawsuit was filed. The lawsuit sought not only return of the documents but a list of all library patrons who had access to them and a description of the nature of those users' research and publications.

The ALA's sister organization, the Freedom to Read Foundation (see p. xxxi–xxxii), identified the case as one of extreme importance, with potential to set positive precedent in favor of First Amendment protection for library-user privacy, and filed an amicus brief explaining the crucial link between library confidentiality and First Amendment rights. Although the case ultimately was resolved without reaching the confidentiality issue, the fact that a request for library-user records was made as part of the lawsuit indicates the breadth of circumstances in which a threat to confidentiality may arise.

Through the Association's various position statements, the profession has established a code of free access to services and materials for all library users. Opposed to using the library as a means of intimidating patrons, the profession strives to enhance the intellectual freedom of the library user by providing not only all materials requested, but also free and equal access to all materials without fear of recrimination for pursuing one's interests.

The Librarian and Intellectual Freedom

Although the profession, through ALA, formulates policies to help ensure a climate favorable to intellectual freedom, the individual librarian is the key to achieving the end result. Adherence to the *Library Bill of Rights* by individual librarians is the only means of effecting the profession's goals. Consequently, the concept of intellectual freedom also considers the individual librarian's intellectual freedom, both in pursuit of professional responsibilities and in personal life. Several agencies within or closely affiliated with ALA, accordingly, encourage and protect the librarian's commitment to the principles of intellectual freedom.

From 1940 until 1967, most of such activities were centered in the Intellectual Freedom Committee. For many years, it not only recommended policies but also directed a variety of educational efforts, including collecting and publicizing information about censorship incidents, sponsoring censorship exhibits at conferences, conducting preconferences on intellectual freedom themes, and planning complementary programs to further the Association's goals regarding intellectual freedom.

One of these complementary programs is the Office for Intellectual Freedom (OIF), established in December 1967. OIF evolved finally from a 1965 preconference on intellectual freedom held in Washington, D.C. That meeting recommended establishing an ALA headquarters unit to conduct and coordinate the Association's intellectual freedom activities and to provide continuity for the total program. The goal of OIF is to educate librarians and the general public on the importance of intellectual freedom, relieving the IFC of this task and allowing it to concentrate on developing policy. The OIF serves as the administrative arm of the Intellectual Freedom Committee and bears the responsibility for implementing ALA policies on intellectual freedom, as approved by the Council. The philosophy of the Office for Intellectual Freedom is based on the premise that if librarians are to appreciate the importance of intellectual freedom they must first understand the concept as it relates to the individual, the institution, and the functioning of society. Believing that with understanding comes the ability to teach others, OIF maintains a broad program of informational publications, projects, and services.

The regular OIF publications are the bimonthly *Newsletter on Intellectual Freedom* and the monthly *Intellectual Freedom Action News.* In addition, the Office prepares special educational materials, including the *Banned Books Week Resource Kit;* monographs such as *Censorship and Selection: Issues and Answers for Schools* (now in its second edition); and *Confidentiality in Libraries: An Intellectual Freedom Modular Education Program.* OIF also distributes documents, articles, brochures, and all ALA policy statements concerning intellectual freedom. As part of its information program, OIF maintains and distributes a banned-books exhibit. The exhibit is available for display at national, state, and local conferences, workshops, seminars, and other meetings.

The Office for Intellectual Freedom advises and consults with librarians confronting potential or actual censorship problems. Telephone and letter requests about materials that have drawn the censorial efforts of an individual or group in the community prompt efforts to give appropriate assistance. A new means of assistance established in 1994 is the Intellectual Freedom Action Network (see part VI, Working for Intellectual Freedom, section 1: "What ALA Can Do to Help Librarians Combat Censorship"), a group of concerned volunteers who have identified themselves as willing to stand up in support of intellectual freedom when controversy comes to their area, and to alert OIF to the activities of censorship pressure groups in their communities. The OIF coordinates the Action Network, calling upon its members when necessary to write letters, attend meetings or provide moral support to librarians fighting censorship in their localities.

OIF also coordinates the Intellectual Freedom Committee's relations with other organizations having similar concerns. These include the intellectual freedom committees of the ALA divisions and state library association intellectual freedom committees. Close contact with nonlibrary organizations—such as the Association of American Publishers, the American Booksellers Association, the American Civil Liberties Union, the National Coalition against Censorship, and others—is also maintained.

As ALA's intellectual freedom program developed, the need for an organizational forum through which individual ALA members could participate in intellectual-freedom activities according to their varying levels of interest began to be felt. At the 1973 Annual Conference in Las Vegas, the Intellectual Freedom Round Table was organized as the Association's membership-activity program for intellectual freedom. The activities of the Round Table supplement OIF's education program and offer opportunities for ALA members to become active in the Association's intellectual freedom efforts.

The IFRT sponsors three intellectual freedom awards. The annual state and regional achievement award, given by the IFRT since 1984, was revised in 1991. Formerly presented to a state Intellectual Freedom Committee, the award has been expanded to include "state educational media association intellectual freedom committee[s], state intellectual freedom coalition[s] legal defense fund[s] or other such group that has implemented the most successful and creative state intellectual freedom project during the calendar year. The award also may be presented for on-going or multiyear projects." IFRT established the John Philip Immroth Memorial Award for Intellectual Freedom, given annually in memory of the cofounder and first chairperson of the Round Table, "to honor notable contributions to intellectual freedom and demonstrations of personal courage in defense of freedom of expression." Biennially, the IFRT sponsors the Eli M. Oboler Award, presented for the best published work in the area of intellectual freedom.

Soon after adoption of the *Library Bill of Rights* and establishment of the Intellectual Freedom Committee, the profession realized that more than just information sources were needed to foster the practice of intellectual freedom in libraries. Some members called for a "policing" effort to publicize censorship problems and bring pressure upon authorities to correct conditions conducive to censorship. As early as the 1948 ALA Annual Conference in Atlantic City, Robert D. Leigh, director of the Public Library Inquiry, addressed the Council and recommended that "some responsible group" be created to investigate reports of library censorship, to make public reports of investigations, to give possible aid to professionals who become victims of censorship, and in extreme cases, to exercise "a professional boycott against the libraries of censoring authorities."[11] Some of Leigh's recommendations were debated for nearly twenty years before a national resolution of the problems began to emerge. As a first substantive step, in 1969 the Association adopted its Program of Action in Support of the *Library Bill of Rights.*

The first Program of Action, developed by the IFC and approved by the Council, created a mechanism whereby complaints about censorship incidents were reported to the Office for Intellectual Freedom and acted upon by the Intellectual Freedom Committee. Such complaints were studied by the OIF and the IFC to determine whether they involved intellectual freedom problems within the scope of the *Library Bill of Rights.* If the complaint fell under the Program of Action, the Office for Intellectual Freedom and the Intellectual Freedom Committee attempted to mediate, arbitrate, or provide appropriate assistance to effect a just resolution of the problem. If these means failed, one prerogative of the Committee was to establish a fact-finding team to investigate further. After such an investigation, the team reported its findings to the IFC for review. Further substantive action required a recommendation by the IFC to the ALA Executive Board. Under a sanctions policy adopted in 1971, the IFC could recommend publication of a summary of the report, it could recommend publication of the entire report, or it could recommend various other sanctions against groups or individuals violating the spirit of the *Library Bill of Rights.* The ALA Executive Board made the final disposition of the Intellectual Freedom Committee's recommendations.

From 1969 to 1971, in response to requests for action, three fact-finding projects were undertaken by the IFC. The first major case was brought by Joan Bodger. An extensive investigation explored Bodger's charge that she had been fired from the Missouri State Library because of her public support of intellectual freedom. She had written a letter to a local newspaper protesting the suppression of an underground newspaper. The IFC concluded that her allegations were correct and recommended publication of the complete report in *American Libraries.* The Executive Board approved, and the report of the Bodger fact-finding team appeared in the July-August 1970 issue of *American Libraries,* vindicating Bodger and deploring the Missouri State Library Commission's actions, which resulted in her firing.

The other two requests for action also entailed fact-finding studies, after which the Intellectual Freedom Committee found it could not support charges contained in the complaints. Reports summarizing the two cases were published in *American Libraries.*[12]

The three complaints investigated under the Program of Action made it clear that cases involving intellectual freedom might also raise issues of tenure, academic status, ethical practices, and a variety of other matters. The difficulty of focusing only on intellectual freedom increased in late 1970 when a complaint was received from J. Michael McConnell, who was denied a position at the University of Minnesota Library shortly after his well-publicized application for a marriage license to marry another male. Charging the university discriminated against him because of his homosexuality, McConnell appealed to the IFC, claiming his case fell under the Program of Action. To support his claim, he cited the 1946 ALA Statement of Principles of Intellectual Freedom and Tenure for Librarians, which states, "Intellectual freedom precludes partisan political control of appointments and makes it possible for librarians to devote themselves to the practice of their profession without fear of interference or of dismissal for political, religious, racial, marital or other unjust reasons."

The IFC did not dispute McConnell's claim that his case fell under the scope of the 1946 policy statement. It disagreed, however, that the case came within the jurisdiction of the Program of Action, because that mechanism dealt only with violations of the *Library Bill of Rights.* The Committee attempted to resolve the problem by rewriting the Program of Action to allow jurisdiction over all ALA policies on intellectual freedom. The revision, completed during a special December 1970 meeting of the IFC, was to come before the Council for approval in January 1971. At its Midwinter Meeting, however, the Committee again revised the document to include all ALA policies on intellectual freedom and tenure. It was then pointed out that both the Library Administration Division (LAD) and the Association of College and Research Libraries (ACRL) claimed vested interests in investigations, particularly those involving tenure of academic librarians. The complex jurisdictional problems resulted in an appeal to ALA President Lillian Bradshaw to take steps immediately to develop a central investigatory agency for the entire Association. Moving swiftly, President Bradshaw appointed a membership group representing various interests. In June 1971, the group presented the Program of Action for Mediation, Arbitration, and Inquiry to the Council, which adopted it and rescinded the first Program of Action.

The new Program of Action established a Staff Committee on Mediation, Arbitration, and Inquiry (SCMAI), which functioned somewhat as the IFC had under the old document. In addition to intellectual freedom problems, however, the new committee handled cases involving tenure, professional status, fair employment practices, ethical practices, and due process as set forth in ALA policies. In June 1990, SCMAI was replaced by the Standing Committee on Review, Inquiry, and Mediation (SCRIM). Lack of funding caused SCRIM to cease operation on September 1, 1992.

The Intellectual Freedom Committee, the Office for Intellectual Freedom, and the Intellectual Freedom Round Table are the primary agencies for establishing and promoting the Association's positions on questions involving intellectual freedom. In addition, the Intellectual Freedom Action Network supports these positions and responds to controversies on the local level. The element in the Association's program in support and defense of intellectual freedom that takes the most aggressive, proactive role, however, is the Freedom to Read Foundation.

Incorporated in November 1969, the Freedom to Read Foundation was ALA's response to librarians who increasingly wanted defense machinery to protect their jobs from jeopardy when they undertook to challenge violations of intellectual freedom. Another primary objective in establishing the Foundation was to have a means through which librarians and other concerned individuals and groups could begin to set legal precedents for the freedom to read. The Foundation was created outside the structure of ALA and, to ensure its full freedom to act with vigor in the legal arena, it remains legally and financially independent. But the Foundation is closely affiliated with ALA through the ex officio membership of ALA officers on its board of trustees. The Foundation's executive director also serves as director of the ALA Office for Intellectual Freedom.

A program of education on the importance of, and the necessity for a commitment to, the principles of intellectual freedom requires assurance that such commitment will not result in reprisals, such as legal prosecution, financial loss, or personal damage. The Freedom to Read Foundation attempts to provide that assurance through financial and legal assistance and legal challenges to restrictive legislation, thereby helping to create a favorable climate for intellectual freedom. Through the provision of financial and legal assistance, the Foundation attempts to negate the necessity for librarians to make the difficult choice between practical expediency (that is, keeping a job) and upholding principles, such as in selecting materials for library collections. Through its various projects and grants, the Foundation hopes to establish those principles enunciated in the *Library Bill of Rights* as legal precedents rather than mere paper policies.

Established by the Freedom to Read Foundation, but now formally independent, the LeRoy C. Merritt Humanitarian Fund was created in 1970. The Merritt Fund was established by the Foundation's board of trustees in recognition of individuals need for subsistence and other support when their positions are jeopardized or lost as a result of defending intellectual freedom. This special fund offers short-term, immediate assistance even prior to the development of all pertinent facts in a particular case, whether or not legal action has been taken.

In the combined forces of the Intellectual Freedom Committee, the Office for Intellectual Freedom, the Intellectual Freedom Round Table, the Intellectual Freedom Action Network, and the Freedom to Read Foundation, along with the LeRoy C. Merritt Humanitarian Fund, the library profession has available a complete program to support the practice of intellectual freedom. The profession, however, has not yet achieved the same success in a closely related area, that of the librarian's personal rather than professional intellectual freedom. The question of what support should be given to librarians who suffer professionally because of personal beliefs and actions has been approached in individual cases but has not been fully resolved.

One of the first instances involving potential recriminations in a professional capacity as a result of personal beliefs occurred in the

late 1940s, with the advent of "loyalty oaths" and "loyalty programs" designed to ferret out communists and "subversives." The
Intellectual Freedom Committee faced the loyalty issue with its
Policy on Loyalty Programs, first adopted by the Council in 1948
and revised in 1951. When another case arose in Florida in 1969, the
Policy on Loyalty Programs was reexamined and again revised. The
last revision, adopted by the Council in January 1971, states in part
the following:

> The American Library Association strongly protests loyalty
> programs which inquire into a library employee's thoughts,
> reading matter, associates, or membership in organizations, un-
> less a particular person's definite actions warrant such investi-
> gation. We condemn loyalty oaths as a condition of employment
> and investigations which permit the discharge of an individual
> without a fair hearing.[13]

In 1969, another incident arose involving a librarian who lost
his position because of actions, based on personal beliefs, taken in
his capacity as a private citizen. T. Ellis Hodgin was fired as city
librarian of Martinsville, Virginia, shortly after he joined a lawsuit
challenging the constitutionality of a religious education course
taught in the city school his daughter attended. He had also been
active in civil rights efforts. Hodgin's situation sparked a controversy among librarians, resulting in a recommendation from the Intellectual Freedom Subcommittee of the Activities Committee on
New Directions for ALA (ACONDA):

> The scope of intellectual freedom encompasses considerably
> more than just the freedom to read. Support must also be ren-
> dered to the librarian who is fired for sporting a beard, for en-
> gaging in civil rights activities, etc., etc. And he should not have
> to claim "poverty" in order to receive it.[14]

The recommendation, however, was not approved as part of
the final ACONDA report.

Some concerned librarians responded to Hodgin's plight by
organizing the National Freedom Fund for Librarians (NFFL),
which collected several thousand dollars to aid him. (When the

NFFL disbanded in 1971, its cash balance was sent to the LeRoy C. Merritt Humanitarian Fund.)

Hodgin also appealed to the Freedom to Read Foundation for assistance to defray the financial hardship he suffered when he lost his position. In June 1970, the Foundation's executive committee awarded him $500

> for having suffered in his defense of freedom of speech as a result
> of which he lost his position as a librarian. Inasmuch as it is the
> obligation of the librarian to protect free speech and a free press
> through his work as a librarian, it is then particularly appropriate
> that, when he is deprived of his job because of his own exercise
> of free speech, the Freedom to Read Foundation assist him in the
> defense of his freedom.[15]

A second grant of $500 was made to Hodgin in January 1971 for the specific purpose of perfecting an appeal of his suit for reinstatement to the U.S. Supreme Court.

The limits of intellectual freedom were again debated by the profession when the previously mentioned case of J. Michael McConnell arose in 1970. The Intellectual Freedom Committee found that McConnell's rights "under the First Amendment have been violated" because he met reprisals for freely expressing his sexual preference.[16] On that basis the LeRoy C. Merritt Humanitarian fund granted $500 to help defray financial hardship occasioned by his inability to find another job.

The question of how far librarians are willing to extend the scope of intellectual freedom for the benefit of their colleagues was raised anew in 1979 by the case of Utah librarian Jeanne Layton. In September 1979, Layton was dismissed from her position as library director in Davis County after she refused to comply with requests to remove the novel *Americana*, by Don DeLillo, from library shelves. The following month she filed suit to regain her job.

The suit was supported from the beginning by the Freedom to Read Foundation, but it soon became clear that the legal battle would be a lengthy and very costly one. Both the Intellectual Freedom Committee and the Freedom to Read Foundation designated the case a priority for 1980. The Utah Library Association rallied librarians and others statewide in support. At the 1980 ALA Annual

Conference in New York, the Freedom to Read Foundation announced that it would match two dollars for every dollar contributed to Jeanne Layton's defense from June 27, 1980, to December 31, 1980, up to a limit of $10,000 in matching funds. The response was, in the words of Foundation President Florence McMullin, "nothing short of overwhelming." When the challenge expired, $6,024 had been received, of which $5,000 was matched "two for one" by the Foundation. Moreover, Jeanne Layton won her suit and regained her job, and one of her main antagonists was defeated for reelection to the county commission.

Although the question of how far librarians will go to support colleagues in defense of intellectual freedom will always be resolvable only on a case-by-case and issue-by-issue basis, the response to Layton's courageous stand surely indicates that in general the library profession takes its responsibilities on this front seriously indeed.

The Library and Intellectual Freedom

Each aspect of intellectual freedom in libraries that has been discussed to this point has involved people—library users and their access to all published materials, as well as librarians and their practice of professional or personal intellectual freedom.

One last branch of intellectual freedom remains to be examined, that being the library as an institution and the nature of its role in social change and education. Continually debated within the profession and the American Library Association, the issue has been summarized as "neutrality versus advocacy." In essence, the question is, Can libraries, as institutions, advocate social or political causes and still maintain their image as providers of views representing all sides of all questions?

Whenever the question is raised, it initiates further queries. For example, what constitutes advocating a cause—biased book selection, biased displays, prejudicial assignment of library meeting rooms? Or, what constitutes a cause—peace, ecology, democracy? If a library sponsors a display of books on peace, in order to maintain neutrality must it also sponsor a display on war? The questions are complex, and the answers have shown no uniformity whatsoever.

The American Library Association itself has vacillated on the main issue, reaching only a partial resolution in the late 1960s and the early 1970s.

At the 1969 Annual Conference in Atlantic City, the membership and the Council debated whether or not the Association should take a public stand opposing the war in Vietnam or opposing deployment of an antiballistic missile system (ABM). It was argued that because political and moral issues are so deeply entangled with education and library issues, institutions such as ALA and libraries are obligated to take such positions. Those who opposed such positions argued in favor of neutrality on questions not directly related to libraries. They argued that intellectual freedom for those librarians opposed to the majority view would be violated if the Association attempted to take stands on social and political issues. They further maintained that they had tradition on their side, since the Association had always declined to take a stand on issues not directly related to libraries. That argument, of course, was incorrect. The Association had previously taken stands in some instances and refused to do so in others.

In June 1921, for example, the ALA Council espoused a very decided position on the question of disarmament after the First World War. In a strong resolution, the Council stated the following:

WHEREAS, The members of the American Library Association had full demonstration of the pain and pinch that belongs to war and the increased cost of all necessities, both personal and professional, caused thereby; and

WHEREAS, The exigencies of international conditions brought about by the cost of war is appalling from every standpoint; and

WHEREAS, We believe the example of the United States in this matter will be followed by the other nations;

THEREFORE BE IT RESOLVED, That the American Library Association urge upon the president of the United States and Congress the initiative of a movement leading to a reduction of armament at the earliest possible moment; and be it further

RESOLVED, That a request be made by the members of the American Library Association to their individual congressman for such action and that a record be made of the replies.[17]

However, in 1928, when faced by a request from the American Civil Liberties Union that ALA adopt "one or more resolutions on civil liberty," the ALA Executive Board declined, saying the Association "does not take actions on questions outside the library and bibliographic field."[18] That was similar to the philosophy that prevailed in 1969, when the Vietnam and ABM resolutions failed to pass the Council. The question arose again, though, at the 1970 and 1971 Midwinter Meetings and Annual Conferences. After a great deal of debate, the Council voted at its 1970 Annual Conference in Detroit to "define the broad social responsibilities of ALA in terms of . . . the willingness of ALA to take a position on current critical issues with the relationship to libraries and library service clearly set forth in the position statements."[19]

In line with this policy a carefully reworded resolution opposing the war in Vietnam was adopted by the Council one year later:

WHEREAS, The stated objective of the American Library Association is the promotion and improvement of library service and librarianship; and

WHEREAS, Continued and improved library service to the American public requires sustained support from the public monies; and

WHEREAS, The continuing U.S. involvement in the conflict in Southeast Asia has so distorted our national priorities as to reduce substantially the funds appropriated for educational purposes, including support for library services to the American people; and

WHEREAS, Continued commitment of U.S. arms, troops, and other military support has not contributed to the solution of this conflict;

BE IT THEREFORE RESOLVED, That the American Library Association calls upon the president of the United States to take immediately

those steps necessary to terminate all U.S. military involvement
in the present conflict in Southeast Asia by December 31, 1971,
and to insure the reallocation of national resources to meet press-
ing domestic needs.[20]

With approval of the Vietnam resolution, the Association
seemed to give broader interpretation to the old "library and bibliographic field." However, this more permissive interpretation still
did not resolve the more basic question of whether libraries themselves should follow the course of neutrality or advocacy.

The contradiction was further focused in July 1974, when ALA
endorsed the Equal Rights Amendment. ALA's support for ERA
went much further than its opposition to U.S. military involvement
in Southeast Asia. In 1977, the Council voted not to hold conferences
in states that had not ratified the amendment. In June 1978, the
Council endorsed the ERA Extension Resolution and, at the 1979
Midwinter Meeting, established an ERA task force charged with
assisting and consulting with "ALA Chapters in carrying out the
commitment to passage of the Equal Rights Amendment in ways
best suited to the individual states."[21]

The Association justified this active support of the proposed
amendment, first, by noting the support already expressed by other
professional associations "by reason of its beneficial implications for
all persons in the American society," and, more specifically, as an
outgrowth of ALA's policy requiring equal employment opportunity in libraries, adopted at the 1974 Midwinter Meeting. The
resolution in support of ERA noted that "women constitute 82 percent of the library profession." Hence, it was argued, "equal employment . . . required support of equal rights for women."[22] None
of the operative resolutions on ERA addressed themselves to the
content of library collections. Opponents of the amendment and
pro-ERA advocates of ALA neutrality, however, were quick to argue
that library users "have a right to expect the library to furnish them
with uncensored information on both sides of this and all other
issues. Adoption of advocacy positions and participation in boycotts
cannot help but strike a blow at the public's confidence in the
fair-mindedness and even-handedness of librarians."[23]

Yet another aspect of the advocacy versus neutrality conun-
drum was addressed by the Association in 1987 at its Annual Con-

ference in San Francisco. David Henington, director of Houston Public Library, brought to the IFC for its response and assistance an antiapartheid ordinance passed and implemented by the City of Houston. This ordinance required that all city agencies obtain certification from suppliers of goods and services that they had no affiliates in, and did no business with, the Republic of South Africa.[24] Henington asserted that this requirement was causing serious acquisition problems for the library. Major information services such as the New York Times Company, the *Wall Street Journal* and leading publishers refused to sign such certificates. Some refused because they have reporters in South Africa, one religious group because it has missionaries there, and on principle, in the belief that the free flow of information both into and out of the Republic of South Africa must be defended and enlarged for the sake of those struggling to dismantle the apartheid system there. Because it did not have a copy of the ordinance in hand and because it had received reports of similar ordinances elsewhere, the IFC voted to explore the matter further.

Two ALA members decided that the issue should be taken to the membership at that Conference, and they presented a resolution at the Membership Meeting. The resolution stressed the intellectual freedom implications of this policy and asked that ideas and information be exempted from the laudable goal of enforcing economic sanctions against the Republic of South Africa for its abhorrent apartheid system. A heated encounter ensued between the presenters and other supporters of the resolution and those who saw it as supportive of apartheid and, therefore, racist. The resolution was resoundingly defeated.

At the 1988 Annual Conference in New Orleans, the membership adopted a resolution reaffirming its commitment to Article 19 of the Universal Declaration of Human Rights: "Everyone has the right to freedom of opinion and expression; this right includes freedom to hold opinions without interference and to seek, receive and impart information and ideas through any media regardless of frontiers."

Measuring the Profession's Response

The foregoing discussion illustrates that anything other than an issue-oriented definition of intellectual freedom is impossible. At the present time the profession uniformly disdains censorship of published materials, print or nonprint. The attitude toward user access is somewhat uniform but contains a great deal of dissent on the question of access for minors to all the materials in a library collection. On the question of the librarian's professional practice of intellectual freedom, there is near agreement that every effort should be made to encourage and protect this aspect of librarianship. The librarian's personal intellectual freedom, on and off the job, presents some points of agreement, but major areas of dissent still exist. The same is true in the area of institutional neutrality versus advocacy.

One conclusion from a review of the history, status, and future of intellectual freedom in libraries is that the American Library Association's positions and programs provide one of the few gauges for measuring the profession's response to the problems of defining, promoting, and defending the concept. ALA's evolving position reflects the steady emergence of a philosophy within the entire library community. Although that philosophy exhibits some loose ends, its core grows firmer, based on a history of trial and error and forced response to a changing social climate. The philosophy is young, too young to be rooted in tradition, but gradually it has gained recognition as the substance of the total philosophy shaping library service in the United States.

At the 1990 Midwinter Meeting, the ALA was asked to review and support an Association of American Publishers (AAP) report on the effect of book boycotts in South Africa titled "The Starvation of Young Black Minds: The Effect of Book Boycotts in South Africa," which recommended that the boycott on books and other educational materials be discontinued. The Intellectual Freedom Committee reported no existing ALA policy upon which to base recommendations regarding the AAP report, and at the 1990 Annual Conference proposed a new Interpretation of the *Library Bill of Rights,* initially called "The Free Flow of Information," to address free expression issues raised in the global arena. The resolution was adopted by Council at the 1991 Midwinter Meeting as "The Universal Right to Free Expression, An Interpretation of the *Library Bill of Rights.*" At the same time, Council adopted Article 19 of the Universal Declaration of Human Rights as official ALA policy. This action superseded a 1988 ALA membership resolution, reaffirming its commitment to Article 19, which reads thus: "Everyone has the right to freedom of opinion and expression; this right includes freedom to hold opinions without interference and to seek, receive and impart information and ideas through any media regardless of frontiers."

Simultaneously with the 1990 AAP request, the Social Responsibilities Round Table (SRRT) proposed Guidelines for Librarians Interacting with South Africa. The Intellectual Freedom Committee responded with a memorandum on guidelines for librarians interacting with South Africa in which the Committee recommended that the guidelines be rewritten to address, among other matters, the intellectual freedom concerns absent from the text. The ALA Council declined to adopt the guidelines as written, following which a motion carried to refer the guidelines back to the IFC, the International Relations Committee (IRC), and the Committee on Professional Ethics. At the 1991 Midwinter Meeting, these committees returned a joint recommendation that no further action be taken until the guidelines were rewritten. The Council then referred the document to the Executive Board.

The subject of including books and informational materials in the sanctions against South Africa was never revisited in light of the new policy, "The Universal Right to Free Expression." With the recent reforms in South Africa and the progress toward democratic majority rule, the issue has been diffused.

Another recent issue to raise the advocacy versus neutrality controversy was the war in the Persian Gulf. At the 1991 Midwinter Meeting, the Council passed a resolution condemning the war. This action provoked strong protest from parts of the ALA membership, many of whom believe the Association should not involve itself in matters of public policy not directly related to library interests and concerns. Many members had loved ones serving in the armed forces in the Persian Gulf region at the time. Also at the 1991 Midwinter Meeting, the new policy "The Universal Right to Free Expression" was inaugurated with the passage of two resolutions calling for the "exemption of publications and other informational materials from sanctions" levied by the United States and by the United Nations against Iraq and Kuwait.

The passage of "The Universal Right to Free Expression" opens new vistas to librarians concerned about intellectual freedom. With the exponential growth in global communications and publications, it will be possible for American librarians to act in support of their colleagues and counterparts in countries where intellectual freedom principles are under fire—China, Turkey, Israel, Syria, Saudi Arabia, Guatemala, El Salvador, Kenya, and many others. Conversely, librarians facing censorship attempts in the United States may benefit from the experience and support of those in other countries who have endured far greater challenges.

Most recently, the Association has revisited the debate over advocacy versus neutrality, or "library related" and "non-library related" matters with its decision to withdraw the 1995 Midwinter Meeting from the city of Cincinnati, where voters repealed a gay rights ordinance. Many ALA members felt it would be outrageous to sponsor a meeting in a city that had withdrawn legal protection from discrimination for their gay colleagues; others felt that ALA was compromising its intellectual freedom principles by taking a political position that implied official disapproval of the opinions of Cincinnati's voters and could have the effect of jeopardizing, in the mind of the library-using public, librarians' neutrality in the provision of information from all points of view on homosexuality and other controversial subjects. The debate is certain to be repeated as new questions raising both social justice and intellectual freedom issues arise.

Undoubtedly, as threats to free expression at home and abroad become more complex and interwoven, the line separating advocacy from neutrality will be crossed many times. Following the best of democratic traditions, a healthy debate on the library's role in the issues of the moment must be encouraged.

NOTES

1. American Library Association, "Minutes of Executive Board Meetings," mimeographed, 3:20 (Sept. 29, 1924).
2. Ibid., 5:11 (Jan. 1, 1930).
3. Ibid., 6:214 (Oct. 15, 1933).
4. Ibid., 7:89 (Dec. 27, 1934).
5. Ibid., 7:48–49 (Dec. 27, 1934).
6. Arthur E. Bostwick, "The Librarian as Censor," *ALA Bulletin* 2:113 (Sept. 1908).

7. American Library Association, "Minutes of Executive Board Meetings," mimeographed, 10:48 (Oct. 5, 1938).

8. "Cincinnati Proceedings—Council," *ALA Bulletin* 34:P-37 (Aug. 1940).

9. American Library Association, *Handbook of Organization, 1971–1972* (Chicago: ALA, n.d.), p.13.

10. No. 90-05-192, 271st Judicial District Court; Wise and Jack Counties, Texas; (Letter Opinion) Judge John R. Lindsey.

11. Robert D. Leigh, "Intellectual Freedom," *ALA Bulletin* 42:369 (Sept. 1948).

12. Rosichan summary, *American Libraries* 1:433 (May 1970); and Scott summary, *American Libraries* 2:316–17 (March 1971).

13. "Resolution on Loyalty Investigations," *American Libraries* 2:270 (March 1971).

14. American Library Association Activities Committee on New Directions for ALA, "Final Report and Subcommittee Reports, June 1970," mimeographed, p. 53.

15. "Hodgin Appeal Rests with U.S. Supreme Court," *Freedom to Read Foundation News* 1:5 (Fall 1971).

16. David K. Berninghausen, "Report of the Intellectual Freedom Committee to Council, Dallas, June 25, 1971," *American Libraries* 2:891 (Sept. 1971).

17. *ALA Bulletin* 15:169 (July 1921).

18. American Library Association, *Minutes of Executive Board Meetings* 4:142 (May 29, 1928).

19. *American Libraries* 1:674 (July-Aug. 1970).

20. "Resolution on Southeast Asia Conflict," *American Libraries* 2:826 (Sept. 1971).

21. News release, American Library Association (Sept. 1979).

22. *ALA Council Minutes*, 1974, p.335.

23. Terence L. Day, Chairman, Neill Public Library Board of Trustees, Letter to the Editor, *Chicago Tribune*, January 21, 1979.

24. The Houston City Council subsequently voted to exempt both the public library and the city zoo from the requirements of the ordinance.

PART I

Library Bill of Rights

1

Library Bill of Rights:
The Policy

The American Library Association affirms that all libraries are forums for information and ideas, and that the following basic policies should guide their services.

I. Books and other library resources should be provided for the interest, information, and enlightenment of all people of the community the library serves. Materials should not be excluded because of the origin, background, or views of those contributing to their creation.

II. Libraries should provide materials and information presenting all points of view on current and historical issues. Materials should not be proscribed or removed because of partisan or doctrinal disapproval.

III. Libraries should challenge censorship in the fulfillment of their responsibility to provide information and enlightenment.

IV. Libraries should cooperate with all persons and groups concerned with resisting abridgment of free expression and free access to ideas.

V. A person's right to use a library should not be denied or abridged because of origin, age, background, or views.

VI. Libraries which make exhibit spaces and meeting rooms available to the public they serve should make such facilities available on an equitable basis, regardless of the beliefs or affiliations of individuals or groups requesting their use.

Adopted June 18, 1948. Amended by the ALA Council February 2, 1961; June 27, 1967; and January 23, 1980.

Library Bill of Rights

The *Library Bill of Rights* constitutes the American Library Association's basic policy on intellectual freedom. The bill derives from a statement originally developed by Forrest Spaulding, librarian of the Des Moines Public Library, and adopted by that library on November 21, 1938, as the *Library's Bill of Rights:*

> Now when indications in many parts of the world point to growing intolerance, suppression of free speech, and censorship, affecting the rights of minorities and individuals, the Board of Trustees of the Des Moines Public Library reaffirms these basic policies governing a free public library to serve the best interests of Des Moines and its citizens.
>
> I. Books and other reading matter selected for purchase from public funds shall be chosen from the standpoint of value and interest to the people of Des Moines, and in no case shall selection be based on the race or nationality, political, or religious views of the writers.
>
> II. As far as available material permits, all sides of controversial questions shall be represented equally in the selection of books on subjects about which differences of opinion exist.

III. Official publications and/or propaganda of organized religious, political, fraternal, class, or regional sects, societies, or similar groups, and of institutions controlled by such, are solicited as gifts and will be made available to library users without discrimination. This policy is made necessary because of the meager funds available for the purchase of books and reading matter. It is obviously impossible to purchase the publications of all such groups and it would be unjust discrimination to purchase those of some and not of others.

IV. Library meeting rooms shall be available on equal terms to all organized nonprofit groups for open meetings to which no admission fee is charged and from which no one is excluded.

The document approved by the ALA Council at the 1939 Annual Conference in San Francisco as the *Library's Bill of Rights* retained the spirit of the Des Moines Public Library policy but differed from the original in several respects. The principal differences concerned Articles II, III, and IV of the Des Moines policy. In Article II, reference to equal representation "in the selection of books on subjects about which differences of opinions exist" was changed to "fair and adequate" representation. This change recognized the impossibility of equal representation in terms of numbers of volumes on a particular subject. Article III of the Des Moines policy was completely deleted because it dealt with the individual budget, needs, and purposes of a specific library. As such, it was inappropriate for a document to be applied nationwide.

Article IV of the Des Moines policy, concerning the use of library meeting rooms, was revised extensively before approval by the Council. An introductory phrase establishing the library as "an institution to educate for democratic living" was added, and references to "nonprofit groups" and "admission fee" were deleted. The resulting article broadened the sense of the original by stating that library meeting rooms be available "on equal terms to all groups in the community regardless of their beliefs or affiliations." As adopted by the ALA Council, the revised *Library's Bill of Rights* read as follows:

Today indications in many parts of the world point to growing intolerance, suppression of free speech, and censorship affecting the rights of minorities and individuals. Mindful of this, the Council of the American Library Association publicly affirms its belief in the following basic policies which should govern the services of free public libraries.

I. Books and other reading matter selected for purchase from the public funds should be chosen because of value and interest to people of the community, and in no case should the selection be influenced by the race or nationality or the political or religious views of the writers.

II. As far as available material permits, all sides of questions on which differences of opinion exist should be represented fairly and adequately in the books and other reading matter purchased for public use.

III. The library as an institution to educate for democratic living should especially welcome the use of its meeting rooms for socially useful and cultural activities and the discussion of current public questions. Library meeting rooms should be available on equal terms to all groups in the community regardless of their beliefs or affiliations.

The three-point declaration approved by the Council was recommended by the Association to governing boards of individual libraries for adoption. ALA could not force individual librarians and boards to take specific action, but this policy statement, as all other Association recommendations and statements, provided a guide.

For five years, the *Library's Bill of Rights* stood without change. In 1944 the Intellectual Freedom Committee, chaired by Leon Carnovsky, recommended that Article I of the document be amended to include the statement, "Further, books believed to be factually correct should not be banned or removed from the library simply because they are disapproved of by some people." Approved by the ALA Council on October 14, 1944, the amendment proclaimed for the first time the Association's position regarding the banning or removal of materials. The addition, however, also introduced the phrase "factually correct," which was later to be a source of controversy, debate, and change.

Four years later, with David K. Berninghausen as chair, the Intellectual Freedom Committee recommended a broad revision of the *Library's Bill of Rights* and called for a considerable expansion of the document's scope. Its introductory passage was pared to a precise statement of the Association's purpose: "The Council of the American Library Association reaffirms its belief in the following basic policies which should govern the services of all libraries." By 1948, there was no longer the pre–World War II need to point out "growing intolerance, suppression of free speech, and censorship affecting the rights of minorities and individuals." In the developing cold war, those factors justifying the 1939 policy were even more evident, and it was recognized that the remedies stated in the *Library's Bill of Rights* were necessary to protect free library service in times of peace as well as of crisis.

Article I was prefaced by the phrase "As a responsibility of library service." Intellectual freedom was thus clearly related to the process of materials selection and, moreover, highlighted by being designated a "responsibility." Reference to purchase from the public funds was deleted, thereby extending application of the policy to all library materials, not just those acquired through purchase. Whereas the 1939 document stated that selection should not be influenced by the race, nationality, or political or religious views of writers, the revision more explicitly said that no materials by any authors should be excluded on those grounds.

The first part of Article II was changed to effect a smoother reading, but there were no substantive alterations. However, the 1944 amendment concerning "books believed to be factually correct" was changed to "books . . . of sound factual authority" and the word "banned" was replaced by "proscribed." Despite their seeming slightness, these subtle changes in the second part of the Article actually enlarged the scope of the policy.

A totally new Article III recognized the need of libraries to challenge "censorship of books, urged or practiced by volunteer arbiters of morals or political opinion or by organizations that would establish a coercive concept of Americanism." A new Article IV recognized the libraries' responsibility to cooperate with "allied groups . . . in science, education, and book publishing in resisting all abridgment of the free access to ideas and full freedom of expression." Article III of the 1939 document, concerning the use of library meeting rooms, became Article V of the new policy. Although the wording was altered, no change was made in the intent.

The entire recommended revision was adopted by the ALA Council on June 18, 1948. In effect, it was a completely different document from its predecessor, the 1939 bill. The new bill's scope and possible applications were broadly expanded, establishing its national significance. For the first time, the policy mentioned censorship, and also for the first time, the Association declared the responsibility of libraries to challenge censorship—alone and with allied organizations. As adopted by the Council, the newly entitled *Library Bill of Rights* read as follows:

> The Council of the American Library Association reaffirms its belief in the following basic policies which should govern the services of all libraries.
>
> I. As a responsibility of library service, books and other reading matter selected should be chosen for values of interest, information and enlightenment of all the people of the community. In no case should any material be excluded because of race or nationality, or the political or religious views of the writer.
>
> II. There should be the fullest practicable provision of material presenting all points of view concerning the problems and issues of our times, international, national, and local; and books or other reading matter of sound factual authority should not be proscribed or removed from library shelves because of partisan or doctrinal disapproval.
>
> III. Censorship of books, urged or practiced by volunteer arbiters of morals or political opinion or by organizations that would establish a coercive concept of Americanism, must be challenged by libraries in maintenance of their responsibility to provide public information and enlightenment through the printed word.
>
> IV. Libraries should enlist the cooperation of allied groups in the fields of science, of education, and of book publishing in resisting all abridgment of the free access to ideas and full freedom of expression that are the tradition and heritage of Americans.
>
> V. As an institution of education for democratic living, the library should welcome the use of its meeting rooms for socially useful and cultural activities and discussion of current public

questions. Such meeting places should be available on equal terms to all groups in the community regardless of the beliefs and affiliations of their members.

Although the text of the 1948 document remained unchanged until 1961, its application was broadened in 1951. On the recommendation of the Intellectual Freedom Committee, with the endorsement of the Audio-Visual Board, the Council unanimously resolved that "the *Library Bill of Rights* shall be interpreted as applying to all materials and media of communication used or collected by libraries." The statement, appended as a footnote to all printings of the *Library Bill of Rights* until June 27, 1967, resulted from a Peoria, Illinois, case of attempted censorship by the American Legion and a local newspaper. The Peoria Public Library was pressured to remove the films *The Brotherhood of Man, Boundary Lines,* and *Peoples of the U.S.S.R.* All three films appeared on the ALA Audio-Visual Committee's 1947 list of films suggested for purchase by small libraries. The Educational Film Library Association urged ALA to combat censorship of library film collections, but some librarians contended that the *Library Bill of Rights* applied only to print on paper. The Council resolved the problem by its action of February 3, 1951. That same year, in response to efforts to suppress allegedly "subversive" publications, Council also adopted the first interpretive statement on the *Library Bill of Rights,* the "Statement on Labeling." Additional Interpretations on a wide variety of issues were to follow in subsequent years. (See part I, section 2.)

In 1961, another major addition to the *Library Bill of Rights* was approved by the Council. From 1948 through February 1961, the library profession had studied the problem of segregation in libraries. A study made by the Association's Special Committee on Civil Liberties recommended that a new Article be added to the *Library Bill of Rights* stating that "the rights of an individual to the use of a library should not be denied or abridged because of his race, religion, national origins, or political views." The recommendation was approved by the Council February 2, 1961. The new statement became Article V; and the old Article V, concerning use of meeting rooms, became Article VI. The revised *Library Bill of Rights* read as follows:

Library Bill of Rights

The Council of the American Library Association reaffirms its belief in the following basic policies which should govern the services of all libraries.

I. As a responsibility of library service, books and other reading matter selected should be chosen for values of interest, information and enlightenment of all the people of the community. In no case should any book be excluded because of the race or nationality or the political or religious views of the writer.

II. There should be the fullest practicable provision of material presenting all points of view concerning the problems and issues of our times, international, national, and local; and books or other reading matter of sound factual authority should not be proscribed or removed from library shelves because of partisan or doctrinal disapproval.

III. Censorship of books, urged or practiced by volunteer arbiters of morals or political opinion or by organizations that would establish a coercive concept of Americanism, must be challenged by libraries in maintenance of their responsibility to provide public information and enlightenment through the printed word.

IV. Libraries should enlist the cooperation of allied groups in the fields of science, of education, and of book publishing in resisting all abridgment of the free access to ideas and full freedom of expression that are the tradition and heritage of Americans.

V. The rights of an individual to the use of a library should not be denied or abridged because of his race, religion, national origins or political views.

VI. As an institution of education for democratic living, the library should welcome the use of its meeting rooms for socially useful and cultural activities and discussion of current public questions. Such meeting places should be available on equal terms to all groups in the community regardless of the beliefs and affiliations of their members.

By official action of the Council on February 3, 1951, the "Library Bill of Rights" shall be interpreted to apply to all materials and media of communication used or collected by libraries.

On June 27, 1967, almost thirty years after its origin, the *Library Bill of Rights* underwent its second thorough revision. The need for change was made explicit during a special preconference, sponsored by the Intellectual Freedom Committee with Ervin Gaines as chair, held prior to the 1965 Midwinter Meeting in Washington, D.C. The primary target in the text was the phrase "of sound factual authority," introduced into Article I in 1944, and revised and transferred to Article II in 1948. Criticism of the phrase arose when a librarian in Belleville, Illinois, used it to exclude a Protestant publication that he, being Catholic, described as lacking "sound factual authority."

In their discussion of the Belleville situation, the preconference participants determined that some of the most profound and influential publications in our culture lack the element of "sound factual authority," and the phrase itself could easily be abused to thwart the intent and purpose of the *Library Bill of Rights*. It was apparent that the phrase also could effectively hold the Association from defending fiction or any of those great works that start from philosophical premises but have nothing to do with fact.

Along with a recommendation that the troublesome phrase be dropped, the Intellectual Freedom Committee also asked that several other textual changes be made. In Articles I and V, the word "social" was a suggested addition because of far-reaching results of the civil rights movement. In Article IV, the Committee recommended eliminating the phrase "that are the tradition and heritage of Americans" because it was both redundant and nationalistic. The Committee further recommended that the reference in Article IV be expanded beyond the groups in science, education, and book publishing to reflect the wider context in which librarians and the Association actually operated.

It was also recommended that Article VI, concerning the use of meeting rooms, be amended to include the phrase, "provided that the meetings be open to the public." This amendment clarified the Association's position regarding the use of library meeting rooms by private groups with restricted attendance. The enlarged scope of the text led the IFC to recommend that "library materials" be substituted for "reading matter," thus making the footnote of 1951 regarding nonprint materials unnecessary.

By the time the Intellectual Freedom Committee's proposed changes came before the Council in 1967, a preconference on Intellectual Freedom and the Teenager had recommended that young people be given free access to all books in a library collection. Accordingly, the Committee included with its previous suggestions the recommendation that Article V include the word "age."

On June 28, 1967, the Council adopted all of the Intellectual Freedom Committee's recommendations. The revision was a statement very different from its 1939 progenitor. Whereas the original document concerned itself primarily with unbiased book selection, a balanced collection, and open meeting rooms, the new version went much further. It recognized that censorship of any materials and in any guise eventually affects the library. It therefore provided libraries with principles for opposing censorship and promoting intellectual freedom, in the broadest sense. The 1967 revision of the *Library Bill of Rights* read as follows:

The Council of the American Library Association reaffirms its belief in the following basic policies which should govern the services of all libraries.

I. As a responsibility of library service, books and other library materials selected should be chosen for values of interest, information and enlightenment of all the people of the community. In no case should library materials be excluded because of the race or nationality or the social, political, or religious views of the authors.

II. Libraries should provide books and other materials presenting all points of view concerning the problems and issues of our times; no library materials should be proscribed or removed from libraries because of partisan or doctrinal disapproval.

III. Censorship should be challenged by libraries in the maintenance of their responsibility to provide public information and enlightenment.

IV. Libraries should cooperate with all persons and groups concerned with resisting abridgment of free expression and free access to ideas.

V. The rights of an individual to the use of a library should not be denied or abridged because of his age, race, religion, national origins or social or political views.

VI. As an institution of education for democratic living, the library should welcome the use of its meeting rooms for socially useful and cultural activities and discussion of current public questions. Such meeting places should be available on equal terms to all groups in the community regardless of the beliefs and affiliations of their members, provided that the meetings be open to the public.

Yet the document, though thoroughly refined, was still not above criticism. During the following decade, questions were raised about its silence with respect to sex discrimination and institutional censorship in college and research libraries, while its unqualified references to "the community" and to "public" meeting rooms made it appear as a document for public libraries only. Moreover, the profound changes in American society that took place in the late 1960s and early 1970s virtually mandated further changes. Hence, in January 1980, the *Library Bill of Rights* underwent a third major revision, the product of nearly three years of careful review.

The initial impetus for revision came in 1977 with a request from the Committee on the Status of Women in Librarianship that the *Library Bill of Rights* be revised to reject sex discrimination in library services and to eliminate sex-linked pronoun usage from the document itself, which the Intellectual Freedom Committee agreed to act upon as part of an overall reassessment of the document. The subsequent review process involved unprecedentedly broad participation from all sectors of the library community.

At the 1978 Midwinter Meeting, the Intellectual Freedom Committee asked a subcommittee of its own members to prepare a new draft. At the 1978 Annual Conference, the Committee received a report from the subcommittee and conducted a membership hearing on the revision process. At the 1979 Midwinter Meeting, a draft *Library Bill of Rights* was approved for distribution and sent for comment to all ALA councilors, divisions, round tables, and committees, and to all chapter intellectual freedom committees, journals, and bulletins. The draft was also published in the national library press. Comments received were then reviewed at the 1979 Annual Conference, where the Committee also held another open hearing. Shortly after the close of this conference, a new draft was approved by mail and circulated by the IFC to all councilors and ALA units and the library press. Final comments were reviewed by the Committee at the 1980 Midwinter Meeting, where Frances C. Dean, its chair, submitted the final revision to the Council.

In addition to eliminating use of sex-linked pronouns, the Committee recommended revision of the preamble to state explicitly the role of libraries in maintaining intellectual freedom. Libraries are described in the revision as "forums for information and ideas," employing the word "forum" to indicate that the library should be open to any opinion or view. During discussion of this revision, it was suggested that the library be defined as in Article VI, as "an institution of education for democratic living." This formulation was rejected because it could imply support for the idea that libraries should censor all materials that it deems antidemocratic.

Democracy, strictly speaking, means "rule by the majority." From the standpoint of intellectual freedom, the library's role in our society is not based on the principle of majority rule but on the principle embodied in the First Amendment, that minority points of view have a right to be heard, no matter how unpopular with, or even detested by, the majority.

In Article I, the Intellectual Freedom Committee recommended elimination of verbiage that seemed to detract from clarity and simplicity of expression and modification of the word "community" to read "the community the library serves," inasmuch as many libraries serve a special public, such as a specific academic or school community. The Committee further recommended replacing the word "author" with the phrase "those contributing to their creation" because the originators of many library materials are today referred to by other terms.

In Article II, the Committee recommended adding that libraries have an obligation to provide information and diverse points of view on historical as well as current issues. In Article III, stylistic changes, as well as elimination of the modifier "public," were suggested. The meaning of that word in the Article's context placed an obligation on nonpublic libraries that such libraries insist they do not have.

Revision of Article V was marked by considerable debate about whether a general statement affirming the rights of all individuals to library use could serve the same function as a more detailed list of all those specific conditions or factors that might lead to infringement of this right. Considering that explicitly designating one or more factors as discriminatory might risk excluding other grounds not specifically mentioned, either by oversight or inability to predict the future; and judging the so-called laundry-list approach stylistically unwieldy, the Committee recommended instead a general statement condemning discrimination according to origin, background, or views. The Committee recommended, however, retaining specific reference to age, because a suitable generic term that would readily be recognized as inclusive of this factor could not be found.

Finally, Article VI was revised to take into account differences among types of libraries and to eliminate any implication that libraries might censor materials and exclude programs on the grounds that they contain antidemocratic ideas or are not socially useful. The revision laid firm emphasis on the principle of equitable and nondiscriminatory application of rules and regulations governing meeting rooms and exhibit space, while permitting libraries broad flexibility in formulating these according to the dictates of their widely varied situations.

On January 23, 1980, the Council adopted the recommendations of the Intellectual Freedom Committee. The resulting document constitutes the present *Library Bill of Rights*.

At the 1988 Annual Conference, the Minority Concerns Committee recommended, and Council approved, that "the *Library Bill of Rights* be reviewed to include the concepts of freedom of access to information and libraries without limitation by language or economic status." During its initial review of this Council action at the 1989 Midwinter Meeting, the Intellectual Freedom Committee suggested that a revision of the Interpretations be undertaken first to address explicitly and immediately the issues raised by the Minority Concerns Committee. The *Library Bill of Rights* would then be reassessed in light of the revised Interpretations. Thus began a review process that resulted in the reworking of all but one of the then-extant Interpretations and the addition of new Interpretations: "The Universal Right to Free Expression" and "Economic Barriers to Information Access." (See part I, section 2, which follows.)

During the process of reviewing the Interpretations, other concerns regarding gender and sexual orientation also were brought to the attention of the Committee. When review of the existing Interpretations was complete, the Intellectual Freedom Committee considered the *Library Bill of Rights* itself in light of the revised Interpretations and the request of the Minority Concerns Committee. The IFC concluded that revision of the basic document not only was unnecessary but that it would be unwise to open a document that had stood the test of time to the "laundry list" approach. To address concerns relating to economic status and fees for library service, the Committee recommended adoption of a new Interpretation, "Economic Barriers to Information Access." To address the issues of equity of service and access and representation in the collection for gays, bisexuals, and lesbians, which had been raised during the process of review, the Committee recommended adoption of another new Interpretation, "Access to Library Resources and Services Regardless of Gender or Sexual Orientation." The new Interpretations were adopted by the ALA Council in 1993.

In 1994, in response to a rapidly changing information environment and the need for guidance expressed by many librarians about how to apply the *Library Bill of Rights* to electronic access to information, the Committee began work on a new Interpretation called "Access to Electronic Information, Services, and Networks." As part of the process of development, the Committee sponsored a hearing at the 1995 Midwinter Meeting in Philadelphia to receive testimony and observations from librarians working in different library settings on the issue of access to information via electronic means. The Committee then met in Chicago in March 1995, to digest and consider all the contributions from the librarians and to prepare a draft Interpretation for circulation. Comments were solicited from all ALA units, and a draft was presented to the ALA Council at the 1995 Annual Conference in Chicago. After concerns were raised on the floor of Council about the effect of some of the language relating to fees and nondiscriminatory access, particularly in academic library settings, the draft was referred to the IFC for further consideration. As of this writing, it is anticipated that the IFC will submit a final version for Council's approval in 1996.

Although there can be little doubt that unforeseen developments will mandate yet further revision or the development of additional interpretive statements, the *Library Bill of Rights* is by no means a product of hasty work and, as its history proves, remains a vibrant statement of principle and a useful guide to action for librarians in all library settings.

2

Library Bill of Rights
Interpretations

Although the Articles of the *Library Bill of Rights* are unambiguous statements of basic principles that should govern the service of all libraries, questions do arise concerning application of these principles to specific library practices. For example, a 1951 Peoria, Illinois, case involving certain films in the public library required the Association to clarify the application of the *Library Bill of Rights* to nonprint materials. A recommendation by the Intellectual Freedom Committee and the Audio-Visual Board resulted in the ALA Council's adding an interpretive footnote explaining that the *Library Bill of Rights* applies to all materials and media of communication used or collected by libraries.

During the 1971 Annual Conference in Dallas, the Intellectual Freedom Committee considered censorship cases that clearly called for Interpretations of the *Library Bill of Rights* to define its application to certain practices. Believing that frequent revisions, amendments, or additions of footnotes weaken the document's effectiveness, the Committee resolved instead to develop statements to be called Interpretations of the *Library Bill of Rights*. The Committee said further that certain documents already in existence should be designated Interpretations of the *Library Bill of Rights*.

After the Council adopted the 1980 revision of the *Library Bill of Rights*, the Intellectual Freedom Committee undertook the first

18

systematic review of all the Interpretations. The initial purpose of this review was to make all policies consistent with both the letter and the spirit of the revised *Library Bill of Rights*. As the process developed, however, the goals became more sweeping. Important gaps in policy were filled, and, taken as a group, the Interpretations were remolded into a unified general guide to application of the *Library Bill of Rights*. Not only were most policies thoroughly rewritten or amended, but new Interpretations were also formulated and outdated or inadequate material eliminated. As with the 1980 revision of the *Library Bill of Rights*, the IFC sought and received extensive comments from ALA councilors, units, and chapters to whom all drafts were circulated in advance. The process of revision was completed at the 1982 Annual Conference in Philadelphia.

In response to a 1988 Minority Concerns Committee report, recommending a revision of the *Library Bill of Rights* to ensure protection against discrimination in library services based on language or economic status, the Intellectual Freedom Committee began the second comprehensive review of the Interpretations. The IFC agreed that each Interpretation would be considered separately and recommended to the Council for adoption upon completion of any necessary revisions. The process resulted in the revision of all but one Interpretation, the addition of new Interpretations, "The Universal Right to Free Expression" and "Economic Barriers to Information Access," and the rescission of an Interpretation no longer deemed relevant. Indirectly, the process spurred the development of two other new Interpretations, "Access to Library Resources and Services Regardless of Gender or Sexual Orientation" and "Access to Electronic Information, Services, and Networks," the latter still in the drafting stages as of this writing.

Following are those documents designated by the Intellectual Freedom Committee as Interpretations of the *Library Bill of Rights* and background statements detailing the philosophy and history of each. For convenience and easy reference, the documents are presented in alphabetical order. These documents are policies of the American Library Association, having been adopted by the ALA Council.

2.1

Access for Children and Young People to Videotapes and Other Nonprint Formats

An Interpretation of the *Library Bill of Rights*

L ibrary collections of videotapes, motion pictures, and other nonprint formats raise a number of intellectual freedom issues, especially regarding minors.

The interests of young people, like those of adults, are not
limited by subject, theme, or level of sophistication. Librarians have
a responsibility to ensure young people have access to materials and
services that reflect diversity sufficient to meet their needs.

To guide librarians and others in resolving these issues, the
American Library Association provides the following guidelines.

Article V of the *Library Bill of Rights* says, "A person's right to
use a library should not be denied or abridged because of origin,
age, background, or views."

ALA's Free Access to Libraries for Minors: An Interpretation of
the *Library Bill of Rights* states:

> The "right to use a library" includes free access to, and unre-
> stricted use of, all the services, materials, and facilities the library
> has to offer. Every restriction on access to, and use of, library
> resources, based solely on the chronological age, educational
> level, or legal emancipation of users violates Article V.
>
> . . . [P]arents—and only parents—have the right and the respon-
> sibility to restrict the access of their children—and only their

children—to library resources. Parents or legal guardians who do not want their children to have access to certain library services, materials, or facilities should so advise their children. Librarians and governing bodies cannot assume the role of parents or the functions of parental authority in the private relationship between parent and child. Librarians and governing bodies have a public and professional obligation to provide equal access to all library resources for all library users.

Policies which set minimum age limits for access to videotapes and/or other audiovisual materials and equipment, with or without parental permission, abridge library use for minors. Further, age limits based on the cost of the materials are unacceptable. Unless directly and specifically prohibited by law from circulating certain motion pictures and video productions to minors, librarians should apply the same standards to circulation of these materials as are applied to books and other materials.

Recognizing that libraries cannot act *in loco parentis*, ALA acknowledges and supports the exercise by parents of their responsibility to guide their own children's reading and viewing. Published reviews of films and videotapes and/or reference works which provide information about the content, subject matter, and recommended audiences can be made available in conjunction with nonprint collections to assist parents in guiding their children without implicating the library in censorship. This material may include information provided by video producers and distributors, promotional material on videotape packaging, and Motion Picture Association of America (MPAA) ratings *if they are included on the tape or in the packaging by the original publisher* and/or if they appear in review sources or reference works included in the library's collection. Marking out or removing ratings information from videotape packages constitutes expurgation or censorship.

MPAA and other rating services are private advisory codes and have no legal standing*. For the library to add such ratings to the

---

*For information on case law, please contact the ALA Office for Intellectual Freedom. *See also* "Statement on Labeling" and "Expurgation of Library Materials," Interpretations of the *Library Bill of Rights*.

materials if they are not already there, to post a list of such ratings with a collection, or to attempt to enforce such ratings through circulation policies or other procedures constitutes labeling, "an attempt to prejudice attitudes" about the material, and is unacceptable. The application of locally generated ratings schemes intended to provide content warnings to library users is also inconsistent with the *Library Bill of Rights.*

Adopted June 28, 1989, by the ALA Council; the quotation from "Free Access to Libraries for Minors" was changed after Council adopted the July 3, 1991, revision of that Interpretation.

Access for Children and Young People to Videotapes and Other Nonprint Formats

In January 1989, the IFC examined the Interpretation "Circulation of Motion Pictures and Video Productions" in response to urgings from the ALA youth divisions and to the Minority Concerns Committee's request for a review of the *Library Bill of Rights* to ensure that it provided for equitable access without regard to language or economic status. The IFC concluded that a new Interpretation was necessary to address fully the issue of minors' access to videos and to provide similar guarantees for nonprint materials resulting from new technologies.

The Committee also sought to provide clearer guidelines for librarians, emphasizing the importance of parent—not librarian—responsibility for guiding a child's viewing or choice of other library materials, opposing the use of cost-based restrictions to inhibit minors' access to materials, and rejecting the imposition of private rating systems and the unapproved editing of films or other copyright materials for classroom use.

The new draft Interpretation was presented to the Committee at the June 1989 ALA Annual Conference. After discussion with representatives from the youth divisions and the Professional Ethics Committee, which resulted in minor editorial changes, the Interpretation was adopted and recommended to the Council. On June 28, 1989, the Council adopted the new Interpretation in place of the former "Circulation of Motion Pictures and Video Productions." The latter was then rescinded by the Council.

[The next page is 23-3.]

23

2.2

Access to Electronic Information, Services, and Networks

An Interpretation of the *Library Bill of Rights*

The world is in the midst of an electronic communications revolution. Based on its constitutional, ethical, and historical heritage, American librarianship is uniquely positioned to address the broad range of information issues being raised in this revolution. In particular, librarians address intellectual freedom from a strong ethical base and an abiding commitment to the preservation of the individual's rights.

Freedom of expression is an inalienable human right and the foundation for self-government. Freedom of expression encompasses the freedom of speech and the corollary right to receive information. These rights extend to minors as well as adults. Libraries and librarians exist to facilitate the exercise of these rights by selecting, producing, providing access to, identifying, retrieving, organizing, providing instruction in the use of, and preserving recorded expression regardless of the format or technology.

The American Library Association expresses these basic principles of librarianship in its *Code of Ethics* and in the *Library Bill of Rights* and its Interpretations. These serve to guide librarians and library governing bodies in addressing issues of intellectual freedom that arise when the library provides access to electronic information, services, and networks.

Issues arising from the still-developing technology of computer-mediated information generation, distribution, and retrieval need to be approached and regularly reviewed from a context of constitutional principles and ALA policies so that fundamental and traditional tenets of librarianship are not swept away.

Electronic information flows across boundaries and barriers despite attempts by individuals, governments, and private entities to channel or control it. Even so, many people, for reasons of technology, infrastructure, or socio-economic status, do not have access to electronic information.

In making decisions about how to offer access to electronic information, each library should consider its mission, goals, objectives, cooperative agreements, and the needs of the entire community it serves.

The Rights of Users

All library system and network policies, procedures, or regulations relating to electronic resources and services should be scrutinized for potential violation of user rights. User policies should be developed according to the policies and guidelines established by the American Library Association, including "Guidelines for the Development and Implementation of Policies, Regulations and Procedures Affecting Access to Library Materials, Services and Facilities."

Users should not be restricted or denied access for expressing or receiving constitutionally protected speech. Users' access should not be changed without due process, including, but not limited to, formal notice and a means of appeal.

Although electronic systems may include distinct property rights and security concerns, such elements may not be employed as a subterfuge to deny users' access to information. Users have the right to be free of unreasonable limitations or conditions set by libraries, librarians, system administrators, vendors, network service providers, or others. Contracts, agreements, and licenses entered into by libraries on behalf of their users should not violate this right. Users also have a right to information, training, and assistance necessary to operate the hardware and software provided by the library.

Users have both the right of confidentiality and the right of privacy. The library should uphold these rights by policy, procedure, and practice. Users should be advised, however, that because security is technically difficult to achieve, electronic transactions and files could become public.

The rights of users who are minors shall in no way be abridged.[1]

Equity of Access

Electronic information, services, and networks provided directly or indirectly by the library should be equally, readily, and equitably accessible to all library users. American Library Association policies oppose the charging of user fees for the provision of information services by all libraries and information services that receive their major support from public funds (50.3; 53.1.14; 60.1; 61.1). It should be the goal of all libraries to develop policies concerning access to electronic resources in light of "Economic Barriers to Information Access: An Interpretation of the Library Bill of Rights" and "Guidelines for the Development and Implementation of Policies, Regulations and Procedures Affecting Access to Library Materials, Services and Facilities."

Information Resources and Access

Providing connections to global information, services, and networks is not the same as selecting and purchasing material for a library collection. Determining the accuracy or authenticity of electronic information may present special problems. Some information accessed electronically may not meet a library's selection or collection development policy. It is, therefore, left to each user to determine what is appropriate. Parents and legal guardians who are concerned about their children's use of electronic resources should provide guidance to their own children.

Libraries and librarians should not deny or limit access to information available via electronic resources because of its allegedly controversial content or because of the librarian's personal beliefs or fear of confrontation. Information retrieved or utilized electronically should be considered constitutionally protected unless determined otherwise by a court with appropriate jurisdiction.

Libraries, acting within their mission and objectives, must support access to information on all subjects that serve the needs or interests of each user, regardless of the user's age or the content of the material. Libraries have an obligation to provide access to government information available in electronic format. Libraries and librarians should not deny access to information solely on the grounds that it is perceived to lack value.

In order to prevent the loss of information, and to preserve the cultural record, libraries may need to expand their selection or collection development policies to ensure preservation, in appropriate formats, of information obtained electronically.

Electronic resources provide unprecedented opportunities to expand the scope of information available to users. Libraries and librarians should provide access to information presenting all points of view. The provision of access does not imply sponsorship or endorsement. These principles pertain to electronic resources no less than they do to the more traditional sources of information in libraries.[2]

Adopted by the ALA Council, January 24, 1996.

NOTES

1. See "Free Access to Libraries for Minors"; "Access to Resources and Services in the School Library Media Program"; and "Access for Children and Young People to Videotapes and Other Nonprint Formats."

2. See "Diversity in Collection Development."

Access to Electronic Information, Services, and Networks

At the 1994 Annual Conference meeting in Miami Beach, the Intellectual Freedom Committee discussed its response to a document titled "Principles for the Development of the National Information Infrastructure," which had been developed by several ALA divisions and other library organizations as a unified statement of the library community's hopes with regard to development of the national "information superhighway." The Committee endorsed the concept of the draft but found many areas of concern, including wording that suggested an acceptance of fees for access to electronic information and distinctions between library service based upon the type or the format of information to be provided. An atmosphere of urgency about issuing a statement on the subject of the national information infrastructure pervaded the 1994 conference. Bills on the subject were pending before Congress. Nevertheless, the Intellectual Freedom Committee felt that ALA's basic intellectual freedom policies were being swept aside, at least to some degree, in the rush by many library organizations to become "players" in the discussions taking place in Washington on the structure of the national information superhighway. It was the compound effect of these concerns, coupled with an increasing volume of requests for guidance from librarians in the field, that solidified the Intellectual Freedom Committee's determination to develop a new Interpretation of the

Library Bill of Rights, "Access to Electronic Information, Services, and Networks." An IFC subcommittee was appointed at the 1994 Annual Conference to prepare a first draft; at the same time, the Committee agreed to sponsor open hearings on the subject at the 1995 Midwinter Meeting in Philadelphia.

Both before and during the hearing, the Committee received comment and testimony from librarians, representing a broad variety of types of libraries and library services, expressing their concerns and questions about access to electronic information. The Committee itself also identified several areas of concern, not the least of which was the definition of *electronic communication.* For example, is the Internet a public forum, or is it not? Are parts of it public fora and parts of it not? Other areas of concern included privacy and confidentiality, attribution or lack thereof of articles and information appearing on the Internet, "flaming" and hate speech, punishment by cutting off information or user accounts, fees, children's access, content and diversity, collection development, language, disability, and restriction of news groups. Recognizing the breadth of issues that needed to be addressed and the urgency of the need, the Committee decided to hold a special meeting to work on and produce a draft Interpretation for circulation prior to the 1995 Annual Conference.

The Committee met in Chicago March 3–5, 1995. An intensive weekend of work resulted in a draft document composed of four sections: an introductory section placing electronic information, services, and networks squarely within the realm of First Amendment rights, freedom of expression, and public-forum concepts; a section on the rights of users; a section on equity of access; and a section on information resources and access issues. The draft was circulated broadly to ALA's Council and Executive Board, all of the Divisions and Round Tables, Chapter Intellectual Freedom Committees and all other interested librarians. It also was posted on the Office for Intellectual Freedom's listserv, ALAOIF, and comments were invited from all participants.

At the 1995 Annual Conference in Chicago, discussions of additional comments received resulted in editorial changes and rearrangement of some of the language of the draft. The sections on equity of access and the rights of users were changed to clarify the Committee's intent that fees not be charged for electronic-information services and that services be provided in a nondiscriminatory manner.

The revised draft was circulated to all ALA units meeting at the conference for additional comments and was endorsed by the Public Library Association and the American Association of School Librarians. Other units, particularly the Association of College and Research Libraries, expressed strong reservations about the draft, especially about its principles on fees and equity of access. In light of these concerns, the draft was referred to the IFC for additional work. As of this writing, it is anticipated that a final version will be presented to Council for adoption in 1996.

2.3

Access to Library Resources and Services Regardless of Gender or Sexual Orientation

An Interpretation of the *Library Bill of Rights*

American libraries exist and function within the context of a body of laws derived from the United States Constitution and the First Amendment. The *Library Bill of Rights* embodies the basic policies which guide libraries in the provision of services, materials, and programs.

In the preamble to its *Library Bill of Rights*, the American Library Association affirms that *all* [emphasis added] libraries are forums for information and ideas. This concept of *forum* and its accompanying principle of *inclusiveness* pervade all six Articles of the *Library Bill of Rights*.

The American Library Association stringently and unequivocally maintains that libraries and librarians have an obligation to resist efforts that systematically exclude materials dealing with any subject matter, including gender, homosexuality, bisexuality, lesbianism, heterosexuality, gay lifestyles, or any facet of sexual orientation:

■ Article I of the *Library Bill of Rights* states that "Materials should not be excluded because of the origin, background, or views of those contributing to their creation." The Association affirms that books and other materials coming from gay presses, gay, lesbian, or bisexual authors or other creators, and materials dealing with gay lifestyles are protected by the *Library Bill of Rights*. Librarians are obligated by the *Library Bill of Rights* to endeavor to select materials without regard to the gender or sexual orientation of their creators by using the criteria identified in their written, approved selection policies. (ALA policy 53.1.5).

■ Article II maintains that "Libraries should provide materials and information presenting all points of view on current and historical issues. Materials should not be proscribed or removed because of partisan or doctrinal disapproval." Library services, materials, and programs representing diverse points of view on gender or sexual orientation should be considered for purchase and inclusion in library collections and programs. (ALA policies 53.1.1, 53.1.9, and 53.1.11). The Association affirms that attempts to proscribe or remove materials dealing with gay or lesbian life without regard to the written, approved selection policy violate this tenet and constitute censorship.

■ Articles III and IV mandate that libraries "challenge censorship" and cooperate with those "resisting abridgement of free expression and free access to ideas."

■ Article V holds that "A person's right to use a library should not be denied or abridged because of origin, age, background or views." In the *Library Bill of Rights* and all its Interpretations, it is intended that: "origin" encompasses all the characteristics of individuals that are inherent in the circumstances of their birth; "age" encompasses all the characteristics of individuals that are inherent in their levels of development and maturity; "background" encompasses all the characteristics of individuals that are a result of their life experiences; and "views" encompasses all the opinions and beliefs held and expressed by individuals.

Therefore, Article V of the *Library Bill of Rights* mandates that library services, materials, and programs be available to all members of the community the library serves, without regard to gender or sexual orientation.

■ Article VI maintains that "Libraries which make exhibit spaces and meeting rooms available to the public they serve should make such facilities available on an equitable basis, regardless of the beliefs or affiliations of individuals or groups requesting their use." This protection extends to all groups and members of the community the library serves, without regard to gender or sexual orientation.

The American Library Association holds that any attempt, be it legal or extra-legal, to regulate or suppress library services, materials, or programs must be resisted in order that protected expression is not abridged. Librarians have a professional obligation to ensure that all library users have free and equal access to the entire range of library services, materials, and programs. Therefore, the Association strongly opposes any effort to limit access to information and ideas. The Association also encourages librarians to proactively support the First Amendment rights of all library users, including gays, lesbians, and bisexuals.

Adopted by the ALA Council, June 30, 1993.

Access to Library Resources and Services Regardless of Gender or Sexual Orientation

The American Library Association held its 1993 Midwinter Meeting in Denver, Colorado, two months after that state had adopted a constitutional amendment repealing legislation protecting the civil rights of gays and lesbians. The amendment, Colorado Constitutional Amendment 2, was one of several such initiatives that sprang up in Western and Pacific Northwestern states in 1992 and reappeared persistently, despite being struck down as unconstitutional in courts or being turned back by voters. Thus, it was in an atmosphere of intolerance and discrimination against individuals based on their sexual orientation that a proposed resolution on gender, sexual orientation, and the *Library Bill of Rights* came before ALA's Council. Specifically, the resolution directed that Article V of the *Library Bill of Rights* be amended to add the words "gender" and "sexual orientation" after the word "age," with the amended section to read thus: "a person's right to use the library should not be denied or abridged because of origin, age, gender, sexual orientation, background, or views." The proposed resolution was referred to the Intellectual Freedom Committee for review and recommendation.

The IFC became concerned with the impulse and momentum for amending the *Library Bill of Rights*, pointing out the long-standing "laundry list" problem in Article V, where it sometimes has been assumed that any characteristic not specifically listed is thereby

31

excluded. The 1980 revisions to the *Library Bill of Rights* deliberately broadened the language of Article V to cover all possibilities; and, in response to a request of the Minority Concerns Committee in 1989 to review the *Library Bill of Rights* to ensure that it addressed language and economic status, the Intellectual Freedom Committee declined to amend the document; it opted instead to incorporate those concerns into revisions of Interpretations. In addition, amending the *Library Bill of Rights* would mean that thousands of libraries across the country that had adopted the document as part of their operating principles and practices would need to readopt a revised version. Ordinarily, this would be a matter of routine. The repressive national atmosphere at the time, however, aroused concern that the process of adopting a revised version of the *Library Bill of Rights* would invite vigorous assault by conservative pressure groups that had identified the document as a target and had worked in various localities to secure its removal from local library policy.

Faced with these concerns, the Intellectual Freedom Committee elected to present a substitute resolution reaffirming that the *Library Bill of Rights* did include gender and sexual orientation. In her Report to Council, Intellectual Freedom Committee chair Candace Morgan explained:

> We took this action for several reasons: first, our Association's commitment to nondiscrimination with regard to gender and sexual orientation has always been part of the meaning of all Articles of the *Library Bill of Rights,* not just Article V; second, terminology in the *Library Bill of Rights,* particularly in Article V, is deliberately broad to prohibit discrimination targeted at any class of individuals on the basis of arbitrary distinctions; third, we have frequently been asked to add language to Article V, and we have refused to do so in the belief that the addition of specific classifications implies that other classes not explicitly included are therefore excluded; and fourth, this organization has never, in our memory, amended the *Library Bill of Rights* without broad distribution for comment from all divisions and other interested bodies.

Council accepted the Intellectual Freedom Committee's substitute resolution. At that same Midwinter Meeting, the IFC also recommended, and Council adopted, a more generic "Resolution on Gay Rights and Materials," designed to be useful and immediately available in localities where antigay initiatives were springing up with regularity.

In addition to adopting these two resolutions, however, Council directed the Intellectual Freedom Committee to bring to the 1993 Annual Conference in New Orleans specific language to revise the *Library Bill of Rights* so as to address the issue of sexual orientation.

In New Orleans, the Committee's concerns about revising the *Library Bill of Rights* were as strong as they had been at the Midwinter Meeting. Battles over maintaining the current version of the *Library Bill of Rights* had just been fought in both North Carolina and Nevada. Given the atmosphere of attack on the *Library Bill of Rights* already evident in many communities, the Committee believed the wiser course would be to present a very strongly worded Interpretation of the *Library Bill of Rights* to Council for its adoption. Such an Interpretation would state specifically that the document already covers gays, lesbians, and anyone else, with regard to both their access to materials and the necessity of maintaining collections that contain materials by and about homosexuals. Council had directed that language to amend the *Library Bill of Rights* be prepared, however. The Intellectual Freedom Committee was faced with the dilemma of responding to Council's directive despite strong reservations about the approach to the problem that Council apparently wanted to take. In addition to proposed language to revise the *Library Bill of Rights,* a draft Interpretation on gender and sexuality was prepared and circulated to all ALA units prior to the Annual Conference soliciting response on this approach to the issue. The draft, and the approach of adopting an Interpretation rather than amending the *Library Bill of Rights* itself, was enthusiastically received and endorsed by a number of ALA's divisions and committees, including ALSC, PLA, ALTA, YALSA, the Committee on Professional Ethics, and the Intellectual Freedom Round Table. Given that response, Intellectual Freedom Committee chair Candace Morgan explained in her 1993 Annual Conference Report to Council that the Committee had decided—with the support of the above-named divisions, committees, and round table—to recommend the option of adopting an Interpretation only and leaving the *Library Bill of Rights* as is. Morgan acknowledged in her report:

There is no question that materials by and about gays, lesbians, and bisexuals, and on the subject of homosexuality in general, are at the top of the agenda of organized pressure groups that are attacking libraries all over the country for including such materials in their collections. There is also no question that gays, lesbians, and bisexuals themselves are the victims and the targets of unprecedented attacks aimed at codifying discrimination against homosexuals into law. Finally, there is no question that the library profession's commitment to intellectual freedom and the responsibility of libraries and librarians to protect and defend access to information from all points of view, requires including materials in libraries on homosexuality to serve the needs of all library users, including gays, lesbians, and bisexuals. This commitment to free expression also mandates that we take positive action to protect the rights of access for all persons regardless of sexuality, gender, or age.

Morgan went on to explain that, ironically, the *Library Bill of Rights* had recently come under attack in Nevada and North Carolina by opponents of intellectual freedom because those opponents assumed that the document, unamended, already protected materials by, about, or of interest to gays, lesbians, and bisexuals. The battles to protect the *Library Bill of Rights* in state and local policy had been hard fought and narrowly won. Many of the fighters, including public and school librarians in many other states, reported that in the current climate of attacks on the freedom to read, adopting a newly amended *Library Bill of Rights* would be politically impossible. Believing that the document would be useless to the profession if not incorporated into local library policy, Morgan explained the Committee's strong belief that it would be unwise to initiate an opportunity to exclude the document from local policy by forcing local libraries to consider readopting an amended version. Issuing an Interpretation for governing bodies and librarians would guide their understanding of the *Library Bill of Rights* as it was already incorporated in policy. Finally, Morgan explained the "laundry list" problem, in which revision of Article V of the *Library Bill of Rights* to include specific characteristics renders it vulnerable to requests that a long list of characteristics be added and creates the implication that any characteristic not explicitly included is, therefore, excluded. One of the first comments the Intellectual Freedom Committee received when the possibility of revision to include gender and sexual orientation was announced was that if disability was not currently covered, as a move to amend implied, the word "ability" should be included to cover mental, emotional, or physical conditions. Health, race, national origin, and language were also suggested as additions to the list. The Committee itself added "financial status" to the language for the proposed amendment because, at the time, it was still considering a request of the Minority Concerns Committee to address economic status and language in the *Library Bill of Rights* while simultaneously working on a proposed Interpretation to do just that.

The Intellectual Freedom Committee's reasoning was persuasive, and Council rejected amendments to the *Library Bill of Rights*. Instead, it adopted a new Interpretation of the *Library Bill of Rights*, "Access to Library Resources and Services Regardless of Gender or Sexual Orientation," which makes absolutely clear that censorship of material based on sexuality, or discrimination against library users based on gender or sexual orientation, is and always has been totally inappropriate and violative of the *Library Bill of Rights*.

2.4

Access to Resources and Services in the School Library Media Program

An Interpretation of the *Library Bill of Rights*

The school library media program plays a unique role in promoting intellectual freedom. It serves as a point of voluntary access to information and ideas and as a learning laboratory for students as they acquire critical thinking and problem solving skills needed in a pluralistic society. Although the educational level and program of the school necessarily shapes the resources and services of a school library media program, the principles of the *Library Bill of Rights* apply equally to all libraries, including school library media programs.

School library media professionals assume a leadership role in promoting the principles of intellectual freedom within the school by providing resources and services that create and sustain an atmosphere of free inquiry. School library media professionals work closely with teachers to integrate instructional activities in classroom units designed to equip students to locate, evaluate, and use a broad range of ideas effectively. Through resources, programming, and educational processes, students and teachers experience the free and robust debate characteristic of a democratic society.

School library media professionals cooperate with other individuals in building collections of resources appropriate to the developmental and maturity levels of students. These collections provide resources which support the curriculum and are consistent with the philosophy, goals, and objectives of the school district. Resources in school library media collections represent diverse points of view on current as well as historical issues.

While English is, by history and tradition, the customary language of the United States, the languages in use in any given community may vary. Schools serving communities in which other languages are used make efforts to accommodate the needs of students for whom English is a second language. To support these efforts, and to ensure equal access to resources and services, the school library media program provides resources which reflect the linguistic pluralism of the community.

Members of the school community involved in the collection development process employ educational criteria to select resources unfettered by their personal, political, social, or religious views. Students and educators served by the school library media program have access to resources and services free of constraints resulting from personal, partisan, or doctrinal disapproval. School library media professionals resist efforts by individuals to define what is appropriate for all students or teachers to read, view, or hear.

Major barriers between students and resources include: imposing age or grade level restrictions on the use of resources, limiting the use of interlibrary loan and access to electronic information, charging fees for information in specific formats, requiring permissions from parents or teachers, establishing restricted shelves or closed collections, and labeling. Policies, procedures, and rules related to the use of resources and services support free and open access to information.

The school board adopts policies that guarantee students access to a broad range of ideas. These include policies on collection development and procedures for the review of resources about which concerns have been raised. Such policies, developed by persons in the school community, provide for a timely and fair hearing and assure that procedures are applied equitably to all expressions of concern. School library media professionals implement district policies and procedures in the school.

Adopted July 2, 1986; amended January 10, 1990, by the ALA Council.

Access to Resources and Services in the School Library Media Program

During the early 1950s, as the anticommunist reaction of McCarthyism swept across the United States, school librarians and school curriculum planners were affected no less than people in journalism, entertainment, and government. Schools were coerced to ban works that were alleged to contain "un-American" thinking.

The issue of selecting school library materials was raised during the meeting of the board of directors of the American Association of School Librarians (AASL) during the 1953 ALA Annual Conference in Los Angeles. Sue Hefley, chair of the school libraries discussion group at the second Conference on Intellectual Freedom (held at Whittier College, June 20–21), reported on her group's consensus concerning the need for a policy statement on the matter of selection. In response to Hefley's report, the board voted

> that a committee be appointed to consider the advisability of preparing a statement on book selection in defense of liberty in schools of a democracy, and in considering this problem to make use of the excellent statement prepared at the Conference on Intellectual Freedom. Furthermore, that this committee make recommendations as to what further action AASL should take in this matter.[1]

In preparation for the AASL meeting at the 1954 Annual Conference in Minneapolis, the Committee on Book Selection in Defense of Liberty in Schools of a Democracy submitted a draft for a *School Library Bill of Rights*. At the 1955 Midwinter Meeting, the AASL officially accepted the *School Library Bill of Rights*, and, on July 8, 1955, it was adopted by the ALA Council.

In the years following the adoption of the *School Library Bill of Rights*, the *Library Bill of Rights* underwent several basic changes. (For full discussion, see part I, section 1, *Library Bill of Rights*). Because of changes in the *Library Bill of Rights*, affirmed by the *School Library Bill of Rights* of 1955, as well as changes in the conception of the range of materials to be provided by libraries, the AASL Board of Directors appointed a committee in 1968 to consider revising the 1955 *School Library Bill of Rights*.

At the 1969 ALA Annual Conference in Atlantic City, the revised *School Library Bill of Rights* was brought before the AASL Board of Directors. Making only minor corrections, the board voted to accept the revised version:

> The American Association of School Librarians reaffirms its belief in the *Library Bill of Rights* of the American Library Association. Media personnel are concerned with generating understanding of American freedoms through the development of informed and responsible citizens. To this end the American Association of School Librarians asserts that the responsibility of the school library media center is:
>
> To provide a comprehensive collection of instructional materials selected in compliance with basic written selection principles, and to provide maximum accessibility to these materials;
>
> To provide materials that will support the curriculum, taking into consideration the individual's needs, and the varied interests, abilities, socioeconomic backgrounds, and maturity levels of the students served;
>
> To provide materials for teachers and students that will encourage growth in knowledge, and that will develop literary, cultural, and aesthetic appreciation, and ethical standards;

To provide materials which reflect the ideas and beliefs of religious, social, political, historical, and ethnic groups and their contribution to the American and world heritage and culture, thereby enabling students to develop an intellectual integrity in forming judgments;

To provide a written statement, approved by the local boards of education, of the procedures for meeting the challenge of censorship of materials in school library media centers; and

To provide qualified professional personnel to serve teachers and students.

It soon became clear, however, that the existence of two documents with very similar titles could be a source of confusion. Moreover, with the 1967 amendment of the *Library Bill of Rights* to oppose discrimination against library users by age, the *School Library Bill of Rights* became largely redundant. As increasing numbers of librarians pointed out, the school document simply repeated in different language the principles enunciated more forcefully in the *Library Bill of Rights*. This served only to detract attention from and, hence, to weaken the impact of the Association's most basic document on intellectual freedom.

The problem was discussed extensively in both the Intellectual Freedom Committee and AASL. At the 1976 Annual Conference in Chicago, the Board of Directors of the American Association of School Librarians withdrew the *School Library Bill of Rights* and endorsed the *Library Bill of Rights*.

Since 1976 and particularly in the 1980s, the challenge to materials in school libraries and media centers has increased in volume and intensity. The need became apparent for an Interpretation of the *Library Bill of Rights* that spoke directly to the unique role of school libraries and media centers in the educational process. A clear statement of the responsibility of school library media professionals for the selection process and of the centrality of intellectual freedom principles in this process was perceived as the central focus for this Interpretation.

In 1985–86, an Interpretation was drafted by the AASL with the cooperation of the IFC. At the 1986 Annual Conference in New York,

"Access to Resources and Services in the School Library Media Program" was adopted by the ALA Council. It read as follows:

The school library media program plays a unique role in promoting intellectual freedom. It serves as a point of voluntary access to information and ideas and as a learning laboratory for students as they acquire critical thinking and problem solving skills needed in a pluralistic society. Although the educational level and program of the school necessarily shape the resources and services of a school library media program, the principles of the *Library Bill of Rights* apply equally to all libraries, including school library media programs.

School library media professionals assume a leadership role in promoting the principles of intellectual freedom within the school by providing resources and services that create and sustain an atmosphere of free inquiry. School library media professionals work closely with teachers to integrate instructional activities in classroom units designed to equip students to locate, evaluate, and use a broad range of ideas effectively. Through resources, programming, and educational processes, students and teachers experience the free and robust debate characteristic of a democratic society.

School library media professionals cooperate with other individuals in building collections of resources appropriate to the developmental and maturity levels of students. These collections provide resources which support the curriculum and are consistent with the philosophy, goals, and objectives of the school district. Resources in school library media collections represent diverse points of view and current as well as historic issues.

Members of the school community involved in the collection development process employ educational criteria to select resources unfettered by their personal, political, social, or religious views. Students and educators served by the school library media program have access to resources and services free of constraints resulting from personal, partisan, or doctrinal disapproval. School library media professionals resist efforts by individuals to define what is appropriate for all students or teachers to read, view, or hear.

Major barriers between students and resources include imposing age or grade level restrictions on the use of resources, limiting the use of interlibrary loan and access to electronic information, charging fees for information in specific formats, requiring permissions from parents or teachers, establishing restricted shelves or closed collections, and labeling. Policies, procedures, and rules related to the use of resources and services support free and open access to information.

The school board adopts policies that guarantee student access to a broad range of ideas. These include policies on collection development and procedures for the review of resources about which concerns have been raised. Such policies, developed by persons in the school community, provide for a timely and fair hearing and ensure that procedures are applied equitably to all expressions of concern. School library media professionals implement district policies and procedures in the school.

A revised Interpretation was circulated for comment in the fall of 1989. The sole substantive change was the addition of a paragraph stating that the school library media program should attempt to accommodate needs of students for whom English is a second language. To ensure equality of access, librarians must provide resources reflecting the linguistic pluralism of the community that they serve.

At the 1990 Midwinter Meeting, comments received from AASL, OLPR, SCOLE, and the Professional Ethics Committee resulted in minor editorial changes. The policy was recommended to the Council and adopted on January 10, 1990.

NOTE

1. *School Libraries* 3, no. 1:8 (Oct. 1953).

2.5

Challenged Materials

An Interpretation of the *Library Bill of Rights*

The American Library Association declares as a matter of firm principle that it is the responsibility of every library to have a clearly defined materials selection policy in written form which reflects the *Library Bill of Rights*, and which is approved by the appropriate governing authority.

Challenged materials which meet the criteria for selection in the materials selection policy of the library should not be removed under any legal or extra-legal pressure. The *Library Bill of Rights* states in Article I that "Materials should not be excluded because of the origin, background, or views of those contributing to their creation," and in Article II, that "Materials should not be proscribed or removed because of partisan or doctrinal disapproval." Freedom of expression is protected by the Constitution of the United States, but constitutionally protected expression is often separated from unprotected expression only by a dim and uncertain line. The Constitution requires a procedure designed to focus searchingly on challenged expression before it can be suppressed. An adversary hearing is a part of this procedure.

Therefore, any attempt, be it legal or extra-legal, to regulate or suppress materials in libraries must be closely scrutinized to the end that protected expression is not abridged.

Adopted June 25, 1971; amended July 1, 1981; amended January 10, 1990, by the ALA Council.

Challenged Materials

The *Library Bill of Rights* states that library materials should not be "excluded because of the origin, background, or views" of their creators. The document states further that "materials should not be proscribed or removed because of partisan or doctrinal disapproval." Nevertheless, libraries are still pressured by many groups and individuals to remove certain materials because they find their sexual, political, or religious content objectionable.

Particularly when sexually explicit materials are the object of censorship efforts, librarians and boards of trustees are often unaware of the legal procedures required to effect the removal of such items. Many attorneys, even when employed by state or local governing bodies, are not aware of the procedures to determine whether or not a work is obscene under the law. According to U.S. Supreme Court decisions, a work is not obscene until found to be so by a court of law and only after an adversary hearing to determine the question of obscenity. Until a work is specifically found to be unprotected by the First Amendment, the title remains a legal library acquisition and need not be removed.

In 1971, several attempts to ban publications from libraries involved charges that the works were obscene and therefore not legal or proper acquisitions for the library. In Groton, Connecticut, in a case involving *Evergreen Review*, the librarian and the board of trustees were threatened with prosecution under a state obscenity statute if they refused to remove the magazine from the library. The board, after several months of resisting efforts to remove the magazine, capitulated in the face of this threat to prosecute them as individuals.

The Groton, Connecticut, case prompted the Intellectual Freedom Committee, with the aid of legal counsel, to study U.S. Supreme Court and federal circuit court decisions concerning procedures whereby materials are determined to be obscene. Three cases in particular were reviewed: *Bantam Books, Inc.* v. *Sullivan* (372 U.S. 58, 83 S. Ct. 631 [1963]); *Marcus* v. *Search Warrants* (367 U.S. 717, 732; 81 S. Ct. 1708, 1716 [1961]); and *A Quantity of Copies of Books* v. *Kansas* (378 U.S. 205, 211; 84 S. Ct. 1723 [1964]).

Using the language of these three decisions as a basis, the Intellectual Freedom Committee developed "Resolution on Challenged Materials." The statement was submitted to the ALA Council during the 1971 Annual Conference in Dallas and was adopted as an ALA policy on June 25, 1971. It read as follows:

WHEREAS, The *Library Bill of Rights* states that no library materials should be proscribed or removed because of partisan or doctrinal disapproval; and

WHEREAS, Constitutionally protected expression is often separated from unprotected expression only by a dim and uncertain line; and

WHEREAS, Any attempt, be it legal or extra-legal, to regulate or suppress material must be closely scrutinized to the end that protected expression is not abridged in the process; and

WHEREAS, The Constitution requires a procedure designed to focus searchingly on the question before speech can be suppressed; and

WHEREAS, The dissemination of a particular work which is alleged to be unprotected should be completely undisturbed until an independent determination has been made by a judicial officer, including an adversary hearing;

THEREFORE, THE PREMISES CONSIDERED, BE IT RESOLVED, That the American Library Association declares as a matter of firm principle that no challenged library material should be removed from any library under any legal or extra-legal pressure, save after an independent determination by a judicial officer in a court of competent jurisdiction and only after an adversary hearing, in accordance with well-established principles of law.

A decade later, legal standards for determining obscenity had changed significantly. Nevertheless, the basic principle—that expression is protected by the First Amendment until it has been determined through an adversary procedure that such expression is obscene, libelous, or otherwise unprotected—remained firmly established in U.S. constitutional law. In reviewing the 1971 resolution in 1981, however, the IFC found that a major revision still was necessary. The principal difficulties were twofold. The first problem was the rather simple matter of format. Written as a formal resolution, with an implementary paragraph preceded by a series of "whereas clauses," "Resolution on Challenged Materials" was inconsistent in form with other Interpretations of the *Library Bill of Rights*, and lacked clarity and force as a document directed toward the general public as well as library professionals.

The second problem was more substantive. The materials selection policies of most libraries correctly provide opportunities for patron comments and citizen requests for reconsideration of library materials. Yet the policy seemed to make a mockery of such procedures by declaring in advance that "no challenged library material should be removed" unless the library were ordered to do so by a court of law. Moreover, many librarians complained that such an inflexible declaration served to tie the library's own hands in its efforts to correct the inevitable mistakes that occur in any selection process.

With these considerations in mind, the IFC presented the Council with a new version of the document, written in a format similar to the other Interpretations of the *Library Bill of Rights* and more appropriate for a broader audience. The new version linked the decision to remove or retain challenged materials to the maintenance of clear guidelines consistent with the *Library Bill of Rights* and established by the library's materials selection policy. The revision

46

designated the maintenance of a "clearly defined" selection policy a "responsibility" of all libraries. The new version offered libraries and patrons alike greater flexibility in the consideration of challenges while at the same time reaffirming the principles of the *Library Bill of Rights,* calling for the closest scrutiny of all efforts to remove materials, and maintaining due process in the reconsideration procedure. On July 1, 1981, the Council adopted the revised statement "Challenged Materials" as a policy of the American Library Association:

> The American Library Association declares as a matter of firm principle that it is the responsibility of every library to have a clearly defined materials selection policy in written form which reflects the *Library Bill of Rights,* and which is approved by the appropriate governing authority.
>
> Challenged materials which meet the materials selection policy of the library should not be removed under any legal or extralegal pressure. The *Library Bill of Rights* states in Article I that "Materials should not be excluded because of the origin, background, or views of those contributing to their creation," and in Article II, that "Materials should not be proscribed or removed because of partisan or doctrinal disapproval." Freedom of expression is protected by the Constitution of the United States, but constitutionally protected expression is often separated from unprotected expression only by a dim and uncertain line. The Constitution requires a procedure designed to focus searchingly on challenged expression before it can be suppressed. An adversary hearing is a part of this procedure.
>
> Therefore, any attempt, be it legal or extra-legal, to regulate or suppress materials in libraries must be closely scrutinized to the end that protected expression is not abridged.

In 1986, in response to inquiries from librarians facing book or material challenges for the first time, the Intellectual Freedom Committee developed the following list of definitions to clarify terminology associated with challenges:

> *Expression of Concern.* An inquiry that has judgmental overtones.

Oral Complaint. An oral challenge to the presence and/or appropriateness of the material in question.

Written Complaint. A formal, written complaint filed with the institution (library, school, etc.), challenging the presence and/or appropriateness of specific material.

Public Attack. A publicly disseminated statement challenging the value of the material, presented to the media and/or others outside the institutional organization in order to gain public support for further action.

Censorship. A change in the access status of material, based on the content of the work and made by a governing authority or its representatives. Such changes include exclusion, restriction, removal, or age/grade level changes.

As part of the Interpretation review process initiated in 1989, one minor change was made in this policy to state explicitly that materials must meet criteria stated in materials selection policies rather than simply meeting the policy, per se. No substantive changes were recommended.

On January 10, at the 1990 Midwinter Meeting, the Council adopted the "Challenged Materials" Interpretation, as amended.

2.6

Diversity in Collection Development

An Interpretation of the *Library Bill of Rights*

Throughout history, the focus of censorship has fluctuated from generation to generation. Books and other materials have not been selected or have been removed from library collections for many reasons, among which are prejudicial language and ideas, political content, economic theory, social philosophies, religious beliefs, sexual forms of expression, and other topics of a potentially controversial nature.

Some examples of censorship may include removing or not selecting materials because they are considered by some as racist or sexist; not purchasing conservative religious materials; not selecting materials about or by minorities because it is thought these groups or interests are not represented in a community; or not providing information on or materials from non-mainstream political entities.

Librarians may seek to increase user awareness of materials on various social concerns by many means, including, but not limited to, issuing bibliographies and presenting exhibits and programs.

Librarians have a professional responsibility to be inclusive, not exclusive, in collection development and in the provision of interlibrary loan. Access to all materials legally obtainable should be assured to the user, and policies should not unjustly exclude materials even if they are offensive to the librarian or the user.

Collection development should reflect the philosophy inherent in Article II of the *Library Bill of Rights:* "Libraries should provide materials and information presenting all points of view on current and historical issues. Materials should not be proscribed or removed because of partisan or doctrinal disapproval." A balanced collection reflects a diversity of materials, not an equality of numbers. Collection development responsibilities include selecting materials in the languages in common use in the community which the library serves. Collection development and the selection of materials should be done according to professional standards and established selection and review procedures.

There are many complex facets to any issue, and variations of context in which issues may be expressed, discussed, or interpreted. Librarians have a professional responsibility to be fair, just, and equitable and to give all library users equal protection in guarding against violation of the library patron's right to read, view, or listen to materials and resources protected by the First Amendment, no matter what the viewpoint of the author, creator, or selector. Librarians have an obligation to protect library collections from removal of materials based on personal bias or prejudice, and to select and support the access to materials on all subjects that meet, as closely as possible, the needs and interests of all persons in the community which the library serves. This includes materials that reflect political, economic, religious, social, minority, and sexual issues.

Intellectual freedom, the essence of equitable library services, provides for free access to all expressions of ideas through which any and all sides of a question, cause, or movement may be explored. Toleration is meaningless without tolerance for what some may consider detestable. Librarians cannot justly permit their own preferences to limit their degree of tolerance in collection development, because freedom is indivisible.

Adopted July 14, 1982; amended January 10, 1990, by the ALA Council.

Diversity in Collection Development

During the 1971 Midwinter Meeting in Los Angeles, the ALA Intellectual Freedom Committee met with representatives of the Executive Board of the International Conference of Police Associations. The meeting was to provide a forum for discussing police efforts to remove William Steig's *Sylvester and the Magic Pebble* from public and school libraries. During the meeting, the officers raised a provocative and embarrassing question for librarians. They asked why some librarians were quick to comply with requests to remove another children's book, *Little Black Sambo,* from their collections when blacks complained that its illustrations were degrading; yet now, when police officers found William Steig's pigs dressed as law-enforcement officers to be degrading, librarians objected vociferously to taking the book out of their collections.

The evasive response from the IFC was generally to the effect that the Committee had difficulty impressing upon members of the library profession the importance of the principles of intellectual freedom. The inability to answer the officers' charge adequately acknowledged the accusation implicit in the question: some librarians do employ a double standard when it comes to their practice of intellectual freedom and their commitment to it. Many librarians express a strong commitment to the principles of intellectual freedom but fail to grasp that the concept of intellectual freedom, in its pure sense, promotes no causes, furthers no movements, and favors no viewpoints. *Little Black Sambo* and *Sylvester and the Magic Pebble* did not bring new issues before the library profession. These books only inherited the cloak of controversy that had already surrounded such diverse works as *The Adventures of Huckleberry Finn, Mother Goose Nursery Rhymes and Fairy Tales, Doctor Doolittle,* and *The Merchant of Venice.*

Article II of the *Library Bill of Rights* states that "no library materials should be proscribed or removed from libraries because of partisan or doctrinal disapproval." The phrase "no library materials" does not appear by accident. Before June 1967, the sentence concluded, "books or other reading matter of sound factual authority should not be proscribed or removed from library shelves because of partisan or doctrinal disapproval." Article II was revised in 1967 because some librarians used alleged lack of "sound factual authority" as a basis for removing library materials. To determine which materials lacked sound factual authority, many deferred to their personal conceptions of *fact* and *authority.* One of the most extreme examples, cited at the time of the revision, was of a Catholic librarian who excluded Protestant publications because they were not of "sound factual authority." Today, the simpler, broader phrase "no library materials" in the *Library Bill of Rights* leaves no room for interpretation. The revised statement reflects the philosophy that freedom is indivisible and that tolerance, if it is to be meaningful, must hold for all points of view.

At the 1972 Midwinter Meeting in Chicago, the Intellectual Freedom Committee reported its intention to prepare a statement making clear the meaning of the *Library Bill of Rights* as it pertains to attempts to censor library materials because of alleged racism, sexism, or any other "isms." The statement was approved by the IFC on June 25, 1972. It was subsequently submitted to the ALA Council at the 1973 Midwinter Meeting in Washington, D.C., and approved as an ALA policy on February 2, 1973. Entitled "Sexism, Racism, and Other -Isms in Library Materials," it read as follows:

> Traditional aims of censorship efforts have been to suppress political, sexual, or religious expressions. The same three subjects have also been the source of most complaints about materials in library collections. Another basis for complaints, however, has

become more and more frequent. Due, perhaps, to increased awareness of the rights of minorities and increased efforts to secure those rights, libraries are being asked to remove, restrict or reconsider some materials which are allegedly derogatory to specific minorities or which supposedly perpetuate stereotypes and false images of minorities. Among the several recurring "isms" used to describe the contents of the materials objected to are "racism" and "sexism."

Complaints that library materials convey a derogatory or false image of a minority strike the personal social consciousness and sense of responsibility of some librarians who—accordingly—comply with the requests to remove such materials. While such efforts to counteract injustices are understandable, and perhaps even commendable as reflections of deep personal commitments to the ideal of equality for all people, they are—nonetheless—in conflict with the professional responsibility of librarians to guard against encroachments upon intellectual freedom.

This responsibility has been espoused and reaffirmed by the American Library Association in many of its basic documents on intellectual freedom over the past thirty years. The most concise statement of the Association's position appears in Article II of the *Library Bill of Rights,* which states that "Libraries should provide books and materials presenting all points of view concerning the problems and issues of our times; no library materials should be proscribed or removed because of partisan or doctrinal disapproval."

While the application of this philosophy may seem simple when dealing with political, religious, or even sexual expressions, its full implications become somewhat difficult when dealing with ideas, such as racism or sexism, which many find abhorrent, repugnant, and inhumane. But, as stated in "The Freedom to Read":

> It is inevitable in the give and take of the democratic process that the political, the moral, or the aesthetic concepts of an individual or group will occasionally collide with those of another individual or group. In a free society each individual is free to determine for himself what he wishes to read, and each group is free to determine what it

will recommend to its freely associated members. But no group has the right to take the law into its own hands, and to impose its own concept of politics or morality upon other members of a democratic society. Freedom is no freedom if it is accorded only to the accepted and the inoffensive. . . . We realize that the application of these propositions may mean the dissemination of ideas and manners of expression that are repugnant to many persons. We do not state these propositions in the comfortable belief that what people read is unimportant. We believe rather that what people read is deeply important; that ideas can be dangerous; but that the suppression of ideas is fatal to a democratic society. Freedom itself is a dangerous way of life, but it is ours.

Some find this creed acceptable when dealing with materials for adults but cannot extend its application to materials for children. Such reluctance is generally based on the belief that children are more susceptible to being permanently influenced—even damaged—by objectionable materials than are adults. The *Library Bill of Rights,* however, makes no distinction between materials and services for children and adults. Its principles of free access to all materials available apply to every person; as stated in Article V, "The rights of an individual to the use of a library should not be denied or abridged because of his age, race, religion, national origins or social or political views."

Some librarians deal with the problem of objectionable materials by labeling them or listing them as "racist" or "sexist." This kind of action, too, has long been opposed by the American Library Association through its Statement on Labeling, which says,

> If materials are labeled to pacify one group, there is no excuse for refusing to label any item in the library's collection. Because authoritarians tend to suppress ideas and attempt to coerce individuals to conform to a specific ideology, the American Library Association opposes such efforts which aim at closing any path to knowledge.

Others deal with the problem of objectionable materials by instituting restrictive circulation or relegating materials to closed or restricted collections. This practice, too, is in violation of the *Library Bill of Rights* as explained in Restricted Access to Library Materials, which says

> Too often only "controversial" materials are the subject of such segregation, leading to the conclusion that factors other than theft and mutilation were the true considerations. The distinction is extremely difficult to make, both for the librarian and the patron. Selection policies, carefully developed on the basis of principles of intellectual freedom and the *Library Bill of Rights*, should not be vitiated by administrative practices such as restricted access.

The American Library Association has made clear its position concerning the removal of library materials because of partisan or doctrinal disapproval, or because of pressures from interest groups, in another policy statement, the Resolution on Challenged Materials:

> The American Library Association declares as a matter of firm principle that no challenged material should be removed from any library under any legal or extra-legal pressure, save after an independent determination by a judicial officer in a court of competent jurisdiction and only after an adversary hearing, in accordance with well-established principles of law.

Intellectual freedom, in its purest sense, promotes no causes, furthers no movements, and favors no viewpoints. It only provides for free access to all ideas through which any and all sides of causes and movements may be expressed, discussed, and argued. The librarian cannot let his own preferences limit his degree of tolerance, for freedom is indivisible. Toleration is meaningless without toleration for the detestable.

It soon became apparent that this lengthy and somewhat unwieldy document had been formulated to address a specific situation arising in the late 1960s and early 1970s. During this time many people of a liberal or leftist political orientation, who in the past had stood in the forefront of the anticensorship battle, were falling, intentionally or not, into the very practice they had previously opposed when espoused by others. By the end of the 1970s, however, although the problem addressed by the policy continued, new instances of censorship had arisen in which other would-be censors also sought to justify their actions by support for broadly accepted social values. In reviewing the policy in the early 1980s, the IFC concluded that a broader statement covering the influence of conflicting values, philosophies, and points of view on library collections, and reaffirming the library's commitment to the inclusion of all, would be more appropriate.

At first the Committee tried to expand the number of "isms" covered by the policy to include such phenomena as anti-Semitism, communism and anticommunism, homosexuality, and the like. It quickly became obvious, however, that this approach would not only be extremely awkward but, like the original policy, would tie the document to the temporal particularities of the period in which it was written. The Committee therefore decided to formulate and present to the Council a new interpretation, expanding more broadly on the call in the *Library Bill of Rights* for libraries "to provide materials and information presenting all points of view on current and historical issues."

The new policy was titled "Diversity in Collection Development." These words were not lightly chosen. Indeed, the IFC initially had preferred the title "Balanced Collections." In the early 1980s, however, several groups and individuals actively involved in increasing censorship pressures, largely from the right of center, also had raised the demand for "balance" in library holdings. Insofar as this was a call for libraries to be more inclusive in collection development, it was welcomed by ALA. Many, however, also saw in the demand for "balance" a dangerous, if hidden, threat of censorship.

The concept of balanced collections may be misunderstood to presuppose a bias toward moderation and to place limitations on the acquisition of materials thought to be "extreme," because these might skew the "balance" of the collection. The requirement that a library collection be "balanced" could be construed to imply for instance, that, leftist materials cannot be acquired if there is no equivalent material from the right, or vice versa. If balance is sought in this formal sense, librarians are placed in a position that requires them to act as validators of opinion by assigning values, or "weights," to differing points of view across the spectrum of opinion. In other words, a misconceived if well-intentioned requirement for balance may also make of the librarian a kind of censor.

Recognizing this possible misapplication of the notion of balance, the Committee opted to emphasize instead the concept of diversity. Not only is the library obliged to include many differing views in its collection, but materials representing the broadest diversity of human thought and creativity should, in general, be actively sought, irrespective of the opinions, prejudices, values, and tastes of the librarian, and whether or not a given numerical or other balance of views can be achieved at a given moment. The Committee completed work on the document at the 1982 Annual Conference in Philadelphia and on July 14, 1982, the Council approved the new interpretation of the *Library Bill of Rights*, noting that it replaced the former policy on "Racism, Sexism, and Other -Isms in Library Materials," which was then rescinded. The new policy read as follows:

> Throughout history, the focus of censorship has vacillated from generation to generation. Books and other materials have not been selected or have been removed from library collections for many reasons, among which are prejudicial language and ideas, political content, economic theory, social philosophies, religious beliefs, and/or sexual forms of expression.
>
> Some examples of this may include removing or not selecting materials because they are considered by some as racist or sexist; not purchasing conservative religious materials; not selecting materials about or by minorities because it is thought these groups or interests are not represented in a community; or not providing information on or materials from nonmainstream political entities.
>
> Librarians may seek to increase user awareness of materials on various social concerns by many means, including, but not limited to, issuing bibliographies and presenting exhibits and programs.
>
> Librarians have a professional responsibility to be inclusive, not exclusive, in collection development and in the provision of interlibrary loan. Access to all materials legally obtainable should be assured to the user, and policies should not unjustly exclude materials even if offensive to the librarian or the user. Collection

development should reflect the philosophy inherent in Article II of the *Library Bill of Rights:* "Libraries should provide materials and information presenting all points of view on current and historical issues. Materials should not be proscribed or removed because of partisan or doctrinal disapproval." A balanced collection reflects a diversity of materials, not an equality of numbers. Collection development and the selection of materials should be done according to professional standards and established selection and review procedures.

There are many complex facets to any issue, and variations of context in which issues may be expressed, discussed, or interpreted. Librarians have a professional responsibility to be fair, just, and equitable and to give all library users equal protection in guarding against violation of the library patrons' liberty to read, view, or listen to materials and resources protected by the First Amendment, no matter what the viewpoint of the author, creator, or selector. Librarians have an obligation to protect library collections from removal of materials based on personal bias or prejudice, and to select and support the access to materials on all subjects that meet, as closely as possible, the needs and interests of all persons in the community which the library serves. This includes materials that reflect political, economic, religious, social, minority, and sexual issues.

Intellectual freedom, the essence of equitable library services, promotes no causes, furthers no movements, and favors no viewpoints. It only provides for free access to all expressions of ideas through which any and all sides of a question, cause, or movement may be explored. Toleration is meaningless without tolerance for what some may consider detestable. Librarians cannot justly permit their own preferences to limit their degree of tolerance in collection development, because freedom is indivisible.

Note: This policy replaces the policy "Racism, Sexism, and Other -Isms in Library Materials."

The Interpretation "Diversity in Collection Development" was revised in 1989 to acknowledge the responsibility of all librarians to be sensitive to the language(s) in common use in the community the library serves. Finally, the phrase claiming that intellectual freedom "promotes no causes, furthers no movements, and favors no viewpoints" was deleted from the text.

The newly revised Interpretation was adopted by the Council on January 10, 1990.

2.7

Economic Barriers to Information Access

An Interpretation of the *Library Bill of Rights*

A democracy presupposes an informed citizenry. The First Amendment mandates the right of all persons to free expression, and the corollary right to receive the constitutionally protected expression of others. The publicly supported library provides free and equal access to information for all people of the community the library serves. While the roles, goals and objectives of publicly supported libraries may differ, they share this common mission.

The library's essential mission must remain the first consideration for librarians and governing bodies faced with economic pressures and competition for funding.

In support of this mission, the American Library Association has enumerated certain principles of library services in the *Library Bill of Rights*.

Principles Governing Fines, Fees, and User Charges

Article I of the *Library Bill of Rights* states:

> Books and other library resources should be provided for the interest, information, and enlightenment of all people of the community the library serves.

Article V of the *Library Bill of Rights* states:

A person's right to use a library should not be denied or abridged because of origin, age, background, or views.

The American Library Association opposes the charging of user fees for the provision of information by all libraries and information services that receive their major support from public funds. All information resources that are provided directly or indirectly by the library, regardless of technology, format, or methods of delivery, should be readily, equally, and equitably accessible to all library users.

Libraries that adhere to these principles systematically monitor their programs of service for potential barriers to access and strive to eliminate such barriers when they occur. All library policies and procedures, particularly those involving fines, fees, or other user charges, should be scrutinized for potential barriers to access. All services should be designed and implemented with care, so as not to infringe on or interfere with the provision or delivery of information and resources for all users. Services should be re-evaluated on a regular basis to ensure that the library's basic mission remains uncompromised.

Librarians and governing bodies should look for alternative models and methods of library administration that minimize distinctions among users based on their economic status or financial condition. They should resist the temptation to impose user fees to alleviate financial pressures, at long-term cost to institutional integrity and public confidence in libraries.

Library services that involve the provision of information, regardless of format, technology, or method of delivery, should be made available to all library users on an equal and equitable basis. Charging fees for the use of library collections, services, programs, or facilities that were purchased with public funds raises barriers to access. Such fees effectively abridge or deny access for some members of the community because they reinforce distinctions among users based on their ability and willingness to pay.

Principles Governing Conditions of Funding

Article II of the *Library Bill of Rights* states:

Materials should not be proscribed or removed because of partisan or doctrinal disapproval.

Article III of the *Library Bill of Rights* states:

Libraries should challenge censorship in the fulfillment of their responsibility to provide information and enlightenment.

Article IV of the *Library Bill of Rights* states:

Libraries should cooperate with all persons and groups concerned with resisting abridgment of free expression and free access to ideas.

The American Library Association opposes any legislative or regulatory attempt to impose content restrictions on library resources, or to limit user access to information, as a condition of funding for publicly supported libraries and information services.

The First Amendment guarantee of freedom of expression is violated when the right to receive that expression is subject to arbitrary restrictions based on content.

Librarians and governing bodies should examine carefully any terms or conditions attached to library funding and should oppose attempts to limit through such conditions full and equal access to information because of content. This principle applies equally to private gifts or bequests and to public funds. In particular, librarians and governing bodies have an obligation to reject such restrictions when the effect of the restriction is to limit equal and equitable access to information.

Librarians and governing bodies should cooperate with all efforts to create a community consensus that publicly supported libraries require funding unfettered by restrictions. Such a consensus supports the library mission to provide the free and unrestricted exchange of information and ideas necessary to a functioning democracy.

The Association's historic position in this regard is stated clearly in a number of Association policies: 50.4, "Free Access to Information"; 50.9, "Financing of Libraries"; 51.2, "Equal Access to Library Service"; 51.3, "Intellectual Freedom"; 53, "Intellectual Freedom Policies"; 59.1, "Policy Objectives"; and 60, "Library Services for the Poor."

Adopted by the ALA Council, June 30, 1993.

Economic Barriers to Information Access

In 1989, the American Library Association's Minority Concerns Committee requested that Council direct the Intellectual Freedom Committee to review the *Library Bill of Rights* to ensure that it included protection for intellectual freedom without regard to language or economic status. The ALA Council issued that directive, thereby launching a three-year process of review of all of the Interpretations of the *Library Bill of Rights*, of which all save one were amended to address the question of language. Throughout its discussions, the IFC discussed whether a separate or new Interpretation, specifically dealing with questions relating to economic status, was needed; it concluded that the prevalence of questions about fees for library services necessitated a new Interpretation.

The process of gathering information for what became "Economic Barriers to Information Access" began at the 1991 Annual Conference in Atlanta, where the IFC sponsored an open hearing on fees for library service to receive comments from librarians working in all areas of library service and types of libraries. A first draft of an Interpretation was developed at the 1992 Midwinter Meeting in San Antonio, and widely circulated for comment prior to and during the 1992 Annual Conference in San Francisco. Continuing its process of receiving comments and suggestions on the draft, the Committee met, at the 1993 Midwinter Meeting in Denver, with representatives of the Library of Congress (LC), who themselves were contemplating charging fees for library services.

Since 1977, the American Library Association has had on the books a policy (50.4) opposing fees for library services, specifically information services. But libraries have always felt pressure both from funding agencies and internally to recover the cost of providing certain types of services, particularly in times of economic hardship. In 1993, the atmosphere of fiscal restraint was being felt by all types of libraries all over the country, and had reached to the Library of Congress itself.

Judith Farley, Daniel Molhollan, and Winston Tabb, representatives of the Library of Congress, met with the IFC at the 1993 Midwinter Meeting to discuss a bill then pending before Congress dealing with LC's funding and fees. While expressing concerns about user charges, they were troubled by statements in the then current draft Interpretation flatly opposing the charging of user fees. At that time, LC was the subject of a funding bill in Congress defining three different types of library service: core, national, and specialized. Core services would be free, national services would have fees related to distribution costs only, and specialized services would be provided on a full cost-recovery basis. The proposal generated intensive discussion at the Intellectual Freedom Committee meeting during that 1993 Midwinter. The net result of the discussion was to solidify the Committee's belief that an Interpretation of the *Library Bill of Rights* addressing economic barriers to information access must be unequivocal with regard to the provision of information in libraries—an information "have and have-not" society, based upon the ability to pay for information services in libraries, must be avoided. As IFC chair Candace Morgan explained in her Report to Council for that Midwinter meeting, the draft was revised to "address the Committee's growing concern over the creeping acceptance, by governing bodies and funding sources, of the idea that libraries should be required to recover some costs through user charges, which have the potential to create barriers to access based on economic status."

Another issue that was raised during the discussion was potential restrictions and conditions imposed upon information access by donors. Libraries sometimes receive donations of money or materials which carry with them conditions imposing restrictions upon access which discriminate against some library users.

Finally, the pervasive atmosphere of fiscal restraint had generated pressures from local government upon libraries to charge fees for services. The Committee noted that much of that pressure reflected a lack of understanding of the unique mission of publicly supported libraries—no other agency serves as a public forum through which the ideals of the First Amendment may be realized. The Committee added introductory language to the draft Interpretation to place libraries "firmly within the realm of essential public services, and to address how libraries, which must compete for funding, can examine their policies to ensure that the essential mission of providing free access to information is protected." The Committee wanted to encourage libraries to educate their funding agencies about their unique role and to urge them to insist on being treated as unique by local governments. The new introductory language in the revised draft Interpretation squarely placed libraries within the arena of First Amendment law—as public forums for access to information subject to First Amendment principles and responsible to their users to provide information access without charge.

Following consideration of testimony presented at the 1991 hearing, comments made on the draft and the concerns of the representatives of the Library of Congress, a substantially revised version was circulated for comment to the ALA Executive Board, the ALA Council, ALA Committees, Divisions, Round Tables, chairs of state intellectual freedom committees, and interested librarians, prior to the 1993 Annual Conference. Additional written and oral comments continued to be received until and during the Conference, where the Committee again met with representatives of the Library of Congress. A final draft was offered to Council for its adoption at that 1993 Annual Conference in New Orleans.

The final version takes a strong position against the charging of fees and urges libraries to examine their policies and practices to ensure that information access is not restricted by being based upon the ability to pay. Although the Interpretation was adopted by Council at the 1993 Annual Conference, the discussion of the principles it states continues. Many libraries, still suffering severe budgetary constraints, have contended that the document is too idealistic and sets a standard that libraries cannot realistically meet. Others acknowledge that the document states central matters of principle in deliberately strong terms, that libraries must stake their ground and refuse to accede to demands to charge fees and become "entrepreneurial." Instead, they should demand that the essential services they provide be adequately funded and new services not be mandated unless appropriate budgets to pay for them are supplied by funding agencies.

The debate over charges for information services is sure to continue as more sophisticated, and more expensive, modes of information access find their way into libraries. Providing patrons with access to the Internet, as well as other electronic networks and database services, some of which are themselves fee-based, will continue to be a budgetary issue for libraries, and the temptation to charge fees for the use of newer technologies is ever present. In the process of developing "Economic Barriers to Information Access," a history of charging fees for new technologies in many libraries emerged. The Intellectual Freedom Committee determined that the best way to describe the resources provided by publicly supported libraries that the Committee believed should be free of all user charges was through the use of the expression "information resources and services." The document does not preclude the possibility of charging fees for noninformation services, such as photocopying. The language of the Interpretation is intentionally broad, however, in order to preclude the possibility of extended bickering over what constitutes, for example, "core" service or the provision of information for which user charges should not be imposed. The final document sets forth an ideal toward which libraries are encouraged to aspire and encourages continuous scrutiny of library policy, procedure, and operation for potential economic barriers to ensure that access to information is not proscribed according to the ability to pay.

2.8

Evaluating Library Collections

An Interpretation of the *Library Bill of Rights*

The continuous review of library materials is necessary as a means of maintaining an active library collection of current interest to users. In the process, materials may be added and physically deteriorated or obsolete materials may be replaced or removed in accordance with the collection maintenance policy of a given library and the needs of the community it serves. Continued evaluation is closely related to the goals and responsibilities of libraries and is a valuable tool of collection development. This procedure is not to be used as a convenient means to remove materials presumed to be controversial or disapproved of by segments of the community. Such abuse of the evaluation function violates the principles of intellectual freedom and is in opposition to the preamble and Articles I and II of the *Library Bill of Rights*, which state:

> The American Library Association affirms that all libraries are forums for information and ideas, and that the following basic policies should guide their services.
>
> I. Books and other library resources should be provided for the interest, information, and enlightenment of all people of the community the library serves. Materials should not be excluded because of the origin, background, or views of those contributing to their creation.

II. Libraries should provide materials and information presenting all points of view on current and historical issues. Materials should not be proscribed or removed because of partisan or doctrinal disapproval.

The American Library Association opposes such "silent censorship" and strongly urges that libraries adopt guidelines setting forth the positive purposes and principles of evaluation of materials in library collections.

Adopted February 2, 1973; amended July 1, 1981, by the ALA Council.

Evaluating Library Collections

In both theory and practice, library collections undergo continual reevaluation to ensure that they fulfill and remain responsive to the goals of the institution and the needs of library patrons. The reevaluation process, however, can also be used to achieve the purposes of the censor, purposes manifestly inconsistent with Articles I and II of the *Library Bill of Rights*.

At the 1972 Midwinter Meeting in Chicago, the Intellectual Freedom Committee realized the necessity of an Interpretation of the *Library Bill of Rights* with regard to the more general issues involved in reevaluating library collections. Accordingly, the Committee announced its intent to prepare a statement on reevaluation. The document was approved by the Intellectual Freedom Committee at the 1972 Annual Conference in Chicago. It was submitted to the ALA Council at the 1973 Midwinter Meeting in Washington, D.C., and was adopted on February 2, 1973, under the title "Reevaluating Library Collections."

> The continuous review of library collections to remove physically deteriorated or obsolete materials is one means to maintain active library collections of current interest to users.* Continued

---

* The traditional term "weeding," implying "the removal of a noxious growth," is purposely avoided because of the imprecise nature of the term.

reevaluation is closely related to the goals and responsibilities of libraries, and is a valuable tool of collection building. This procedure, however, is sometimes used as a convenient means to remove materials thought to be too controversial or disapproved of by segments of the community. Such abuse of the reevaluation function violates the principles of intellectual freedom and is in opposition to Articles I and II of the *Library Bill of Rights*, which state that:

> As a responsibility of library service, books and other library materials selected should be chosen for values of interest, information, and enlightenment of all the people of the community. In no case should library materials be excluded because of the race or nationality or the social, political, or religious views of the authors.
>
> Libraries should provide books and other materials presenting all points of view concerning the problems and issues of our times; no library materials should be proscribed or removed from libraries because of partisan or doctrinal disapproval.

The American Library Association opposes such "silent censorship," and recommends that libraries adopt guidelines setting forth the positive purposes and principles for reevaluation of materials in library collections.

In 1981, the policy was rewritten by the IFC to reflect the changes that had been made in the 1980 version of the *Library Bill of Rights*. In the process, a number of editorial changes were made in the text with the aim of increasing its forcefulness. The most significant amendment recommended by the IFC was a change in the title of the document from "Reevaluating Library Collections" to "Evaluating Library Collections." The change was suggested because the process of evaluating library materials for acquisition or retention is a single ongoing process and, in principle, is never completed and then redone. Moreover, the Intellectual Freedom Committee thought that it could be falsely inferred from the word "reevaluating" that initial evaluations of works had been incorrect. The revision was approved by the Council on July 1, 1981.

2.9

Exhibit Spaces and Bulletin Boards

An Interpretation of the *Library Bill of Rights*

Libraries often provide exhibit spaces and bulletin boards. The uses made of these spaces should conform to the *Library Bill of Rights:* Article I states, "Materials should not be excluded because of the origin, background, or views of those contributing to their creation." Article II states, "Materials should not be proscribed or removed because of partisan or doctrinal disapproval." Article VI maintains that exhibit space should be made available "on an equitable basis, regardless of the beliefs or affiliations of individuals or groups requesting their use."

In developing library exhibits, staff members should endeavor to present a broad spectrum of opinion and a variety of viewpoints. Libraries should not shrink from developing exhibits because of controversial content or because of the beliefs or affiliations of those whose work is represented. Just as libraries do not endorse the viewpoints of those whose works are represented in their collections, libraries also do not endorse the beliefs or viewpoints of topics which may be the subject of library exhibits.

Exhibit areas often are made available for use by community groups. Libraries should formulate a written policy for the use of these exhibit areas to assure that space is provided on an equitable basis to all groups which request it.

Written policies for exhibit space use should be stated in inclusive rather than exclusive terms. For example, a policy that the library's exhibit space is open "to organizations engaged in educational, cultural, intellectual, or charitable activities" is an inclusive statement of the limited uses of the exhibit space. This defined limitation would permit religious groups to use the exhibit space because they engage in intellectual activities, but would exclude most commercial uses of the exhibit space.

A publicly supported library may limit use of its exhibit space to strictly "library-related" activities, provided that the limitation is clearly circumscribed and is viewpoint neutral.

Libraries may include in this policy rules regarding the time, place, and manner of use of the exhibit space, so long as the rules are content-neutral and are applied in the same manner to all groups wishing to use the space. A library may wish to limit access to exhibit space to groups within the community served by the library. This practice is acceptable provided that the same rules and regulations apply to everyone, and that exclusion is not made on the basis of the doctrinal, religious, or political beliefs of the potential users.

The library should not censor or remove an exhibit because some members of the community may disagree with its content. Those who object to the content of any exhibit held at the library should be able to submit their complaint and/or their own exhibit proposal to be judged according to the policies established by the library.

Libraries may wish to post a permanent notice near the exhibit area stating that the library does not advocate or endorse the viewpoints of exhibits or exhibitors.

Libraries which make bulletin boards available to public groups for posting notices of public interest should develop criteria for the use of these spaces based on the same considerations as those outlined above. Libraries may wish to develop criteria regarding the size of material to be displayed, the length of time materials may remain on the bulletin board, the frequency with which material may be posted for the same group, and the geographic area from which notices will be accepted.

Adopted July 2, 1991, by the ALA Council.

Exhibit Spaces and Bulletin Boards

Use of library exhibit spaces and meeting rooms became a subject of developing controversy in the 1970s. These years saw several publicized efforts to deny access to such facilities to controversial groups or exhibitors. In North Carolina, for example, an exhibit sponsored by the Ku Klux Klan at a public library sparked a violent confrontation with protestors. At the University of California library at Berkeley, Turkish students protested the "one-sidedness" of an exhibit on the early twentieth-century massacre of Armenians by Turks, which had been placed in the library by students of Armenian ancestry. In several places, attempts were made to deny use of such facilities to certain groups on the grounds either that the groups themselves were advocates of violence or that the threat of violence associated with their meetings—including threats made against these meetings by the groups' opponents—posed a danger to library employees and patrons or to library property. At the same time, exhibits mounted by libraries themselves sometimes came under fire. In Virginia, for instance, an exhibit of books about homosexuality in a public library collection was accused of promoting this practice and of obscenity. All these efforts to censor library exhibits were in violation of Article VI of the *Library Bill of Rights*.

Yet the 1970s were also marked by some confusion within ALA about the applicability of Article VI, as it was formulated in the 1967 version of the *Library Bill of Rights*. In particular, academic and school libraries pointed out that the provision was written to apply in reality only to public libraries, and public librarians noted that not enough flexibility existed even to accommodate the varying situations of public libraries.

The 1980 revision of the *Library Bill of Rights* took account of these objections, and the revision of Article VI in that year successfully remedied its major defects. (See part I, section 1: "*Library Bill of Rights:* History.") At the 1980 Annual Conference in New York, however, the IFC, with Frances C. Dean as chair, decided that, given both the increasing number of incidents and the admitted complexity of applying even the revised Article in practice, a written policy interpreting the Article would be desirable.

The Intellectual Freedom Committee agreed that the key to applying the Article was the need to maintain flexibility, while upholding a standard of fairness. On this basis a policy was prepared and, at the 1981 Midwinter Meeting in Washington, D.C., presented to the Council, which adopted it as an ALA policy on February 4, 1981. It read as follows:

> As part of their program of service, many libraries provide meeting rooms and exhibit spaces for individuals and groups. Article VI of the *Library Bill of Rights* states that such facilities should be made available to the public served by the given library "on an equitable basis, regardless of the beliefs or affiliations of individuals or groups requesting their use."
>
> In formulating this position, the American Library Association sought to accommodate the broad range of practices among public, academic, school and other libraries, while upholding a standard of fairness. Libraries maintaining exhibit and meeting room facilities for outside groups and individuals should develop and publish policy statements governing their use. These statements can properly define and restrict eligibility for use as long as the qualifications do not pertain to the content of a meeting or exhibit or to the beliefs or affiliations of the sponsors.
>
> It is appropriate for a library to limit access to meeting rooms or exhibit space to members of the specific community served by the library or to groups of a specific category. It is not proper to apply such limitations in ways which favor points of

view or organizations advocating certain viewpoints. For example, some libraries permit religious groups to use meeting facilities, while others do not. According to Article VI, both policies are acceptable as long as all religious groups are treated in the same way, irrespective of their doctrines.

Exhibits and meetings sponsored by the library itself should be organized in a manner consistent with the *Library Bill of Rights*, especially Article II which states that "libraries should provide materials and information presenting all points of view." However, in granting meeting or exhibit space to outside individuals and groups, the library should make no effort to censor or amend the content of the exhibit or meeting. Those who object to or disagree with the content of any exhibit or meeting held at the library should be entitled to submit their own exhibit or meeting proposals which should be judged according to the policies established by the library.

The library may properly limit the use of its meeting rooms to meetings which are open to the public, or it may make space available for both public and private sessions. Again, however, the same standard should be applicable to all.

In 1989, revisions were undertaken to reflect nondiscrimination on the basis of language or economic status. Discussion on appropriate changes in the Interpretation continued through June 26, 1990, at which time the Committee voted to rescind two sentences of the Interpretation as an interim measure.

For example, some libraries permit religious groups to use meeting facilities, while others do not. According to Article VI, both policies are acceptable as long as all religious groups are treated in the same way, irrespective of their doctrines.

The sentences were rescinded in light of a recent court decision in favor of a religious organization that had been denied use of a library meeting room. (See part V, section 4: "Public Libraries as Limited Public Fora.") The policy then read as follows:

As part of their program of service, many libraries provide meeting rooms and exhibit spaces for individuals and groups. Article VI of the *Library Bill of Rights* states that such facilities should be made available to the public served by the given library "on an equitable basis, regardless of the beliefs or affiliations of individuals or groups requesting their use."

In formulating this position, the American Library Association sought to accommodate the broad range of practices among public, academic, school and other libraries, while upholding a standard of fairness. Libraries maintaining exhibit and meeting room facilities for outside groups and individuals should develop and publish policy statements governing their use. These statements can properly define and restrict eligibility for use as long as the qualifications do not pertain to the content of a meeting or exhibit or to the beliefs or affiliations of the sponsors.

It is appropriate for a library to limit access to meeting rooms or exhibit space to members of the specific community served by the library or to groups of a specific category. The library may properly limit the use of its meeting rooms to meetings which are open to the public, or it may make space available for both public and private sessions. It is not proper to apply such limitations in ways which favor points of view or organizations advocating certain viewpoints.

Exhibits and meetings sponsored by the library itself should be organized in a manner consistent with the *Library Bill of Rights*, especially Article II which states that "libraries should provide materials and information presenting all points of view." However, in granting meeting or exhibit space to outside individuals and groups, the library should make no effort to censor or amend the content of the exhibit or meeting. Those who object to or disagree with the content of any exhibit or meeting held at the library should be entitled to submit their own exhibit or meeting proposals which should be judged according to the policies established by the library.

Following adoption of the interim language, continuing concerns about the meaning of "viewpoint neutral restrictions," the rules governing designated public forums, and commercial uses of library meeting rooms led to a consensus decision to rewrite the policy totally.

In January 1991, two separate Interpretations—"Meeting Rooms" and "Exhibit Spaces and Bulletin Boards"—were introduced. Recent court decisions supporting the right of religious groups to have access to public forums for their meetings raised questions that were best dealt with in a discrete meeting-room policy, rather than under the same policy rubric that included meeting rooms, exhibit spaces, and bulletin boards. After additional discussion about fees, commercial uses, and disclaimers to clarify the library's position as a neutral host and not an advocate of particular meetings or exhibits, the Committee voted to adopt the two Interpretations for circulation to all ALA units, the Council, and the executive Board for comment.

The two policies were adopted as revised on July 2, 1991, at the Annual Conference. (For the policy "Meeting Rooms," see part I, section 2.13.)

2.10

Expurgation of Library Materials

An Interpretation of the *Library Bill of Rights*

Expurgating library materials is a violation of the *Library Bill of Rights*. Expurgation as defined by this Interpretation includes any deletion, excision, alteration, editing, or obliteration of any part(s) of books or other library resources by the library, its agent, or its parent institution (if any). By such expurgation, the library is in effect denying access to the complete work and the entire spectrum of ideas that the work intended to express. Such action stands in violation of Articles I, II, and III of the *Library Bill of Rights*, which state that "Materials should not be excluded because of the origin, background, or views of those contributing to their creation," that "Materials should not be proscribed or removed because of partisan or doctrinal disapproval," and that "Libraries should challenge censorship in the fulfillment of their responsibility to provide information and enlightenment."

The act of expurgation has serious implications. It involves a determination that it is necessary to restrict access to the complete work. This is censorship. When a work is expurgated, under the assumption that certain portions of that work would be harmful to minors, the situation is no less serious.

Expurgation of any books or other library resources imposes a restriction, without regard to the rights and desires of all library users, by limiting access to ideas and information.

Further, expurgation without written permission from the holder of the copyright on the material may violate the copyright provisions of the United States Code.

Adopted February 2, 1973; amended July 1, 1981; amended January 10, 1990, by the ALA Council.

Expurgation of Library Materials

The December 1971 issue of *School Library Journal* (page 7) carried the following report submitted by one of its readers:

> Maurice Sendak might faint but a staff member of Caldwell Parish Library [Louisiana], knowing that the patrons of the community might object to the illustrations in *In the Night Kitchen*, solved the problem by diapering the little boys with white tempera paint. Other libraries might wish to do the same.

In response, Ursula Nordstrom, publisher of Harper Junior Books, sent a statement to more than 380 librarians, professors, publishers, authors, and artists throughout the United States:

> [The news item sent to *School Library Journal*] is representative of several such reports about Maurice Sendak's *In the Night Kitchen*, a book for children, that have come out of public and school libraries throughout the country.
>
> At first, the thought of librarians painting diapers or pants on the naked hero of Sendak's book might seem amusing, merely a harmless eccentricity on the part of some prim few. On reconsideration, however, this behavior should be recognized for what it is: an act of censorship by mutilation rather than by obvious suppression.

More than 425 persons signed the statement of protest circulated by Miss Nordstrom.

The expurgation of *In the Night Kitchen* was brought to the attention of the Intellectual Freedom Committee by the Children's Book Council in June 1972. During its meeting at the 1972 ALA Annual Conference in Chicago, the Committee decided, after considering whether expurgation was already covered by the *Library Bill of Rights*, that a statement should be issued specifically on expurgation. During the 1973 Midwinter Meeting in Washington, D.C., the Committee approved a statement on expurgation of library materials and sent it to the ALA Council for approval. The statement which was adopted by the Council as an ALA policy on February 2, 1973, read as follows:

> Library materials are chosen for their value and interest to the community the library serves. If library materials were acquired for these reasons and in accordance with a written statement on materials selection, then to expurgate must be interpreted as a violation of the *Library Bill of Rights*. For purposes of this statement, expurgation includes deletion, excision, alteration or obliteration. By such expurgation, the library is in effect denying access to the complete work and the full ideas that the work was intended to express; such action stands in violation of Article II of the *Library Bill of Rights*, which states that "no library materials should be proscribed or removed from libraries because of partisan or doctrinal disapproval."
>
> The act of expurgation has serious implications. It involves a determination by an individual that it is necessary to restrict the availability of that material. It is, in fact, censorship.
>
> When a work is expurgated, under the assumption that certain sections of that work would be harmful to minors, the situation is no less serious. Expurgation of any library materials imposes a restriction, without regard to the rights and desires of all library users.

In 1981, during the review of all the Interpretations of the *Library Bill of Rights*, the IFC reviewed the policy on expurgation and made several changes designed to add clarity to and strengthen the document. Most important, the IFC recommended basing the argument of the Interpretation not only on Article II of the *Library Bill of*

Rights but on Articles II and III as well. The revision was adopted by the Council on July 1, 1981, and read as follows:

> Books and other library resources are selected for their value, interest, and importance to the people of the community the library serves. Since books and other library resources are acquired for these reasons and in accordance with a written statement on materials selection, then expurgating them must be interpreted as a violation of the *Library Bill of Rights*. Expurgation as defined by this Interpretation includes any deletion, excision, alteration, or obliteration of any part(s) of books or other library resources by the library. By such expurgation, the library is in effect denying access to the complete work and the entire spectrum of ideas that the work intended to express; such action stands in violation of Articles I, II, and III of the *Library Bill of Rights*, which state that "Materials should not be excluded because of the origin, background, or views of those contributing to their creation"; that "Materials should not be proscribed or removed because of partisan or doctrinal disapproval"; and that "Libraries should challenge censorship in the fulfillment of their responsibility to provide information and enlightenment."
>
> The act of expurgation has serious implications. It involves a determination that it is necessary to restrict complete access to that material. This is censorship. When a work is expurgated, under the assumption that certain portions of that work would be harmful to minors, the situation is no less serious.
>
> Expurgation of any books or other library resources imposes a restriction, without regard to the rights and desires of all library users, by limiting access to ideas and information.

At the June 1989 Annual Conference in Dallas, the Interpretation "Expurgation of Library Materials" was revised in accordance with the request of the Minority Concerns Committee for review of the *Library Bill of Rights* to ensure that discrimination on the basis of language and economic status would be addressed. The IFC adopted a revised version, which was subsequently circulated for comments.

At the January 1990 ALA Midwinter Meeting, minor editorial changes were made, and the new draft was adopted and recommended to the Council. On January 10, 1990, the Interpretation became ALA policy.

2.11

Free Access to Libraries
for Minors

An Interpretation of the *Library Bill of Rights*

Library policies and procedures which effectively deny minors equal access to all library resources available to other users violate the *Library Bill of Rights*. The American Library Association opposes all attempts to restrict access to library services, materials, and facilities based on the age of library users.

Article V of the *Library Bill of Rights* states, "A person's right to use a library should not be denied or abridged because of origin, age, background, or views." The "right to use a library" includes free access to, and unrestricted use of, all the services, materials, and facilities the library has to offer. Every restriction on access to, and use of, library resources, based solely on the chronological age, educational level, or legal emancipation of users violates Article V.

Libraries are charged with the mission of developing resources to meet the diverse information needs and interests of the communities they serve. Services, materials, and facilities which fulfill the needs and interests of library users at different stages in their personal development are a necessary part of library resources. The needs and interests of each library user, and resources appropriate to meet those needs and interests, must be determined on an individual basis. Librarians cannot predict what resources will best fulfill the needs and interests of any individual user based on a single criterion such as chronological age, level of education, or legal emancipation.

The selection and development of library resources should not be diluted because of minors having the same access to library resources as adult users. Institutional self-censorship diminishes the credibility of the library in the community, and restricts access for all library users.

Librarians and governing bodies should not resort to age restrictions on access to library resources in an effort to avoid actual or anticipated objections from parents or anyone else. The mission, goals, and objectives of libraries do not authorize librarians or governing bodies to assume, abrogate, or overrule the rights and responsibilities of parents or legal guardians. Librarians and governing bodies should maintain that parents—and only parents—have the right and the responsibility to restrict the access of their children—and only their children—to library resources. Parents or legal guardians who do not want their children to have access to certain library services, materials or facilities, should so advise their children. Librarians and governing bodies cannot assume the role of parents or the functions of parental authority in the private relationship between parent and child. Librarians and governing bodies have a public and professional obligation to provide equal access to all library resources for all library users.

Librarians have a professional commitment to ensure that all members of the community they serve have free and equal access to the entire range of library resources regardless of content, approach, format, or amount of detail. This principle of library service applies equally to all users, minors as well as adults. Librarians and governing bodies must uphold this principle in order to provide adequate and effective service to minors.

Adopted June 30, 1972; amended July 1, 1981; July 3, 1991, by the ALA Council.

Free Access to Libraries for Minors

The question of whether or not intellectual freedom in libraries applies to children and young adults has been debated by librarians since the early years of the profession's involvement with intellectual freedom. The question was considered many times by the Intellectual Freedom Committee and led to the preconference institute titled Intellectual Freedom and the Teenager, held in San Francisco, June 23–25, 1967.

Sponsored jointly by the Intellectual Freedom Committee, the Young Adult Services Division, and the American Association of School Librarians, and attended by approximately four hundred librarians, the preconference featured a variety of speakers of national reputation, including author Kenneth Rexroth, attorneys Stanley Fleishman and Alex P. Allain, book-review editor Robert Kirsh, and library young-adult consultant Esther Helfand. The most outspoken panelist was Edgar L. Freidenberg, author of *Coming of Age in America*, who told participants:

> The library is just one more place where the kids are taught they are second-class citizens. They learn this not only from the books pressed upon them by the helpful librarian but even more so from the very atmosphere of the place.[1]

In his summary of the three-day meeting, Ervin Gaines, chair of the IFC, dwelt at length on Freidenberg's comments:

> He made the assumption that intellectual freedom was an in-alienable right and that age is not a morally relevant factor and that adults have themselves no right to determine for youth access to ideas. This assumption which came at the very beginning of this talk echoed and re-echoed throughout the conference. There was surprising unanimity of opinion on this particular point.[2]

As the preconference progressed, there was also surprising unanimity on the position that not only teenagers, but all young people, were the focus of the discussions. This was reflected in one of the major recommendations of the institute, "that free access to all books in a library collection be granted to young people."[3]

Later, during the 1967 Annual Conference, Gaines moved that the Council adopt a revised version of the *Library Bill of Rights*. He introduced his motion with the following remarks:

> At a meeting of the Intellectual Freedom Committee yesterday two minor amendments were suggested to this text [the revised *Library Bill of Rights*]. In section 5 we suggest that the word "age" be inserted. . . . This suggestion comes as a result of recommendations from the preconference on Intellectual Freedom and the Teenager, which was held last week.

The change was approved by the Council, and the Association, well in advance of society in general, took a significant stand, approving free access for minors to all the materials in a library collection.

After 1967, the word "age" in the *Library Bill of Rights* was a constant source of confusion. Did it mean children should be able to take home any materials in a library collection, or were some restrictions permissible? What about double card systems or multiple card systems, restricting minors to use of only part of the collection? These and other questions accrued until the IFC's 1972 Midwinter Meeting. Twenty hours of meetings were dominated by discussions of minors and library access problems, all related to the word "age" in the *Library Bill of Rights*.

After the meeting, the Committee announced plans to develop a position statement concerning access to libraries for minors. A draft was subsequently sent, in the spring of 1972, to the boards of the Public Library Association, the American Association of School Librarians, the Children's Services Division, the Young Adult Services Division, and the American Library Trustee Association. At its annual meeting in June 1972, the IFC approved the statement and recommended it to the ALA Council, which adopted it on June 30, 1972, as an ALA policy titled "Free Access to Libraries for Minors." The statement read as follows:

Some library procedures and practices effectively deny minors access to certain services and materials available to adults. Such procedures and practices are not in accord with the *Library Bill of Rights* and are opposed by the American Library Association.

Restrictions take a variety of forms, including, among others, restricted reading rooms for adult use only, library cards limiting circulation of some materials to adults only, closed collections for adult use only, and interlibrary loan service for adult use only.

All limitations in minors' access to library materials and services violate Article V of the *Library Bill of Rights,* which states, "The rights of an individual to the use of a library should not be denied or abridged because of age. . . ." Limiting access to some services and materials to only adults abridges the use of libraries for minors. "Use of the library" includes use of, and access to, all library materials and services.

Restrictions are often initiated under the assumption that certain materials are "harmful" to minors, or in an effort to avoid controversy with parents who might think so. The librarian who would restrict the access of minors to materials and services because of actual or suspected parental objection should bear in mind that he is not in loco parentis in his position as librarian. Individual intellectual levels and family backgrounds are significant factors not accommodated by a uniform policy based upon age.

In today's world, children are exposed to adult life much earlier than in the past. They read materials and view a variety of media on the adult level at home and elsewhere. Current emphasis upon early childhood education has also increased opportunities for young people to learn and to have access to materials, and has decreased the validity of using chronological age as an index to the use of libraries. The period of time during which children are interested in reading materials specifically designed for them grows steadily shorter, and librarians must recognize and adjust to this change if they wish to maintain the patronage of young people.

The American Library Association holds that it is the parent—and only the parent—who may restrict his children—and only his children—from access to library materials and services. The parent who would rather his child did not have access to certain materials should so advise the child.

The word "age" was incorporated into Article V of the *Library Bill of Rights* as a direct result of a preconference titled Intellectual Freedom and the Teenager, held in San Francisco in June 1967. One recommendation of the preconference participants was "that free access to all books in a library collection be granted to young people." The preconference generally concluded that young people are entitled to the same access to libraries and to the materials in libraries as are adults and that materials selection should not be diluted on that account.

This does not mean, for instance, that issuing different types of borrowers' cards to minors and adults is, per se, contrary to the *Library Bill of Rights*. If such practices are used for purposes of gathering statistics, the various kinds of cards carry no implicit or explicit limitations on access to materials and services. Neither does it mean that maintaining separate children's collections is a violation of the *Library Bill of Rights*, provided that no patron is restricted to the use of only certain collections.

The Association's position does not preclude isolating certain materials for legitimate protection of irreplaceable or very costly works from careless use. Such "restricted-use" areas as rare book rooms are appropriate if the materials so classified are genuinely rare, and not merely controversial.

Unrestrictive selection policies, developed with care for principles of intellectual freedom and the *Library Bill of Rights*, should not be vitiated by administrative practices which restrict minors to the use of only part of a library's collections and services.

Following adoption of the 1980 revision of the *Library Bill of Rights*, the IFC reviewed the document anew. Working closely with the intellectual freedom Committees of the Young Adult Services Division and the Association for Library Service to Children (previously the Children's Services Division), at the 1981 Midwinter Meeting and Annual Conference, the Committee made several changes aimed not only at eliminating sex-linked language but also at strengthening the impact of the Interpretation. Reference to the 1967 preconference was deleted as a historical detail irrelevant to a broad public statement of policy, and several key paragraphs were rewritten to communicate the Association's stand with greater force and clarity.

The Intellectual Freedom Committee also decided to delete from the document all references to specific administrative practices such as dual-card systems and restricted-use areas—which, although not always in violation of the principles of the *Library Bill of Rights,* have been employed at times in ways that unfairly limit minors' access to library resources. Limiting discussion of the intellectual freedom implications of such administrative practices to their effects on minors' access in itself tended to legitimize their misuse; and, the Committee concluded, the treatment in the document weakened its overall thrust by appearing to qualify the policy and limit its application. The Committee therefore decided to discuss such practices separately and in a more all-sided way by developing a new Interpretation, to be titled "Administrative Policies and Procedures Affecting Access to Library Resources and Services." That Interpretation was adopted in 1982 but rescinded in 1992, when the Committee adopted "Guidelines for the Development and Implementation of Policies, Regulations and Procedures Affecting Access to Library Materials, Services and Facilities." (See part II, section 6.)

On July 1, 1981, the revision of "Free Access to Libraries for Minors" was adopted by the Council. It read as follows:

> Some library procedures and practices effectively deny minors access to certain services and materials available to adults. Such procedures and practices are not in accord with the *Library Bill of Rights* and are opposed by the American Library Association.

Restrictions take a variety of forms, including, among others, restricted reading rooms for adult use only, library cards limiting circulation of some materials to adults only, closed collections for adult use only, collections limited to teacher use, or restricted according to a student's grade level, and interlibrary loan service for adult use only.

Article V of the *Library Bill of Rights* states that, "A person's right to use a library should not be denied or abridged because of origin, age, background, or views." All limitations on minors' access to library materials and services violate that Article. The "right to use a library" includes use of, and access to, all library materials and services. Thus, practices which allow adults to use some services and materials which are denied to minors abridge the use of libraries based on age.

Material selection decisions are often made and restrictions are often initiated under the assumption that certain materials may be "harmful" to minors, or in an effort to avoid controversy with parents. Libraries or library boards which would restrict the access of minors to materials and services because of actual or suspected parental objections should bear in mind that they do not serve in loco parentis. Varied levels of intellectual development among young people and differing family background and child-rearing philosophies are significant factors not accommodated by a uniform policy based upon age.

In today's world, children are exposed to adult life much earlier than in the past. They read materials and view a variety of media on the adult level at home and elsewhere. Current emphasis upon early childhood education has also increased opportunities for young people to learn and to have access to materials, and has decreased the validity of using chronological age as an index to the use of libraries. The period of time during which children are interested in reading materials specifically designed for them grows steadily shorter, and librarians must recognize and adjust to this change if they wish to serve young people effectively. Librarians have a responsibility to ensure that young people have access to a wide range of informational and recreational materials and services that reflects sufficient diversity to meet the young person's needs.

The American Library Association opposes libraries restricting access to library materials and services for minors and holds that it is the parents—and only parents—who may restrict their children—and only their children—from access to library materials and services. Parents who would rather their children did not have access to certain materials should so advise their children. The library and its staff are responsible for providing equal access to library materials and services for all library users.

The word "age" was incorporated into Article V of the *Library Bill of Rights* because young people are entitled to the same access to libraries and to the materials in libraries as are adults. Materials selection should not be diluted on that account.

Ten years later, at the 1991 Midwinter Meeting, a further revised "Free Access to Libraries for Minors" was adopted by the IFC. The Committee had extensively reworked the document to make the protections for minors' access more explicit and to outline with greater precision librarians' responsibilities toward minors and all library users. The new policy emphasized the role of librarians as information providers and placed the burden of guiding minors squarely on the shoulders of parents.

The definition of library usage was expanded to include use of facilities as well as materials and services. Library trustees were implicated in the new policy as being coresponsible with librarians for providing equal access to all library resources for all library users.

The Midwinter version also included a list of practices that librarians have used to restrict indirectly minors' access to expensive, controversial, or otherwise objectionable materials, including issuing limited-access cards; barring entry to stacks, reserve areas, or reading rooms; charging fees; and simply refusing to perform a service based solely on the age or educational level of the user. This list was intended to alert librarians to specific practices that inhibited minors' access to library materials, services, and facilities, and to discourage these all-too-common practices.

At the 1991 Annual Conference, the Council deleted the list of examples from the final Interpretation before approving it as ALA policy. Many councilors believed that ALA's official position would be more effective and adaptable to changing societal circumstances if the Interpretation were written in broad terms, without a list of potential violations of the principle.

The list of examples that follows is not comprehensive, but suggestive of some of the most commonly used practices that violate the *Library Bill of Rights*. Copies are available upon request from the Office for Intellectual Freedom.

Examples of Age-Based Access Limitations

Some specific examples of denial of equal access include, but are not limited to, the following:

> restricting access to reading or reference rooms, or to otherwise open stack areas, on the basis of the age or school grade level of the user;
> issuing limited access library cards, or otherwise restricting the circulation of materials, on the basis of the age or school grade level of the user;
> assigning materials to special collections, such as parenting, teacher-professional, historical-genealogical collections, and restricting access to these collections, on the basis of the age or school grade level of the user;
> using manual or computerized registration or circulation systems that restrict access to materials, on the basis of the age or school grade level of the user;
> sequestering or otherwise restricting access to material because of its content, on the basis of the age or school grade level of the user;
> requiring or soliciting written permission from a parent or guardian to gain or restrict access to materials because of their content, on the basis of the age or school grade level of the user;
> restricting access to interlibrary loan, FAX, and electronic reference services, on the basis of the age or school grade level of the user;
> restricting access to materials because of their format or their cost—such as computer software, compact discs, periodi-

cals, microfilm-fiche, and videocassettes, on the basis of
the age or school grade level of the user;

charging fees or requiring deposits to gain access to services,
materials, or facilities, on the basis of the age or school
grade level of the user;

refusing to process interlibrary loans, reserves, or reference requests for materials classified as juvenile;

assigning professional-nonprofessional staff to reference
searches, on the basis of the age or school grade level of the
user;

restricting access to library-sponsored programs or events
otherwise designed for general audiences, on the basis of
the age or school grade level of the user;

restricting access to public facilities, such as meeting rooms,
display cases, and notice boards, on the basis of the age or
school grade level of the user.

NOTES

1. *San Francisco Examiner and Chronicle,* June 25, 1967.
2. *Newsletter on Intellectual Freedom* 16:54 (Sept. 1967).
3. Ibid., p.55.

2.12

Library-Initiated Programs as a Resource

An Interpretation of the *Library Bill of Rights*

L ibrary-initiated programs support the mission of the library by
providing users with additional opportunities for information,
education, and recreation. Article I of the *Library Bill of Rights* states:
"Books and other library resources should be provided for the
interest, information, and enlightenment of all people of the community the library serves."

Library-initiated programs take advantage of library staff expertise, collections, services, and facilities to increase access to information and information resources. Library-initiated programs introduce
users and potential users to the resources of the library and to the
library's primary function as a facilitator of information access. The
library may participate in cooperative or joint programs with other
agencies, organizations, institutions, or individuals as part of its
own effort to address information needs and to facilitate information access in the community the library serves.

Library-initiated programs on site and in other locations include,
but are not limited to, speeches, community forums, discussion
groups, demonstrations, displays, and live or media presentations.

Libraries serving multilingual or multicultural communities
make efforts to accommodate the information needs of those for
whom English is a second language. Library-initiated programs
across language and cultural barriers introduce otherwise unserved

populations to the resources of the library and provide access to information.

Library-initiated programs "should not be proscribed or removed (or canceled) because of partisan or doctrinal disapproval" of the contents of the program or the views expressed by the participants, as stated in Article II of the *Library Bill of Rights*. Library sponsorship of a program does not constitute an endorsement of the content of the program or the views expressed by the participants, any more than the purchase of material for the library collection constitutes an endorsement of the contents of the material or the views of its creator.

Library-initiated programs are a library resource, and as such, are developed in accordance with written guidelines, as approved and adopted by the library's policy-making body. These guidelines include an endorsement of the *Library Bill of Rights* and set forth the library's commitment to free and open access to information and ideas for all users.

Library staff select topics, speakers and resource materials for library-initiated programs based on the interests and information needs of the community. Topics, speakers and resource materials are not excluded from library-initiated programs because of possible controversy. Concerns, questions or complaints about library-initiated program are handled according to the same written policy and procedures which govern reconsiderations of other library resources.

Library-initiated programs are offered free of charge and are open to all. Article V of the *Library Bill of Rights* states: "A person's right to use a library should not be denied or abridged because of origin, age, background, or views."

The "right to use a library" encompasses all of the resources the library offers, including the right to attend library-initiated programs. Libraries do not deny or abridge access to library resources, including library-initiated programs, based on an individual's economic background and ability to pay.

Adopted January 27, 1982. Amended June 26, 1990, by the ALA Council.

Library-Initiated Programs as a Resource

A s libraries have sought in recent years to broaden their appeal and to strengthen their ties with the communities they serve, library-initiated programs such as invited public speeches, film showings, reading clubs, and children's game groups, have become an increasingly important and visible part of library service. Such programming, however, also has increasingly become a target for would-be censors. In the 1970s, many communities witnessed efforts to ban controversial speakers from appearing in libraries. Elsewhere, showings of R-rated or allegedly "explicit" films were attacked. In New Rochelle, New York, an Italian-American group objected to a library showing of *The Godfather*, and in North Carolina a French comedy about a homosexual couple, *La Cage aux Folles*, was successfully banned from a public library.

In the early 1980s, some parents' groups objected to several library-sponsored "theme" programs for children, especially those emphasizing magic or the occult. In a few communities, citizens concerned about the alleged spread of occultism and witchcraft sought to terminate use of library facilities for organized playing of the popular game "Dungeons and Dragons."

In response to incidents of this sort and a growing number of inquiries from librarians and library users about the applicability of the *Library Bill of Rights* to such programs, in 1981, at the urging of the Intellectual Freedom Committees of the Young Adult Services Division and the Association for Library Service to Children, the IFC, with J. Dennis Day as chair, decided to develop a policy statement. At the 1982 Midwinter Meeting in Denver, the Committee approved the statement and recommended it to the Council, which adopted it on January 27, 1982, as an Interpretation of the *Library Bill of Rights*, entitled "Library-Initiated Programs as a Resource." It read as follows:

> Library-initiated programming is a library resource that provides information, education, and recreation to library users. Library-initiated programming utilizes library staff, books, library and community resources, resource people, displays, and media presentations. The library often incorporates cooperative programming with other agencies, organizations, and educational institutions, as well as other resources, to communicate with library users. Library-initiated programs should provide "for the interest, information, and enlightenment of all the people of the community the library serves," as stated in Article I of the *Library Bill of Rights*.
>
> The American Library Association believes that library-sponsored programs, as well as library resources, "should not be proscribed or removed (or canceled) because of partisan or doctrinal disapproval" (Article II of the *Library Bill of Rights*).
>
> A person's right to attend a library-initiated program "should not be denied or abridged because of origin, age, background, or views" (Article V of the *Library Bill of Rights*).
>
> A written policy on library-initiated programming, approved by the library's policy-making body, should reflect the library's philosophy regarding free access to information and ideas. Similarly, concerns expressed regarding library-initiated programs should be handled as they are for library resources.
>
> Selection of library program topics, speakers, courses, classes, and resource materials should be made by library staff on the basis of the interests and needs of library users and the community. Library programming should not exclude topics, books, speakers, media, and other resources because they might be controversial.

Review of the Interpretation "Library-Initiated Programs as a Resource" began in January, 1989. A draft of a revised document was circulated in the spring of 1990. Comments received on the proposed draft raised questions of fees, access for handicapped and deaf patrons, and the practical problems of abolishing age-based restrictions on program attendance.

As a result of these comments, the Interpretation was expanded to include library programs held on- and off-site, and those produced in cooperation with other groups. Provisions were included to encourage librarians to formulate written policies on programming that conform to the intellectual freedom standards set by the *Library Bill of Rights*.

In addition, librarians were exhorted to consider the multicultural or multilingual composition of their communities in planning library events and not to shrink from addressing controversial topics. A special provision was added to emphasize the librarian's duty to assure equal access to all patrons, explicitly stating that economic background and ability to pay cannot be used to restrict access to library-sponsored events.

The new Interpretation was adopted by the Council on June 26, 1990.

2.13

Meeting Rooms

An Interpretation of the *Library Bill of Rights*

Many libraries provide meeting rooms for individuals and groups as part of a program of service. Article VI of the *Library Bill of Rights* states that such facilities should be made available to the public served by the given library "on an equitable basis, regardless of the beliefs or affiliations of individuals or groups requesting their use."

Libraries maintaining meeting room facilities should develop and publish policy statements governing use. These statements can properly define time, place, or manner of use; such qualifications should not pertain to the content of a meeting or to the beliefs or affiliations of the sponsors. These statements should be made available in any commonly used language within the community served.

If meeting rooms in libraries supported by public funds are made available to the general public for nonlibrary sponsored events, the library may not exclude any group based on the subject matter to be discussed or based on the ideas that the group advocates. For example, if a library allows charities and sports clubs to discuss their activities in library meeting rooms, then the library should not exclude partisan political or religious groups from discussing their activities in the same facilities. If a library opens its meeting rooms to a wide variety of civic organizations, then the library may not deny access to a religious organization. Libraries may wish to post a permanent notice near the meeting room stating that the library does not advocate or endorse the viewpoints of meetings or meeting room users.

Written policies for meeting room use should be stated in inclusive rather than exclusive terms. For example, a policy that the library's facilities are open "to organizations engaged in educational, cultural, intellectual, or charitable activities" is an inclusive statement of the limited uses to which the facilities may be put. This defined limitation would permit religious groups to use the facilities because they engage in intellectual activities, but would exclude most commercial uses of the facility.

A publicly supported library may limit use of its meeting rooms to strictly "library-related" activities, provided that the limitation is clearly circumscribed and is viewpoint neutral.

Written policies may include limitations on frequency of use, and whether or not meetings held in library meeting rooms must be open to the public. If state and local laws permit private as well as public sessions of meetings in libraries, libraries may choose to offer both options. The same standard should be applicable to all.

If meetings are open to the public, libraries should include in their meeting room policy statement a section which addresses admission fees. If admission fees are permitted, libraries shall seek to make it possible that these fees do not limit access to individuals who may be unable to pay, but who wish to attend the meeting. Article V of the *Library Bill of Rights* states that "a person's right to use a library should not be denied or abridged because of origin, age, background, or views." It is inconsistent with Article V to restrict indirectly access to library meeting rooms based on an individual's or group's ability to pay for that access.

Adopted July 2, 1991, by the ALA Council.

HISTORY

Meeting Rooms

The Interpretation "Meeting Rooms" was developed concurrently with the Interpretation "Exhibit Spaces and Bulletin Boards." See part I, section 2.9, for that history.

2.14

Restricted Access to Library Materials

An Interpretation of the *Library Bill of Rights*

Libraries are a traditional forum for the open exchange of information. Attempts to restrict access to library materials violate the basic tenets of the *Library Bill of Rights*.

Historically, attempts have been made to limit access by relegating materials into segregated collections. These attempts are in violation of established policy. Such collections are often referred to by a variety of names, including "closed shelf," "locked case," "adults only," "restricted shelf," or "high demand." Access to some materials also may require a monetary fee or financial deposit. In any situation which restricts access to certain materials, a barrier is placed between the patron and those materials. That barrier may be age related, linguistic, economic, or psychological in nature.

Because materials placed in restricted collections often deal with controversial, unusual, or "sensitive" subjects, having to ask a librarian or circulation clerk for them may be embarrassing or inhibiting for patrons desiring the materials. Needing to ask for materials may pose a language barrier or a staff service barrier. Because restricted collections often are composed of materials which some library patrons consider "objectionable," the potential user may be predisposed to think of the materials as "objectionable" and, therefore, are reluctant to ask for them.

103

Barriers between the materials and the patron which are psychological, or are affected by language skills, are nonetheless limitations on access to information. Even when a title is listed in the catalog with a reference to its restricted status, a barrier is placed between the patron and the publication. (See also "Statement on Labeling.")

There may be, however, countervailing factors to establish policies to protect library materials—specifically, for reasons of physical preservation including protection from theft or mutilation. Any such policies must be carefully formulated and administered with extreme attention to the principles of intellectual freedom. This caution is also in keeping with ALA policies, such as "Evaluating Library Collections," "Free Access to Libraries for Minors," and the "Preservation Policy."

Finally, in keeping with the "Joint Statement on Access" of the American Library Association and Society of American Archivists, restrictions that result from donor agreements or contracts for special collections materials must be similarly circumscribed. Permanent exclusions are not acceptable. The overriding impetus must be to work for free and unfettered access to all documentary heritage.

Adopted February 2, 1973; amended July 1, 1981; July 3, 1991, by the ALA Council.

Restricted Access to Library Materials

On January 11, 1971, the City Council of San Jose, California, received a formal request from T. J. Owens, president of the San Jose branch of the National Association for the Advancement of Colored People (NAACP), that the book *Epaminondas and His Auntie* be removed from general circulation in the San Jose libraries. Owens charged that the book depicts a black child in a manner that makes him look "completely idiotic and stupid."[1]

Subsequent to a discussion of the book with Owens, Homer L. Fletcher, city librarian, recommended to the city council that *Epaminondas and His Auntie* be retained on open shelf in all the city's libraries and that the option remain for children's librarians to reorder the book should they choose to do so. Fletcher's recommendation was based on his view that any other action would be inconsistent with the *Library Bill of Rights,* which stated that "no library materials should be proscribed or removed from libraries because of partisan or doctrinal disapproval." Despite the recommendation of the city librarian, the San Jose City Council voted to remove the book from general circulation in city libraries, and to put the book on reserve, thereby necessitating that each individual who wished to use it make a special request to the librarian. On March 29, 1971, however, the City Council reconsidered its action and, upon recommendation of the Library Commission, adopted the *Library Bill of Rights* as city policy and removed the restrictions on the book.

An advisory statement concerning restricted circulation of library materials, drafted in response to the problem in San Jose, was approved by the Intellectual Freedom Committee during the 1971 ALA Annual Conference in Dallas. This statement, in slightly amended form, was submitted to the Council at the 1973 Midwinter Meeting in Washington, D.C., and approved as an ALA policy on February 2, 1973:

> Restricting access of certain titles and certain classes of library materials is a practice common to many libraries in the United States. Collections of these materials are referred to by a variety of names such as "closed shelf," "locked case," "adults only," or "restricted shelf" collections.
>
> Three reasons generally advanced to justify restricted access are:
>
> 1. It provides a refuge for materials that belong in the collection but which may be considered "objectionable" by some library patrons.
>
> 2. It provides a means for controlling distribution of materials which allegedly should not be read by those who are not "prepared" for such materials by experience, education, or age.
>
> 3. It provides a means to protect certain materials from theft and mutilation.
>
> Though widely used—and often practical—restricted access to library materials is frequently in opposition to the principles of intellectual freedom. While the limitation differs from direct censorship activities, such as removal of library materials or refusal to purchase certain publications, it nonetheless constitutes censorship, albeit in a subtle form. As a form of censorship, restricted access violates the spirit of the *Library Bill of Rights* in the following ways:
>
> 1. It violates that portion of Article II which states that "no library materials should be proscribed . . . because of partisan or doctrinal disapproval."

The word "proscribed," as used in Article II, means "suppressed." Restricted access achieves de facto suppression of certain materials.

Even when a title is listed in the card catalog with a reference to its restricted shelf status, a barrier is placed between the patron and the publication. Because a majority of materials placed in restricted collections deal with controversial, unusual, or "sensitive" subjects, asking a librarian or circulation clerk for them is an embarrassment for patrons desiring the materials. Because restricted collections are often composed of materials which some library patrons consider "objectionable," the potential user is predisposed to thinking of the materials as "objectionable," and is accordingly inhibited from asking for them. Although the barrier between the materials and the patron is psychological, it is nonetheless a tangible limitation on his access to information.

2. It violates Article V, which states that "the rights of an individual to the use of a library should not be denied or abridged because of his age. . . ."

Limiting access of certain materials to adults only abridges the use of the library for minors. "Use of the library" includes use of, and access to, library materials. Such restrictions are generally instituted under the assumption that certain materials are "harmful" to minors, or in an effort to avoid controversy with parents who might think so.

The librarian who would restrict the availability of materials to minors because of actual or suspected parental objection should bear in mind that he is not in loco parentis in his position as librarian. The American Library Association holds that it is the parent—and only the parent—who may restrict his children—and only his children—in reading matter. The parent who would rather his child did not read certain materials or certain kinds of materials should so advise the child.*

---

*See also "Free Access to Libraries for Minors," adopted June 30, 1972, by the ALA Council.

When restricted access is implemented to protect materials from theft or mutilation, the use of the practice may be legitimate. However, segregation of materials to protect them must be administered with extreme attention to the rationale for restricting access. Too often only "controversial" materials are the subject of such segregation, leading to the conclusion that factors other than theft and mutilation were the true considerations. The distinction is extremely difficult to make, for both the librarian and the patron.

Selection policies, carefully developed on the basis of principles of intellectual freedom and the *Library Bill of Rights,* should not be vitiated by administrative practices such as restricted access.

As part of the overall review of all Interpretations of the *Library Bill of Rights* following that document's revision in 1980, the IFC recommended several relatively minor changes in the policy on restricted access, mainly aimed at removing sex-linked pronoun usage and strengthening the arguments against restricting access for minors. The recommendations were presented to the Council, which adopted the revised policy on July 1, 1981. It read as follows:

> Restricting access of certain titles and classes of library materials is a practice common to many libraries in the United States. Collections of these materials are referred to by a variety of names such as "closed shelf," "locked case," "adults only," or "restricted shelf."
>
> Three reasons generally advanced to justify restricted access are:
>
> > 1. It provides a refuge for materials that belong in the collection but which may be considered "objectionable" by some library patrons;
> >
> > 2. It provides a means for controlling distribution of materials, to those who are allegedly not "prepared" for such materials or who have been labeled less responsible, because of experience, education, or age;
> >
> > 3. It provides a means to protect certain materials from theft and mutilation.
>
> Restricted access to library materials is frequently in opposition to the principles of intellectual freedom. While the limitation differs from direct censorship activities, such as removal of

library materials or refusal to purchase certain publications, it nonetheless constitutes censorship, albeit in a subtle form. Restricted access often violates the spirit of the *Library Bill of Rights* in the following ways:

1. It violates that portion of Article II which states that "no library materials should be proscribed . . . because of partisan or doctrinal disapproval."

"Materials . . . proscribed" as used in Article II includes "suppressed" materials. Restricted access achieves de facto suppression of certain materials.

Even when a title is listed in the catalog with a reference to its restricted status, a barrier is placed between the patron and the publication. Because a majority of materials placed in restricted collections deal with controversial, unusual, or "sensitive" subjects, asking a librarian or circulation clerk for them may be embarrassing for patrons desiring the materials. Because restricted collections are often composed of materials which some library patrons consider "objectionable" the potential user is predisposed to thinking of the materials as "objectionable" and may be reluctant to ask for them. Although the barrier between the materials and the patron is psychological, it is nonetheless a limitation on access to information.

2. It violates Article V, which states that, "A person's right to use a library should not be denied or abridged because of . . . age."

Limiting access of certain materials only to adults abridges the use of the library for minors. Access to library materials is an integral part of the right to use a library. Such restrictions are generally instituted under the assumption that certain materials are "harmful" to minors, or in an effort to avoid controversy with adults who might think so.

Libraries and library boards who would restrict the availability of materials to minors because of actual or anticipated parental objection should bear in mind that they do not serve in loco parentis. The American Library Association holds that it is parents—and only parents—who may restrict their children—and only their children—from access to library materials and services. Parents who would rather their children not have access to certain materials should so advise their children.

When restricted access is implemented solely to protect materials from theft or mutilation, the practice may be legitimate. However, segregation of materials to protect them must be administered with extreme attention to the reason for restricting access. Too often only "controversial" materials are the subject of such segregation, indicating that factors other than theft and mutilation—including content—were the true considerations. When loss rates of items popular with young people are high, this cannot justify the labeling of all minors as irresponsible and the adoption of prejudiced restrictions on the right of minors to use library services and materials.

Selection policies, carefully developed to include principles of intellectual freedom and the *Library Bill of Rights*, should not be vitiated by administrative practices such as restricted access.

Note: See also "Free Access to Libraries for Minors," adopted June 30, 1972; amended July 1, 1981, by ALA Council.

In 1990, "Restricted Access to Library Materials" was substantially revised. Barriers between materials and patrons which were deemed psychological, linguistic, or related to other patron characteristics were addressed. New language relating to preservation of library materials, referencing related Interpretations of the *Library Bill of Rights*, including "Evaluating Library Collections" and "Free Access to Libraries for Minors," as well as ALA's "Preservation Policy," was added. Also added was an explanation of how the *Library Bill of Rights* applies to restrictions resulting from agreements made with donors of materials or contracts for special collections materials. The new version of "Restricted Access to Library Materials" was adopted by the Council on July 3, 1991.

NOTE

1. *San Jose News*, March 2, 1971.

2.15

Statement on Labeling

An Interpretation of the *Library Bill of Rights*

Labeling is the practice of describing or designating materials by affixing a prejudicial label and/or segregating them by a prejudicial system. The American Library Association opposes these means of predisposing people's attitudes toward library materials for the following reasons:

1. Labeling is an attempt to prejudice attitudes and as such, it is a censor's tool.
2. Some find it easy and even proper, according to their ethics, to establish criteria for judging publications as objectionable. However, injustice and ignorance rather than justice and enlightenment result from such practices, and the American Library Association opposes the establishment of such criteria.
3. Libraries do not advocate the ideas found in their collections. The presence of books and other resources in a library does not indicate endorsement of their contents by the library.

A variety of private organizations promulgate rating systems and/or review materials as a means of advising either their members or the general public concerning their opinions of the contents and suitability or appropriate age for use of certain books, films, recordings, or other materials. For the library to adopt or enforce any of these private systems, to attach such ratings to library materials, to include them in bibliographic records, library catalogs, or other finding aids, or otherwise to endorse them would violate the *Library Bill of Rights.*

While some attempts have been made to adopt these systems into law, the constitutionality of such measures is extremely questionable. If such legislation is passed which applies within a library's jurisdiction, the library should seek competent legal advice concerning its applicability to library operations.

Publishers, industry groups, and distributors sometimes add ratings to material or include them as part of their packaging. Librarians should not endorse such practices. However, removing or obliterating such ratings—if placed there by or with permission of the copyright holder—could constitute expurgation, which is also unacceptable.

The American Library Association opposes efforts which aim at closing any path to knowledge. This statement, however, does not exclude the adoption of organizational schemes designed as directional aids or to facilitate access to materials.

Adopted July 13, 1951; amended June 25, 1971; July 1, 1981; June 26, 1990, by the ALA Council.

Statement on Labeling

In late 1950, the Intellectual Freedom Committee received a report that the Montclair, New Jersey, chapter of the Sons of the American Revolution (SAR) was exerting pressure on New Jersey libraries to put a prominent label or inscription on "publications which advocate or favor communism, or which are issued or distributed by any communist organization or any other organization formally designated by any authorized government official or agency as communistic or subversive." The SAR said further that such publications "should not be freely available in libraries to readers or in schools to pupils, but should be obtainable only by signing suitable applications."[1]

Rutherford D. Rogers, at the time chair of the IFC, reported the matter to the ALA Council on July 13, 1951, and said groups other than the SAR have tried to use such labeling as a means of limiting the freedom to read. He cited religious groups that sometimes asked libraries to label publications "objectionable," and he mentioned that other "patriotic" organizations were moving toward similar proposals. Rogers also reported that in April 1951 the Association received a letter from the Montclair chapter of the SAR requesting ALA to adopt a policy advocating that communistic and subversive materials not only be labeled but also be segregated from other materials in the library collection and given out only upon written and signed application.

The Intellectual Freedom Committee believed that such practices violated the principles of intellectual freedom and that the labeling of books according to points of view should not be undertaken by any library. The Committee also noted that it was not clear who would do such labeling, who would decide what is communistic or subversive, or by what criteria such decisions would be made. In addition, the process was envisioned as expensive and time consuming, involving examination of all materials in a library collection. The impracticality and financial problems of such a project, however, were not deemed relevant to the Association's policy concerning the practice. As Rogers pointed out, policy was to be based on the principle involved.

The IFC's study of the SAR proposal resulted in a six-point statement. Before presenting the statement to the Council for adoption as an ALA policy, the Committee conducted an informal survey of twenty-four libraries around the country. Twenty responded, all agreeing that labeling violated basic principles of intellectual freedom and should not be practiced by libraries. The IFC's six-point "Statement on Labeling" was approved by the Council as an ALA policy on July 13, 1951:

> 1. Although totalitarian states find it easy and even proper, according to their ethics, to establish criteria for judging publications as "subversive," injustice and ignorance rather than justice and enlightenment result from such practices, and the American Library Association has a responsibility to take a stand against the establishment of such criteria in a democratic state.
>
> 2. Libraries do not advocate the ideas found in their collections. The presence of a magazine or book in a library does not indicate an endorsement of its contents by the library.
>
> 3. No one person should take the responsibility of labeling publications. No sizeable group of persons would be likely to agree on the types of materials which should be labeled or the sources of information which should be regarded with suspicion. As a practical consideration, a librarian who labeled a book or magazine procommunist might be sued for libel.
>
> 4. Labeling is an attempt to prejudice the reader, and as such, it is a censor's tool.
>
> 5. Labeling violates the spirit of the *Library Bill of Rights.*

6. Although we are all agreed that communism is a threat to the free world, if materials are labeled to pacify one group, there is no excuse for refusing to label any item in the library's collection. Because communism, fascism, or other authoritarian-isms tend to suppress ideas and attempt to coerce individuals to conform to a specific ideology, American librarians must be op-posed to such "isms." We are, then, anticommunist, but we are also opposed to any other group which aims at closing any path to knowledge.

The 1951 "Statement on Labeling" was adopted as policy by many libraries and, over the years, was a useful tool in combating this brand of censorship. One incident involving an attempt to label library materials occurred at the St. Charles County Library, St. Charles, Missouri, in 1968 and concluded with a unique twist. The case began when Nina S. Ladof, the librarian, was presented with a petition requesting the removal of *Ramparts* magazine. The library dismissed the petition, explaining that *Ramparts* was purchased in accordance with the library's book selection policy, which included the *Library Bill of Rights* and *The Freedom to Read*.

After the initial attempt to remove *Ramparts*, several months passed. Eventually, though, the original complainant presented the librarian with a sheaf of petitions from the Veterans of Foreign Wars, the American Legion, the Lions Club, and a church. With variations, the petitions read as follows:

> We, the undersigned, do hereby petition the Library Board of the County of St. Charles, requesting that any book or publication on file in the St. Charles County Library System authored, pub-lished, or edited by any individual or group of individuals having been cited by any official Federal or State UnAmerican Activities Committee or Fact-Finding Committee as subversive or unAmerican in nature or belonging to any organization having been cited as subversive or unAmerican, be so explicitly labeled in a conspicuous manner for the information of the patrons of the St. Charles County Libraries.

Ladof pointed out that Dr. Benjamin Spock, author of *The Common Sense of Baby Care*, was sentenced on charges of aiding

115

young men to avoid military service. Would this book require a label? Pursuing this example further, Ladof wrote to Spock's publishers to ask what action they would take if she did, in fact, affix a label to his works. Two replied that they would consider it possible grounds for legal action against the library. Dr. Spock's own attorney concurred.

Both the American Civil Liberties Union and the Freedom of Information Center at the University of Missouri provided Nina Ladof with the legal opinion that labeling a work, as requested in the petition, would be grounds for a libel action by the author whose works were involved because of the injury to the sale of his works that might result. Even if the label were factual, such as "so-and-so was a member of the Communist Party in 1941," he would have grounds to prove such injury. In fact, injury need not actually occur; it need only be a possibility for a court to award substantial damages to a plaintiff in such a case. And, since library boards of trustees cannot be sued as a body, each member would be liable for the damages awarded.

Armed with this information, and with the board's unanimous belief that labels are forms of censorship—and, as such, are completely opposed to basic library policies—the library issued a firm statement rejecting the proposed labeling. The statement included information from legal sources and paraphrased and expanded the six points of the ALA "Statement on Labeling." All persons interested in the matter were sent copies with an explanatory letter. *Ramparts* and other literature written by so-called subversives continued to circulate unlabeled.

The 1951 "Statement on Labeling" stood without revision until 1971. At that time, study of the policy confirmed that some sections were framed in language that reflected the Association's response to a specific threat—the labeling as "subversive" or "communist" specific materials. The Intellectual Freedom Community concluded that, although these sections once met a particular need, they limited the document's usefulness.

To make the "Statement on Labeling" application to a broader range of labeling problems, even encompassing "harmful matter," the Intellectual Freedom Committee recommended a revised version to the Council. The 1971 revision was designated an Interpretation of the *Library Bill of Rights* to emphasize the relationship between Articles I, II, and III of that document and the "Statement on Labeling." The revision was adopted by the Council on June 25, 1971:

> Because labeling violates the spirit of the *Library Bill of Rights*, the American Library Association opposes the technique of labeling as a means of predisposing readers against library materials for the following reasons:
>
> 1. Labeling* is an attempt to prejudice the reader, and as such it is a censor's tool.
>
> 2. Although some find it easy and even proper, according to their ethics, to establish criteria for judging publications as objectionable, injustice and ignorance rather than justice and enlightenment result from such practices, and the American Library Association must oppose the establishment of such criteria.
>
> 3. Libraries do not advocate the ideas found in their collections. The presence of a magazine or book in a library does not indicate an endorsement of its contents by the library.
>
> 4. No one person should take the responsibility of labeling publications. No sizeable group of persons would be likely to agree either on the types of material which should be labeled or the sources of information which should be regarded with suspicion. As a practical consideration, a librarian who labels a book or magazine might be sued for libel.
>
> 5. If materials are labeled to pacify one group, there is no excuse for refusing to label any item in the library's collection. Because authoritarians tend to suppress ideas and attempt to coerce individuals to conform to a specific ideology, the American Library Association opposes such efforts which aim at closing any path to knowledge.

Following the 1980 revision of the *Library Bill of Rights*, the IFC again reviewed the statement, recommending three major changes.

---

*"Labeling," as it is referred to in the "Statement on Labeling," is the practice of describing or designating certain library materials, by affixing a prejudicial label to them or segregating them by a prejudicial system, so as to predispose readers against the materials.

First, the Committee noted that relegating definition of the labeling practice to a footnote detracted from the policy's unity and effectiveness and suggested incorporating the definition in the opening paragraph. Second, the Committee recommended that points 4 and 5 be dropped, because these were not considerations of principle but, rather, "practical" objections to labeling.

Although librarians should certainly be aware that the labeling of library materials could provoke legal action, and although it is certainly true that adoption of labels at the instigation of one group might open a veritable Pandora's box of labeling demands by others, neither of these considerations lies at the basis of the Association's opposition to labeling. The American Library Association opposes labeling of library materials not because this is impractical or legally dangerous but because this practice flagrantly violates both the spirit and the letter of the *Library Bill of Rights* and stands in fundamental opposition to the most basic principles of intellectual freedom.

In addition, the Committee recommended adding a sentence to the statement indicating that the Association's objections to labeling should not be construed as opposition to legitimate organizational schemes designed to facilitate access. The second revision of the "Statement on Labeling" was adopted by the Council on July 1, 1981. It read as follows:

Labeling is the practice of describing or designating certain library materials by affixing a prejudicial label to them or segregating them by a prejudicial system. The American Library Association opposes this as a means of predisposing people's attitudes towards library materials for the following reasons:

1. Labeling is an attempt to prejudice attitudes and as such, it is a censor's tool.

2. Some find it easy and even proper, according to their ethics, to establish criteria for judging publications as objectionable. However, injustice and ignorance rather than justice and enlightenment result from such practices, and the American Library Association opposes the establishment of such criteria.

3. Libraries do not advocate the ideas found in their collections. The presence of books and other resources in a library does not indicate endorsement of their contents by the library.

Statement on Labeling

The American Library Association opposes efforts which aim at closing any path to knowledge. This statement does not, however, exclude the adoption of organizational schemes designed as directional aids or to facilitate access to materials.

In keeping with the review of *Library Bill of Rights* Interpretations, undertaken in response to the 1988 Minority Concerns Committee resolution, the Statement on Labeling was the first to be revised by the Intellectual Freedom Committee at the June 1989 Annual Conference. The importance of this policy increased significantly in light of attempts, in 1990, to pass legislation in Congress requiring warning labels for musical recordings with allegedly obscene lyrics or lyrics deemed offensive or unsuitable for minors.

Policy revisions made clear the ALA's opposition to labeling, and emphasized librarians' responsibility to prevent the imposition of private or voluntary labeling schemes on library materials, while leaving permanently affixed labels intact to avoid expurgation of copyrighted material. The new Interpretation also encourages librarians to become familiar with local laws and regulations on the issue.

Following adoption by the IFC in June 1989, the revised "Statement on Labeling" was circulated to other ALA units. At the 1990 Midwinter Meeting, the revision was reconsidered in light of comments received from the other units. The final version of this Interpretation was accepted by the Committee and then adopted by the Council on June 26, 1990.

NOTE

1. *ALA Bulletin* 45:241 (July–Aug. 1951).

2.16

The Universal Right to Free Expression

An Interpretation of the *Library Bill of Rights*

Freedom of expression is an inalienable human right and the foundation for self-government. Freedom of expression encompasses the freedoms of speech, press, religion, assembly, and association, and the corollary right to receive information.

The American Library Association endorses this principle, which is also set forth in the Universal Declaration of Human Rights, adopted by the United Nations General Assembly. The Preamble of this document states that "... recognition of the inherent dignity and of the equal and inalienable rights of all members of the human family is the foundation of freedom, justice, and peace in the world ..." and "... the advent of a world in which human beings shall enjoy freedom of speech and belief and freedom from fear and want has been proclaimed as the highest aspiration of the common people. ..."

Article 18 of this document states:

Everyone has the right to freedom of thought, conscience, and religion; this right includes freedom to change his religion or belief, and freedom, either alone or in community with others and in public or private, to manifest his religion or belief in teaching, practice, worship, and observance.

Article 19 states:

Everyone has the right to freedom of opinion and expression; this right includes freedom to hold opinions without interference and to seek, receive and impart information and ideas through any media regardless of frontiers.

Article 20 states:

1. Everyone has the right to freedom of peaceful assembly and association.
2. No one may be compelled to belong to an association.

We affirm our belief that these are inalienable rights of every person, regardless of origin, age, background, or views. We embody our professional commitment to these principles in the *Library Bill of Rights* and *Code of Ethics*, as adopted by the American Library Association.

We maintain that these are universal principles and should be applied by libraries and librarians throughout the world. The American Library Association's policy on International Relations reflects these objectives: ". . . to encourage the exchange, dissemination, and access to information and the unrestricted flow of library materials in all formats throughout the world."

We know that censorship, ignorance, and limitations on the free flow of information are the tools of tyranny and oppression. We believe that ideas and information topple the walls of hate and fear and build bridges of cooperation and understanding far more effectively than weapons and armies.

The American Library Association is unswerving in its commitment to human rights and intellectual freedom; the two are inseparably linked and inextricably entwined. Freedom of opinion and expression is not derived from or dependent on any form of government or political power. This right is inherent in every individual. It cannot be surrendered, nor can it be denied. True justice comes from the exercise of this right.

We recognize the power of information and ideas to inspire justice, to restore freedom and dignity to the oppressed, and to change the hearts and minds of the oppressors.

Courageous men and women, in difficult and dangerous circumstances throughout human history, have demonstrated that freedom lives in the human heart and cries out for justice even in the face of threats, enslavement, imprisonment, torture, exile, and death. We draw inspiration from their example. They challenge us to remain steadfast in our most basic professional responsibility to promote and defend the right of free expression.

There is no good censorship. Any effort to restrict free expression and the free flow of information aids the oppressor. Fighting oppression with censorship is self-defeating.

Threats to the freedom of expression of any person anywhere are threats to the freedom of all people everywhere. Violations of human rights and the right of free expression have been recorded in virtually every country and society across the globe.

In response to these violations, we affirm these principles:

> The American Library Association opposes any use of governmental prerogative that leads to the intimidation of individuals which prevents them from exercising their rights to hold opinions without interference, and to seek, receive, and impart information and ideas. We urge libraries and librarians everywhere to resist such abuse of governmental power, and to support those against whom such governmental power has been employed.

> The American Library Association condemns any governmental effort to involve libraries and librarians in restrictions on the right of any individual to hold opinions without interference, and to seek, receive, and impart information and ideas. Such restrictions pervert the function of the library and violate the professional responsibilities of librarians.

> The American Library Association rejects censorship in any form. Any action which denies the inalienable human rights of individuals only damages the will to resist oppression, strengthens the hand of the oppressor, and undermines the cause of justice.

> The American Library Association will not abrogate these principles. We believe that censorship corrupts the cause of justice, and contributes to the demise of freedom.

Adopted by the ALA Council, January 16, 1991.

The Universal Right to Free Expression

Out of a long and emotional debate about support for sanctions— including books and informational materials—against South Africa, a new Interpretation of the *Library Bill of Rights* was created. Modeled after Article 19 of the United Nations Universal Declaration of Human Rights, the "Universal Right to Free Expression" advocates the free flow of information within all countries across national boundaries.

In 1989, the ALA was asked to support the Association of American Publishers in its efforts to end the book boycott against South Africa. The Council asked the IFC for its recommendation. Concurrently, the Social Responsibilities Round Table (SRRT) had proposed a set of guidelines for librarians interacting with South Africa that were opposed by the IFC. The debate within the ALA over South African policy was emotional, vigorous, and sometimes vituperative. It became clear that no extant ALA policy provided an adequate framework from which to respond fully to the complicated international intellectual freedom and human rights questions raised during the course of the debate.

In 1990, the IFC began work on an international free flow of information policy to address this glaring need. The new policy was to provide a secure foundation from which to respond to the AAP's request and from which to address other international intellectual freedom issues. The drafters used Articles 18, 19, and 20 of the Universal Declaration of Human Rights as models for the new policy.

In January 1991, the IFC considered comments on the "Free Flow of Information" draft. The title of the Interpretation was changed to "The Universal Right to Free Expression," and the IFC voted to seek endorsements of other units of the ALA and to present the Interpretation to the Council.

On January 16, 1991, the Council voted to adopt the policy as the most recent addition to the *Library Bill of Rights* and its Interpretations.

PART II

Protecting the Freedom to Read

1

The Freedom to Read: Policy Statement

The freedom to read is essential to our democracy. It is continuously under attack. Private groups and public authorities in various parts of the country are working to remove books from sale, to censor textbooks, to label "controversial" books, to distribute lists of "objectionable" books or authors, and to purge libraries. These actions apparently rise from a view that our national tradition of free expression is no longer valid; that censorship and suppression are needed to avoid the subversion of politics and the corruption of morals. We, as citizens devoted to the use of books and as librarians and publishers responsible for disseminating them, wish to assert the public interest in the preservation of the freedom to read.

We are deeply concerned about these attempts at suppression. Most such attempts rest on a denial of the fundamental premise of democracy: that the ordinary citizen, by exercising critical judgment, will accept the good and reject the bad. The censors, public and private, assume that they should determine what is good and what is bad for their fellow citizens.

We trust Americans to recognize propaganda, and to reject it. We do not believe they need the help of censors to assist them in this task. We do not believe they are prepared to sacrifice their heritage of a free press in order to be "protected" against what others think may be bad for them. We believe they still favor free enterprise in ideas and expression.

We are aware, of course, that books are not alone in being subjected to efforts at suppression. We are aware that these efforts are related to a larger pattern of pressures being brought against education, the press, films, radio and television. The problem is not only one of actual censorship. The shadow of fear cast by these pressures leads, we suspect, to an even larger voluntary curtailment of expression by those who seek to avoid controversy.

Such pressure toward conformity is perhaps natural to a time of uneasy change and pervading fear. Especially when so many of our apprehensions are directed against an ideology, the expression of a dissident idea becomes a thing feared in itself, and we tend to move against it as against a hostile deed, with suppression.

And yet suppression is never more dangerous than in such a time of social tension. Freedom has given the United States the elasticity to endure strain. Freedom keeps open the path of novel and creative solutions, and enables change to come by choice. Every silencing of a heresy, every enforcement of an orthodoxy, diminishes the toughness and resilience of our society and leaves it the less able to deal with stress.

Now as always in our history, books are among our greatest instruments of freedom. They are almost the only means for making generally available ideas or manners of expression that can initially command only a small audience. They are the natural medium for the new idea and the untried voice from which come the original contributions to social growth. They are essential to the extended discussion which serious thought requires, and to the accumulation of knowledge and ideas into organized collections.

We believe that free communication is essential to the preservation of a free society and a creative culture. We believe that these pressures towards conformity present the danger of limiting the range and variety of inquiry and expression on which our democracy and our culture depend. We believe that every American community must jealously guard the freedom to publish and to circulate, in order to preserve its own freedom to read. We believe that publishers and librarians have a profound responsibility to give validity to that freedom to read by making it possible for the readers to choose freely from a variety of offerings.

The freedom to read is guaranteed by the Constitution. Those with faith in free people will stand firm on these constitutional guarantees of essential rights and will exercise the responsibilities that accompany these rights.

We therefore affirm these propositions:

1. *It is in the public interest for publishers and librarians to make available the widest diversity of views and expressions, including those which are unorthodox or unpopular with the majority.*

   Creative thought is by definition new, and what is new is different. The bearer of every new thought is a rebel until that idea is refined and tested. Totalitarian systems attempt to maintain themselves in power by the ruthless suppression of any concept which challenges the established orthodoxy. The power of a democratic system to adapt to change is vastly strengthened by the freedom of its citizens to choose widely from among conflicting opinions offered freely to them. To stifle every nonconformist idea at birth would mark the end of the democratic process. Furthermore, only through the constant activity of weighing and selecting can the democratic mind attain the strength demanded by times like these. We need to know not only what we believe but why we believe it.

2. *Publishers, librarians and booksellers do not need to endorse every idea or presentation contained in the books they make available. It would conflict with the public interest for them to establish their own political, moral, or aesthetic views as a standard for determining what books should be published or circulated.*

   Publishers and librarians serve the educational process by helping to make available knowledge and ideas required for the growth of the mind and the increase of learning. They do not foster education by imposing as mentors the patterns of their own thought. The people should have the freedom to read and consider a broader range of ideas than those that may be held by any single librarian or publisher or government or church. It is wrong that what one can read should be confined to what another thinks proper.

3. *It is contrary to the public interest for publishers or librarians to determine the acceptability of a book on the basis of the personal history or political affiliations of the author.*

A book should be judged as a book. No art or literature can flourish if it is to be measured by the political views or private lives of its creators. No society of free people can flourish which draws up lists of writers to whom it will not listen, whatever they may have to say.

4. *There is no place in our society for efforts to coerce the taste of others, to confine adults to the reading matter deemed suitable for adolescents, or to inhibit the efforts of writers to achieve artistic expression.*

To some, much of modern literature is shocking. But is not much of life itself shocking? We cut off literature at the source if we prevent writers from dealing with the stuff of life. Parents and teachers have a responsibility to prepare the young to meet the diversity of experiences in life to which they will be exposed, as they have a responsibility to help them learn to think critically for themselves. These are affirmative responsibilities, not to be discharged simply by preventing them from reading works for which they are not yet prepared. In these matters taste differs, and taste cannot be legislated; nor can machinery be devised which will suit the demands of one group without limiting the freedom of others.

5. *It is not in the public interest to force a reader to accept with any book the prejudgment of a label characterizing the book or author as subversive or dangerous.*

The idea of labeling presupposes the existence of individuals or groups with wisdom to determine by authority what is good or bad for the citizen. It presupposes that individuals must be directed in making up their minds about the ideas they examine. But Americans do not need others to do their thinking for them.

6. *It is the responsibility of publishers and librarians, as guardians of the people's freedom to read, to contest encroachments upon that freedom by individuals or groups seeking to impose their own standards or tastes upon the community at large.*

It is inevitable in the give and take of the democratic process that the political, the moral, or the aesthetic concepts of an individual or group will occasionally collide with those of another individual or group. In a free society individuals are free to determine for themselves what they wish to read, and each group is free to determine what it will recommend to its freely associated members. But no group has the right to take the law into its own hands, and to impose its own concept of politics or morality upon other members of a democratic society. Freedom is no freedom if it is accorded only to the accepted and the inoffensive.

7. *It is the responsibility of publishers and librarians to give full meaning to the freedom to read by providing books that enrich the quality and diversity of thought and expression. By the exercise of this affirmative responsibility, they can demonstrate that the answer to a bad book is a good one, the answer to a bad idea is a good one.*

The freedom to read is of little consequence when expended on the trivial; it is frustrated when the reader cannot obtain matter fit for that reader's purpose. What is needed is not only the absence of restraint, but the positive provision of opportunity for the people to read the best that has been thought and said. Books are the major channel by which the intellectual inheritance is handed down, and the principal means of its testing and growth. The defense of their freedom and integrity, and the enlargement of their service to society, requires of all publishers and librarians the utmost of their faculties, and deserves of all citizens the fullest of their support.

We state these propositions neither lightly nor as easy generalizations. We here stake out a lofty claim for the value of books. We do so because we believe that they are good, possessed of enormous variety and usefulness, worthy of cherishing and keeping free. We realize that the application of these propositions may mean the dissemination of ideas and manners of expression that are repugnant to many persons. We do not state these propositions in the comfortable belief that what people read is unimportant. We believe rather that what people read is deeply important; that ideas can be dangerous; but that the suppression of ideas is fatal to a democratic society. Freedom itself is a dangerous way of life, but it is ours.

This statement was originally issued in May of 1953 by the Westchester Conference of the American Library Association and the American Book

Publishers Council, which in 1970 consolidated with the American Educational Publishers Institute to become the Association of American Publishers.

Adopted June 25, 1953; revised January 28, 1972, January 16, 1991, by the ALA Council and the AAP Freedom to Read Committee.

A Joint Statement by

American Library Association
Association of American Publishers

Subsequently Endorsed by

American Booksellers Association
American Booksellers Foundation for Free Expression
American Civil Liberties Union
American Federation of Teachers AFL-CIO
Anti-Defamation League of B'nai B'rith
Association of American University Presses
Children's Book Council
Freedom to Read Foundation
International Reading Association
Thomas Jefferson Center for the Protection of Free Expression
National Association of College Stores
National Council of Teachers of English
P.E.N.—American Center
People for the American Way
Periodical and Book Association of America
Sex Information and Education Council of the U.S.
Society of Professional Journalists
Women's National Book Association
YWCA of the U.S.A.

The Freedom to Read

T*he Freedom to Read*, best known of the American Library Association's documents supporting the principles of intellectual
freedom as embodied in the *Library Bill of Rights*, had it beginnings
during the Intellectual Freedom Committee's 1953 Midwinter Meeting in Chicago.[1] At that meeting, Chair William S. Dix suggested the
committee "discuss the current wave of censorship and attacks on
books and libraries" and "help clarify the stand which libraries
might take and point to ways in which our own position might be
strengthened in the minds of the public." The committee directed
Dix to consider a small, off-the-record conference with in-depth discussion of the matter.

Dix's efforts resulted in a conference on the freedom to read,
sponsored jointly by the American Library Association and the
American Book Publishers Council, held at the Westchester Country
Club, Rye, New York, May 2–3, 1953. The object of the meeting was
to bring together nationally known figures representing librarians,
publishers, and the public interest. Spokesmen for the public interest, viewed as vitally important to the success of the conference,
included representatives of business, foundations, law, and education. Luther Evans, former Librarian of Congress—and head of the
United Nations Educational, Scientific and Cultural Organization—
served as chair of the conference.

133

In their invitation to potential participants, the joint sponsors said:

> Recent months have seen the emergence in our country of a pattern of pressures whose effect must be to limit the range and variety of expression. This pattern has affected in one way or another all the media of communications and indeed the entire area of free inquiry. Books are the last of the communications media to be affected by these pressures toward conformity. They remain preeminently the medium for the free expression of facts, ideas, and human experience in all its varieties. Librarians and publishers feel a deep responsibility for doing their part to see that this continues to be so, and they share with thoughtful men in every profession a conviction that freedom of communication is indispensable to a creative culture and a free society.

The objectives of the conference were the following:

> 1. To define the rights and responsibilities of publishers and librarians in maintaining the freedom of Americans to read what they choose;
> 2. To assay recent developments tending to restrict this freedom;
> 3. To consider where lines should be drawn between permissible expression and impermissible expression, and who is to draw the lines; and
> 4. To ascertain the public interest in this area and, if the group agrees, consider ways of asserting it.

Debate at the conference focused on the specific problem areas of obscenity and pornography and disloyalty and subversive materials. The participants considered a number of questions: What is the function of publishers and librarians in circulating ideas? Should they be responsible guides or simply caterers to public taste? Do they have a special responsibility to make available nonconforming expression and unpopular views? Do citizens have a right to read everything not expressly prohibited by law? Should a book be judged only by its content, and the political and personal background of the author ignored? Is the role of the public library entirely neutral? Can books be subversive?

The conference resulted in substantial agreement on principles. A Continuations Committee was appointed to draft a statement based on the proceedings and to consider action and research projects designed to publicize and explore further the matters discussed. The Continuations Committee consisted of Arthur A. Houghton, Jr., president of Steuben Glass; Harold D. Lasswell, professor of law and political science at Yale Law School; Bernard Berelson, director of the Behavioral Sciences Division at the Ford Foundation; William S. Dix, librarian at Princeton University; and Dan Lacy, managing director of the American Book Publishers Council.

By the end of May, the Continuations Committee, with the assistance of other individuals, produced a final version of *The Freedom to Read* for the approval of the Westchester Conference participants. On June 18, 1953, the following statement was endorsed by the Board of Directors of the American Book Publishers Council and on June 25, 1953, by the Council of the American Library Association:

> The freedom to read is essential to our democracy. It is under attack. Private groups and public authorities in various parts of the country are working to remove books from sale, to censor textbooks, to label "controversial" books, to distribute lists of "objectionable" books or authors, and to purge libraries. These actions apparently rise from a view that our national tradition of free expression is no longer valid; that censorship and suppression are needed to avoid the subversion of politics and the corruption of morals. We, as citizens devoted to the use of books and as librarians and publishers responsible for disseminating them, wish to assert the public interest in the preservation of the freedom to read.
>
> We are deeply concerned about these attempts at suppression. Most such attempts rest on a denial of the fundamental premise of democracy: that the ordinary citizen, by exercising his critical judgment, will accept the good and reject the bad. The censors, public and private, assume that they should determine what is good and what is bad for their fellow-citizens.
>
> We trust Americans to recognize propaganda, and to reject obscenity. We do not believe they need the help of censors to assist them in this task. We do not believe they are prepared to

sacrifice their heritage of a free press in order to be "protected" against what others think may be bad for them. We believe they still favor free enterprise in ideas and expression.

We are aware, of course, that books are not alone in being subjected to efforts at suppression. We are aware that these efforts are related to a larger pattern of pressures being brought against education, the press, films, radio, and television. The problem is not only one of actual censorship. The shadow of fear cast by these pressures leads, we suspect, to an even larger voluntary curtailment of expression by those who seek to avoid controversy.

Such pressure toward conformity is perhaps natural to a time of uneasy change and pervading fear. Especially when so many of our apprehensions are directed against an ideology, the expression of a dissident idea becomes a thing feared in itself, and we tend to move against it as against a hostile deed, with suppression.

And yet suppression is never more dangerous than in such a time of social tension. Freedom has given the United States the elasticity to endure strain. Freedom keeps open the path of novel and creative solutions, and enables change to come by choice. Every silencing of a heresy, every enforcement of an orthodoxy, diminishes the toughness and resilience of our society and leaves it the less able to deal with stress.

Now as always in our history, books are among our greatest instruments of freedom. They are almost the only means for making generally available ideas or manners of expression that can initially command only a small audience. They are the natural medium for the new idea and the untried voice from which come the original contributions to social growth. They are essential to the extended discussion which serious thought requires and to the accumulation of knowledge and ideas into organized collections.

We believe that free communication is essential to the preservation of a free society and a creative culture. We believe that these pressures towards conformity present the danger of limiting the range and variety of inquiry and expression on which our democracy and our culture depend. We believe that every American community must jealously guard the freedom to publish and to circulate, in order to preserve its own freedom to read. We believe that publishers and librarians have a profound responsibility to give validity to that freedom to read by making it possible for the reader to choose freely from a variety of offerings.

The freedom to read is guaranteed by the Constitution. Those with faith in free men will stand firm on these constitutional guarantees of essential rights and will exercise the responsibilities that accompany these rights.

We therefore affirm these propositions:

1. *It is in the public interest for publishers and librarians to make available the widest diversity of views and expressions, including those which are unorthodox or unpopular with the majority.*

   Creative thought is by definition new, and what is new is different. The bearer of every new thought is a rebel until that idea is refined and tested. Totalitarian systems attempt to maintain themselves in power by the ruthless suppression of any concept which challenges the established orthodoxy. The power of a democratic system to adapt to change is vastly strengthened by the freedom of its citizens to choose widely from among conflicting opinions offered freely to them. To stifle every nonconformist idea at birth would mark the end of the democratic process. Furthermore, only through the constant activity of weighing and selecting can the democratic mind attain the strength demanded by times like these. We need to know not only what we believe but why we believe it.

2. *Publishers and librarians do not need to endorse every idea or presentation contained in the books they make available. It would conflict with the public interest for them to establish their own political, moral, or aesthetic views as the sole standard for determining what books should be published or circulated.*

   Publishers and librarians serve the educational process by helping to make available knowledge and ideas required for the growth of the mind and the increase of learning. They do not foster education by imposing as mentors the patterns of their own thought. The people should have the freedom to read and consider a broader range of ideas than those that may be held by any single librarian or publisher or government or church. It is wrong that what one man can read should be confined to what another thinks proper.

3. *It is contrary to the public interest for publishers or librarians to determine the acceptability of a book solely on the basis of the personal history or political affiliations of the author.*

A book should be judged as a book. No art or literature can flourish if it is to be measured by the political views or private lives of its creators. No society of free men can flourish which draws up lists of writers to whom it will not listen, whatever they may have to say.

4. *The present laws dealing with obscenity should be vigorously enforced. Beyond that, there is no place in our society for extra-legal efforts to coerce the taste of others, to confine adults to the reading matter deemed suitable for adolescents, or to inhibit the efforts of writers to achieve artistic expression.*

To some, much of modern literature is shocking. But is not much of life itself shocking? We cut off literature at the source if we prevent serious artists from dealing with the stuff of life. Parents and teachers have a responsibility to prepare the young to meet the diversity of experiences in life to which they will be exposed, as they have a responsibility to help them learn to think critically for themselves. These are affirmative responsibilities, not to be discharged simply by preventing them from reading works for which they are not yet prepared. In these matters taste differs, and taste cannot be legislated; nor can machinery be devised which will suit the demands of one group without limiting the freedom of others. We deplore the catering to the immature, the retarded, or the maladjusted taste. But those concerned with freedom have the responsibility of seeing to it that each individual book or publication, whatever its contents, price or method of distribution, is dealt with in accordance with due process of law.

5. *It is not in the public interest to force a reader to accept with any book the prejudgment of a label characterizing the book or author as subversive or dangerous.*

The idea of labeling presupposes the existence of individuals or groups with wisdom to determine by authority what is good or bad for the citizen. It presupposes that each individual must be directed in making up his mind about the ideas he examines. But Americans do not need others to do their thinking for them.

6. *It is the responsibility of publishers and librarians, as guardians of the people's freedom to read, to contest encroachments upon that freedom by individuals or groups seeking to impose their own standards or tastes upon the community at large.*

It is inevitable in the give and take of the democratic process that the political, the moral, or the aesthetic concepts of an individual or group will occasionally collide with those of another individual or group. In a free society each individual is free to determine for himself what he wishes to read, and each group is free to determine what it will recommend to its freely associated members. But no group has the right to take the law into its own hands, and to impose its own concept of politics or morality upon other members of a democratic society. Freedom is no freedom if it is accorded only to the accepted and the inoffensive.

7. *It is the responsibility of publishers and librarians to give full meaning to the freedom to read by providing books that enrich the quality of thought and expression. By the exercise of this affirmative responsibility, bookmen can demonstrate that the answer to a bad book is a good one, the answer to a bad idea is a good one.*

The freedom to read is of little consequence when expended on the trivial; it is frustrated when the reader cannot obtain matter fit for his purpose. What is needed is not only the absence of restraint, but the positive provision of opportunity for the people to read the best that has been thought and said. Books are the major channel by which the intellectual inheritance is handed down, and the principal means of its testing and growth. The defense of their freedom and integrity, and the enlargement of their service to society, requires of all bookmen the utmost of their faculties, and deserves of all citizens the fullest of their support.

From a deceptively comfortable position in the middle of the 1960s, most librarians looked forward to the 1970s with optimism, hoping for a favorable climate for intellectual freedom. The U.S. Supreme Court extended constitutional support and protection in many areas of human and civil rights. Very encouraging to librarians was the expansion of freedom of expression and other First Amendment rights to allow publications that could not have been found fifteen years earlier. An unfettered climate in which all ideas could be freely exchanged seemed imminent.

But the sense of optimism was soon undercut as increased American involvement in the Vietnam war prompted rancorous divisions among citizens and members of the government. And then came 1968: On April 4, Dr. Martin Luther King was assassinated in Memphis, and the riots provoked in Washington, D.C., and elsewhere led President Johnson to call out troops to restore order. By April 14, violence had erupted in twenty-nine states. On June 6, Robert F. Kennedy died in Los Angeles, also a victim of an assassin's bullet. From August 25 to 29, the Democratic National Convention in Chicago became the scene for violent clashes between the police and National Guard troops on one side and more than ten thousand antiwar demonstrators on the other. This period of violent dissent, countered by equally violent reactions, continued into 1970 with the Kent State and Jackson, Mississippi, incidents and battles between the Black Panther Party and police, and between the radical Weathermen group and police.

It became increasingly clear that such incidents of violent dissent and violent reactions were gradually eroding prospects for the open society many had envisioned. The "permissive" atmosphere collided with demands for law and order. One effect of the collision was that, little by little, the supports for intellectual freedom in the society at large were weakened.

In the form of subpoenas, pressure was brought against news reporters, photographers, and television broadcasting corporations to divulge sources of information and to produce unpublished materials deleted from final reports. Vice President Spiro Agnew gave a series of speeches condemning the news media for biased reporting and calling on citizens to protest such reporting. President Richard Nixon promised to appoint conservatives to the Supreme Court.

Recognizing the increasing conservatism of the nation, and mindful that *The Freedom to Read* might be tied too closely to the McCarthy era, the IFC began, in the fall of 1968, to consider the need for and desirability of a new statement to serve the 1970s. A careful view of the document resulted in the following points:

> 1. Article 4, urging the vigorous enforcement of "the present laws dealing with obscenity," should be revised or deleted entirely.
> 2. The basic sentiments expressed in *The Freedom to Read* remain valid and should not be distorted.
> 3. The document has historical significance.
> 4. A new statement is needed dealing specifically with the pressures on today's society and those foreseen arising during the next decade.

Believing a new statement should at least be attempted, the IFC asked the National Book Committee (NBC) and the American Book Publishers Council (ABPC), cosponsor of *The Freedom to Read*, whether they were interested in joining the undertaking. Both replied affirmatively. Theodore Waller and Peter Jennison met with the IFC during the 1969 Midwinter Meeting in Washington, D.C., and formed a subcommittee composed of representatives from ABPC, ALA, and NBC, charged with determining content and preparing a draft document.

Meeting during the Atlantic City Conference, June 1969, the subcommittee—composed of Edwin Castagna, Peter Jennison, Judith F. Krug, Dan Lacy, and Theodore Waller—discussed the two major items: (1) Should *The Freedom to Read* be revised, or should a new document be produced? (As the IFC did, they decided to design a new statement meeting the challenge of the seventies); and (2) What kind of ammunition is needed to meet the challenge of the seventies? The subcommittee also considered such questions as Can freedom to read be separated from intellectual freedom? Is a broader concept of intellectual freedom, embracing the First Amendment together with other aspects of the Bill of Rights, such as the invasion of privacy, needed? Should all media, not just books, be considered? Should complete intellectual freedom be called for, or must one retreat in the end to the principle of the freedom to read?

The subcommittee next met in August of that year, with a membership augmented by the presence of William DeJohn, Freeman Lewis, Harriet Pilpel, and Richard Sullivan. They drafted several statements and asked Jennison to assemble them into one cohesive document. Five drafts were subsequently produced, and the IFC, in a ten-to-one mail vote, approved the fifth draft. At the time of the 1970 Midwinter Meeting, however, a sixth draft had been prepared.

The ABPC Board of Directors received the draft and approved it by acclamation January 28. The sixth draft was resubmitted to the IFC, which approved it in a ten-to-one vote.

Following the 1970 Midwinter Meeting, the staff of the Office for Intellectual Freedom carefully reviewed the sixth draft of the document, tentatively entitled *The Promise of the First Freedom: A Statement of Free Men*. The staff could not join with the IFC in endorsing this document and recommended to the IFC that *The Freedom to Read* be revised, as opposed to rewritten, to meet comtemporary needs. This decision was based on several factors:

1. The major part of *The Freedom to Read* remained valid.

2. Among those parts that needed change were the specific references to books, for libraries were concerned with all types of materials.

3. Although *The Freedom to Read* had historical significance, subsequent policy statements, as well as actions, of the Association were in opposition to a few parts, primarily Article 4.

4. The few parts in opposition were believed to be serious matters and should not be permitted to stand.

The revision was undertaken by the Office for Intellectual Freedom and W. Lester Smith of the Association of American Publishers (AAP), successor to the combined ABPC and the American Educational Publishers Institute. The new document differed from the 1953 version on only a few significant points: the earlier call for "vigorous enforcement of present obscenity laws" was omitted, as was the reference to "the immature, the retarded, and the maladjusted taste."

The revised *Freedom to Read* was approved by the ALA Council at the 1972 Midwinter Meeting and by the AAP as follows:

The freedom to read is essential to our democracy. It is continuously under attack. Private groups and public authorities in various parts of the country are working to remove books from sale, to censor textbooks, to label "controversial" books, to distribute lists of "objectionable" books or authors, and to purge libraries. These actions apparently rise from a view that our national tradition of free expression is no longer valid; that censorship and suppression are needed to avoid the subversion of politics and the corruption of morals. We, as citizens devoted to the use of books and as librarians and publishers responsible for disseminating them, wish to assert the public interest in the preservation of the freedom to read.

We are deeply concerned about these attempts at suppression. Most such attempts rest on a denial of the fundamental premise of democracy: that the ordinary citizen, by exercising his critical judgment, will accept the good and reject the bad. The censors, public and private, assume that they should determine what is good and what is bad for their fellow-citizens.

We trust Americans to recognize propaganda and to reject it. We do not believe they need the help of censors to assist them in this task. We do not believe they are prepared to sacrifice their heritage of a free press in order to be "protected" against what others think may be bad for them. We believe they still favor free enterprise in ideas and expression.

We are aware, of course, that books are not alone in being subjected to efforts at suppression. We are aware that these efforts are related to a larger pattern of pressures being brought against education, the press, films, radio, and television. The problem is not only one of actual censorship. The shadow of fear cast by these pressures leads, we suspect, to an even larger voluntary curtailment of expression by those who seek to avoid controversy.

Such pressure toward conformity is perhaps natural to a time of uneasy change and pervading fear. Especially when so many of our apprehensions are directed against an ideology, the expression of a dissident idea becomes a thing feared in itself, and we tend to move against it as against a hostile deed, with suppression.

And yet suppression is never more dangerous than in such a time of social tension. Freedom has given the United States the elasticity to endure strain. Freedom keeps open the path of novel and creative solutions, and enables change to come by choice. Every silencing of a heresy, every enforcement of an orthodoxy, diminishes the toughness and resilience of our society and leaves it the less able to deal with stress.

Now as always in our history, books are among our greatest instruments of freedom. They are almost the only means for making generally available ideas or manners of expression that can initially command only a small audience. They are the natural medium for the new idea and the untried voice from which come the original contributions to social growth. They are essential to the extended discussion which serious thought requires, and to the accumulation of knowledge and ideas into organized collections.

We believe that free communication is essential to the preservation of a free society and a creative culture. We believe that these pressures towards conformity present the danger of limiting the range and variety of inquiry and expression on which our democracy and our culture depend. We believe that every American community must jealously guard the freedom to publish and to circulate, in order to preserve its own freedom to read. We believe that publishers and librarians have a profound responsibility to give validity to that freedom to read by making it possible for the readers to choose freely from a variety of offerings.

The freedom to read is guaranteed by the Constitution. Those with faith in free people will stand firm on these constitutional guarantees of essential rights and will exercise the responsibilities that accompany these rights.

The Freedom to Read

We therefore affirm these propositions:

1. *It is in the public interest for publishers and librarians to make available the widest diversity of views and expressions, including those which are unorthodox or unpopular with the majority.*

    Creative thought is by definition new, and what is new is different. The bearer of every new thought is a rebel until that idea is refined and tested. Totalitarian systems attempt to maintain themselves in power by the ruthless suppression of any concept which challenges the established orthodoxy. The power of a democratic system to adapt to change is vastly strengthened by the freedom of its citizens to choose widely from among conflicting opinions offered freely to them. To stifle every nonconformist idea at birth would mark the end of the democratic process. Furthermore, only through the constant activity of weighing and selecting can the democratic mind attain the strength demanded by times like these. We need to know not only what we believe but why we believe it.

2. *Publishers, librarians, and booksellers do not need to endorse every idea or presentation contained in the books they make available. It would conflict with the public interest for them to establish their own political, moral, or aesthetic views as a standard for determining what books should be published or circulated.*

    Publishers and librarians serve the educational process by helping to make available knowledge and ideas required for the growth of the mind and the increase of learning. They do not foster education by imposing as mentors the patterns of their own thought. The people should have the freedom to read and consider a broader range of ideas than those that may be held by any single librarian or publisher or government or church. It is wrong that what one can read should be confined to what another thinks proper.

3. *It is contrary to the public interest for publishers or librarians to determine the acceptability of a book on the basis of the personal history or political affiliations of the author.*

A book should be judged as a book. No art or literature can flourish if it is to be measured by the political views or private lives of its creators. No society of free men can flourish which draws up lists of writers to whom it will not listen, whatever they may have to say.

4. *There is no place in our society for efforts to coerce the taste of others, to confine adults to the reading matter deemed suitable for adolescents, or to inhibit the efforts of writers to achieve artistic expression.*

To some, much of modern literature is shocking. But is not much of life itself shocking? We cut off literature at the source if we prevent writers from dealing with the stuff of life. Parents and teachers have a responsibility to prepare the young to meet the diversity of experiences in life to which they will be exposed, as they have a responsibility to help them learn to think critically for themselves. These are affirmative responsibilities, not to be discharged simply by preventing them from reading works for which they are not yet prepared. In these matters taste differs, and taste cannot be legislated; nor can machinery be devised which will suit the demands of one group without limiting the freedom of others.

5. *It is not in the public interest to force a reader to accept with any book the prejudgment of a label characterizing the book or author as subversive or dangerous.*

The idea of labeling presupposes the existence of individuals or groups with wisdom to determine by authority what is good or bad for the citizen. It presupposes that each individual must be directed in making up his mind about the ideas he examines. But Americans do not need others to do their thinking for them.

146

6. *It is the responsibility of publishers and librarians, as guardians of the people's freedom to read, to contest encroachments upon that freedom by individuals or groups seeking to impose their own standards or tastes upon the community at large.*

It is inevitable in the give and take of the democratic process that the political, the moral, or the aesthetic concepts of an individual or group will occasionally collide with those of another individual or group. In a free society each individual is free to determine for himself what he wishes to read, and each group is free to determine what it will recommend to its freely associated members. But no group has the right to take the law into its own hands, and to impose its own concept of politics or morality upon other members of a democratic society. Freedom is no freedom if it is accorded only to the accepted and the inoffensive.

7. *It is the responsibility of publishers and librarians to give full meaning to the freedom to read by providing books that enrich the quality and diversity of thought and expression. By the exercise of this affirmative responsibility, bookmen can demonstrate that the answer to a bad book is a good one, the answer to a bad idea is a good one.*

The freedom to read is of little consequence when expended on the trivial; it is frustrated when the reader cannot obtain matter fit for his purpose. What is needed is not only the absence of restraint, but the positive provision of opportunity for the people to read the best that has been thought and said. Books are the major channel by which the intellectual inheritance is handed down, and the principal means of its testing and growth. The defense of their freedom and integrity, and the enlargement of their service to society, requires of all bookmen the utmost of their faculties, and deserves of all citizens the fullest of their support.

We state these propositions neither lightly nor as easy generalizations. We here stake out a lofty claim for the value of books. We do so because we believe that they are good, possessed of enormous variety and usefulness, worthy of cherishing and keeping free. We realize that the application of these propositions may mean the dissemination of ideas and manners of expression that are repugnant to many persons. We do not state these propositions in the comfortable belief that what people read is unimportant. We believe rather that what people read is deeply important; that ideas can be dangerous; but that the suppression of ideas is fatal to a democratic society. Freedom itself is a dangerous way of life, but it is ours.

The document was subsequently endorsed by many other organizations: American Booksellers Association; American Civil Liberties Union; American Federation of Teachers, AFL-CIO; Anti-Defamation League of B'nai B'rith; Association of American University Presses; Bureau of Independent Publishers and Distributors; Children's Book Council; Freedom of Information Center; Freedom to Read Foundation; Magazine Publishers Association; Motion Picture Association of America; National Association of College Stores; National Board of the Young Women's Christian Association of the U.S.A.; National Book Committee; National Council of Negro Women; National Council of Teachers of English; National Library Week Program; P.E.N.—American Center; Periodical and Book Association of America; Sex Information and Education Council of the U.S.; and Women's National Book Association.

By 1990, both the IFC and the AAP Freedom to Read Committee were in agreement that *The Freedom to Read* needed minor revisions. In addition, it recently had gone out of print. At the Annual Conference in June, Richard Kleeman of the Association of American Publishers recommended minor changes, including removal of gender-specific language. It was also suggested that the new draft incorporate international concerns about the freedom to read.

A major question in regard to a revised statement was whether it should be more explicitly inclusive of the arts and music—targets of many then-recent censorship battles. Again, the view was strongly expressed that the statement had stood the test of time and would only be diminished by major revisions. The IFC agreed to proceed with a review and report back at the 1991 Midwinter Meeting. Richard Kleeman said the AAP Freedom to Read Committee would follow the same timetable.

In January 1991, the Committee considered two new drafts: one without gender-specific language and the other with a new international focus. Ultimately, the Committee decided to adopt only the first version and to address international and other concerns in separate documents. On January 16, 1991, the Committee adopted *The Freedom to Read* as revised and so informed the Council. Given the editorial nature of the changes, no action by the Council was required. On the same date, at its regular monthly meeting, the AAP Freedom to Read Committee adopted the same revision.

NOTE

1. For full details of national and international events surrounding the development of *The Freedom to Read*, see Everett T. Moore, "Intellectual Freedom," in *Research Librarianship: Essays in Honor of Robert B. Downs*, ed. Jerrold Orne (New York: Bowker, 1971).

2

Policy on Confidentiality of Library Records: Policy Statement

The Council of the American Library Association strongly recommends that the responsible officers of each library, cooperative system, and consortium in the United States:

1. Formally adopt a policy which specifically recognizes its circulation records and other records identifying the name of library users to be confidential in nature.*

2. Advise all librarians and library employees that such records shall not be made available to any agency of state, federal, or local government except pursuant to such process, order, or subpoena as may be authorized under the authority of, and pursuant to, federal, state, or local law relating to civil, criminal, or administrative discovery procedures or legislative investigative power.

3. Resist the issuance or enforcement of any such process, order, or subpoena until such time as a proper showing of good cause has been made in a court of competent jurisdiction.**

---

*Note: See also ALA "Code of Ethics," point III: "We protect each library user's right to privacy and confidentiality with respect to information sought or received and materials consulted, borrowed, acquired or transmitted."

**Note: Point 3, above, means that upon receipt of such process, order, or subpoena, the library's officers will consult with their legal counsel to

150

determine if such process, order, or subpoena is in proper form and if there is a showing of good cause for its issuance; if the process, order, or subpoena is not in proper form or if good cause has not been shown, they will insist that such defects be cured.

Adopted January 20, 1971; revised July 4, 1975, and July 2, 1986, by the ALA Council.

Suggested Procedures
for Implementing
"Policy on Confidentiality
of Library Records"

When drafting local policies, libraries should consult with their legal counsel to insure these policies are based upon and consistent with applicable federal, state, and local law concerning the confidentiality of library records, the disclosure of public records, and the protection of individual privacy.

Suggested procedures include the following:

1. The library staff member receiving the request to examine or obtain information relating to circulation or other records identifying the names of library users will immediately refer the person making the request to the responsible officer of the institution, who shall explain the confidentiality policy.

2. The director, upon receipt of such process, order, or subpoena, shall consult with the appropriate legal officer assigned to the institution to determine if such process, order, or subpoena is in good form and if there is a showing of good cause for its issuance.

3. If the process, order, or subpoena is not in proper form or if good cause has not been shown, insistence shall be made that such defects be cured before any records are released. (The legal process requiring the production of circulation or other library records shall ordinarily be in the form of *subpoena duces tecum* [bring your records] requiring the responsible officer to attend court or the taking

of his/her disposition and may require him/her to bring along certain designated circulation or other specified records.)

4. Any threats or unauthorized demands (i.e., those not supported by a process, order, or subpoena) concerning circulation and other records identifying the names of library users shall be reported to the appropriate legal officer of the institution.

5. Any problems relating to the privacy of circulation and other records identifying the names of library users which are not provided for above shall be referred to the responsible officer.

Adopted by the ALA Intellectual Freedom Committee, January 9, 1983; revised January 11, 1988.

Policy on Confidentiality of Library Records

During the spring of 1970, the Milwaukee Public Library was visited by agents of the U.S. Treasury Department, requesting permission to examine the circulation records of books and materials on explosives. Initially rebuffed by the assistant librarian, the agents later returned with an opinion from the city attorney's office that circulation records were public records and that the agents should be allowed access to the files. The library complied. At about the same time, the ALA Office for Intellectual Freedom received reports of similar visits from treasury agents at public libraries in Cleveland, Ohio, and Richmond, California. On July 1 of that year, a report was received from Atlanta, Georgia, stating that in the Atlanta area, twenty-seven libraries and branches were visited.

On July 21, the ALA Executive Board issued an emergency advisory statement urging all libraries to make circulation records confidential as a matter of policy. The advisory statement read:

> The American Library Association has been advised that the Internal Revenue Service of the Treasury Department has requested access to the circulation records of public libraries in Atlanta, Georgia, and Milwaukee, Wisconsin, for the purpose of determining the identity of persons reading matter pertaining to the construction of explosive devices. The Association is further

advised that such requests were not based on any process, order, or subpoena authorized by federal, civil, criminal, or administrative discovery procedures.

The Executive Board of the ALA believes that the efforts of the federal government to convert library circulation records into "suspect lists" constitute an unconscionable and unconstitutional invasion of the right of privacy of library patrons and, if permitted to continue, will do irreparable damage to the educational and social value of the libraries of this country.

Accordingly, the Executive Board of the American Library Association strongly recommends that the responsible officers in each U.S. library:

1. Formally adopt a policy which specifically recognizes its circulation records to be confidential in nature.

2. Advise all librarians and library employees that such records shall not be made available to any agency of state, federal, or local government except pursuant to such process, order, or subpoena as may be authorized under the authority of, and pursuant to, federal, state, or local law relating to civil, criminal, or administrative discovery procedures or legislative investigatory power.

3. Resist the issuance or enforcement of any such process, order, or subpoena until such time as a proper showing of good cause has been made in a court of competent jurisdiction.

David H. Clift, ALA executive director, and staff members met with Randolph W. Thrower, commissioner of the Internal Revenue Service (IRS), on August 5, 1970, to discuss their mutual concern over the inquiries. Little was agreed upon at the meeting except that "efforts would begin, in a spirit of cooperation, to develop guidelines acceptable to the American Library Association and the Internal Revenue Service." That afternoon, Clift received a copy of a letter sent to Senator Sam J. Ervin, Jr., chair of the Senate Subcommittee on Constitutional Rights, by Secretary of the Treasury David M. Kennedy in response to Senator Ervin's earlier expressed concern about the IRS inquiries. Secretary David M. Kennedy's letter stated that the visits had been conducted to "determine the advisability of the use of library records as an investigative technique to assist in quelling bombings. That survey . . . has terminated and will not be repeated." But the door was not being closed on future surveys. The secretary added that "it is our judgment that checking such records in certain limited circumstances is an appropriate investigative technique" and that the Alcohol, Tobacco, and Firearms Division of the Treasury Department has the authority, under federal statute, to conduct limited investigations in specific cases.[1]

ALA indicated its awareness of the Internal Revenue Service's responsibility to enforce the statutes, but noted that the Association's primary concern was not the enforcement itself but, rather, the means by which this enforcement was undertaken regarding libraries. While not intending to hinder effective enforcement of federal statutes, the Association made it clear that circulation records were "not to be made available to any agency of state, federal, or local government except pursuant to such process, order, or subpoena as may be authorized under the authority of, and pursuant to, federal, state, or local law relating to civil, criminal, or administrative discovery procedures or legislative investigatory power."

In anticipation of presenting the matter to the ALA Council at the 1971 Midwinter Meeting in Los Angeles, Intellectual Freedom Committee members were polled by telegram in October 1970, concerning a proposed draft of a policy statement. Suggestions for modification of the July statement were made by the IFC and the Executive Board at the latter's 1970 fall meeting. The board suggested that the original introductory paragraph be shortened, that the phrase "and other records identifying the names of library users with specific materials" be added to Article 1, and that Article 3 be clarified.

The "Policy on Confidentiality of Library Records" was formally adopted by the IFC at a special meeting in December 1970. It was submitted to the ALA Council at the 1971 Midwinter Meeting in Los Angeles, and was approved on January 20, 1971. On that date, in his progress report to the Council, IFC Chair David K. Berninghausen stated the following:

> When the time comes in any society that government officials seek information as to what people are reading, it must be presumed that they expect to use these records as evidence of dangerous thinking. And when a government takes action to

control what its citizens are thinking, it is a tell-tale sign that all is not well in that society.

We recognize that the U.S. Treasury agents probably did not realize that their investigations would be viewed as an invasion of privacy of readers or as an infringement on the freedom of thought guaranteed by the U.S. Constitution and Bill of Rights. But it is such small, beginning steps that lead a nation down the road to tyranny. We are pleased to note that these programs of inquiry have been stopped. We are proud of ALA's prompt action which helped to bring the investigations to an end.[2]

At the 1975 Annual Conference in San Francisco, a new problem of confidentiality was considered by the IFC. Earlier, the Intellectual Freedom Committee of the Washington Library Association had called ALA's attention to the fact that the policy on the confidentiality of library records "identifying the names of library users with specific materials" had been used to justify the release of other kinds of library records on patrons to police officers.

After reviewing this issue, the IFC voted to recommend to Council that the phrase "with specific materials" be deleted from the policy, thus making it applicable to all patron records. The IFC's recommendation was accepted by Council at its meeting on July 4, 1975.

During the 1980–82 revision of ALA's intellectual freedom policies, the IFC considered several suggested revisions of the "Policy on Confidentiality of Library Records." After considerable discussion and consultation with ALA counsel, however, the Committee decided not to recommend any changes in the policy. At the 1983 Midwinter Meeting in San Antonio, however, it was voted to append to the document a note referring to point 3 of the ALA "Code of Ethics" protecting the library user's right to privacy. At San Antonio, the IFC also adopted a series of "suggested procedures" for implementing the confidentiality policy.

At the 1988 Midwinter Meeting in San Antonio, the IFC amended the suggested procedures. The emendations were made to bring the language in this document into conformance with the language in the policy, to stress the need for a court order before any records are released, and to emphasize the need for libraries to consult applicable federal, state, and local law when drafting such a policy for local use.

Later in 1988, responding to concerns about whether the language in the "Policy on Confidentiality of Library Records" was sufficient to cover all records, rather than just registration or circulation records, the IFC reviewed both the policy and the procedures for implementing it. The Committee decided that the language of the policy was sufficient but that the language in the procedures was not uniformly inclusive and should be revised. The Committee chair noted that the procedures should include a direction to librarians to ascertain the status of their state law on confidentiality of library records. In addition, the chair suggested that all state IFCs be encouraged to review their state statutes to determine the inclusivity of the records covered.

A new draft incorporating the above-mentioned concerns was adopted by the Committee on January 11, 1988. Procedures for implementing policy are institutional in nature and not official ALA policy; action by the Council, therefore, was not needed.

NOTES

1. David M. Kennedy, letter to Sen. Sam J. Ervin, Jr., July 29, 1970 (copy in ALA files).
2. American Library Association, "Minutes of Council Meetings," vol. 14, 1971–1972, p. 76.

3

Policy concerning Confidentiality of Personally Identifiable Information about Library Users: Policy Statement

The ethical responsibilities of librarians, as well as statutes in most states and the District of Columbia, protect the privacy of library users. Confidentiality extends to "information sought or received, and materials consulted, borrowed or acquired," and includes database search records, reference interviews, circulation records, interlibrary loan records, and other personally identifiable uses of library materials, facilities, or services.

The First Amendment's guarantee of freedom of speech and of the press requires that the corresponding rights to hear what is spoken and read what is written be preserved, free from fear of government intrusion, intimidation, or reprisal. The American Library Association reaffirms its opposition to "any use of government prerogatives which lead to the intimidation of the individual or the citizenry from the exercise of free expression . . . [and] encourages resistance to such abuse of government power. . . ." (ALA Policy 53.4). In seeking access or in the pursuit of information, confidentiality is the primary means of providing the privacy that will free the individual from fear of intimidation or retaliation.

Libraries are one of the great bulwarks of democracy. They are living embodiments of the First Amendment because their collections include voices of dissent as well as assent. Libraries are impartial resources providing information on all points of view, available to all persons regardless of age, race, religion, national origin, social

159

or political views, economic status, or any other characteristic. The role of libraries as such a resource must not be compromised by an erosion of the privacy rights of library users.

The American Library Association regularly receives reports of visits by agents of federal, state, and local law enforcement agencies to libraries, where it is alleged they have asked for personally identifiable information about library users. These visits, whether under the rubric of simply informing libraries of agency concerns or for some other reason, reflect an insensitivity to the legal and ethical bases for confidentiality, and the role it plays in the preservation of First Amendment rights, rights also extended to foreign nationals while in the United States. The government's interest in library use reflects a dangerous and fallacious equation of what a person reads with what that person believes or how that person is likely to behave. Such a presumption can and does threaten the freedom of access to information. It also is a threat to a crucial aspect of First Amendment rights: that freedom of speech and of the press include the freedom to hold, disseminate, and receive unpopular, minority, "extreme," or even "dangerous" ideas.

The American Library Association recognizes that, under limited circumstances, access to certain information might be restricted due to a legitimate "national security" concern. However, there has been no showing of a plausible probability that national security will be compromised by any use made of *unclassified* information available in libraries. Thus, the right of access to this information by individuals, including foreign nationals, must be recognized as part of the librarian's legal and ethical responsibility to protect the confidentiality of the library user.

The American Library Association also recognizes that law enforcement agencies and officers may occasionally believe that library records contain information which would be helpful to the investigation of criminal activity. If there is a reasonable basis to believe such records are *necessary* to the progress of an investigation or prosecution, the American judicial system provides the mechanism for seeking release of such confidential records: the issuance of a court order, following a showing of *good cause* based on *specific facts*, by a court of competent jurisdiction.

Adopted July 2, 1991, by the ALA Council.

Policy concerning Confidentiality of Personally Identifiable Information about Library Users

In 1989, the Intellectual Freedom Committee prepared a statement sent to then-FBI director William Sessions, outlining ALA's concerns about the FBI Library Awareness Program. (For more on the FBI Library Awareness Program, see "ALA and Intellectual Freedom: A Historical Overview.") Although the FBI had indicated it would exchange a similar statement of its own about the program, none was ever received by ALA. Inquiries to the OIF from librarians seeking assistance in handling law enforcement requests for confidential information about library users continued.

In response to the increasing number of inquiries, the lack of cooperation from the FBI, and concern about law enforcement requests for personally identifiable information about patrons whether found in library records per se or not, the ALA Council requested that a policy addressing the FBI and law enforcement issues be drafted.

The IFC revised and reformatted the statement prepared for the FBI in 1989 to explain library concerns about confidentiality to produce the "Policy concerning Confidentiality of Personally Identifiable Information about Library Users."

In 1991, the first draft was further revised to broaden the language concerning what constitutes personally identifiable information about library users. This was done in response to a case in Oregon, where law enforcement officials took fingerprints from library materials as part of a criminal investigation. Members questioned whether fingerprints could be considered personally identifiable information according to the policy.

The new draft also included a statement expressing the ALA's contention that the use of unclassified materials in libraries cannot reasonably be deemed a national security threat, as alleged by the FBI in an attempt to justify the Library Awareness Program. The final version of the new policy was adopted by the Council on July 2, 1991.

4

Policy on Governmental Intimidation: Policy Statement

The American Library Association opposes any use of governmental prerogatives which leads to the intimidation of the individual or the citizenry from the exercise of free expression. ALA encourages resistance to such abuse of governmental power and supports those against whom such governmental power has been employed.

Adopted February 2, 1973; amended July 1, 1981, by the ALA Council.

Policy on Governmental Intimidation

The issue of the federal government's abuse of authority was brought before the ALA membership at the Association's 1971 Annual Conference in Dallas. At the general membership meeting on June 23, Zoia Horn and Patricia Rom (then librarians at Bucknell University in Lewisburg, Pennsylvania) introduced a resolution on governmental intimidation. Approved by the membership and two days later amended and approved by the ALA Council, the original ALA statement on governmental intimidation read as follows:

WHEREAS, ALA is concerned with the preservation of intellectual freedom; and

WHEREAS, The freedom to think, to communicate, and discuss alternatives are essential elements of intellectual freedom; and

WHEREAS, These freedoms have been threatened by actions of the federal government through the use of informers, electronic surveillance, grand juries, and indictments under the Conspiracy Act of 1968 as demonstrated in the case of the Harrisburg 6;

NOW THEREFORE BE IT RESOLVED,

1. That the ALA Membership Meeting at Dallas recognizes the

danger to intellectual freedom presented by the use of spying in libraries by government agencies;

2.   That ALA go on record against the use of the grand jury procedure to intimidate anti–Vietnam War activists and people seeking justice for minority communities;

3.   That ALA deplore and go on record against the use of the Conspiracy Act of 1968 as a weapon against the citizens of this country who are being indicted for such overt acts as meeting, telephoning, discussing alternative methods of bringing about change, and writing letters;

4.   That the ALA Membership at Dallas assert the confidentiality of the professional relationships of librarians to the people they serve, that these relationships be respected in the same manner as medical doctors to their patients, lawyers to their clients, priests to the people they serve; and

5.   That ALA assert that no librarian would lend himself to a role as informant, whether of voluntarily revealing circulation records or identifying patrons and their reading habits.

In March 1972, the Social Responsibilities Round Table asked the Executive Board to give the Association's moral support and financial aid to a librarian who had been called to testify in a federal court and, after refusing, had been jailed for civil contempt. The Social Responsibilities Round Table held that the "Dallas Resolution on Governmental Intimidation" committed the ALA to supporting this librarian. The Executive Board directed the IFC to review the resolution and "develop a statement which would interpret the resolution in terms of guidance for possible action."

At the 1972 Annual Conference in Chicago, the IFC spent a great portion of its scheduled meetings trying to fulfill this charge. The Committee felt that it was unable to develop an interpretive statement because, in the Committee's words, the 1971 statement was "good in intent, but inoperable . . . due to its narrowness of focus." Because the 1971 statement was tied to a specific piece of legislation and a specific incident, the Intellectual Freedom Committee felt the document was difficult to apply. Rather than develop an interpretive statement, the Committee promised to develop a new resolution, expressing similar concerns, for presentation to the ALA Council at the Association's 1973 Midwinter Meeting. The IFC turned its full attention to preparing a new statement at the 1973 Midwinter Meeting. The new document was presented to the Council on February 2, 1973.

The Committee originally moved that the resolution be adopted and substituted in its entirety for the 1971 Dallas statement. However, the Council felt that the new resolution omitted one important concern: an affirmation of the confidential nature of the librarian-patron relationship, covered by Articles 4 and 5 of the Dallas resolution. To ensure that this point would be retained as part of official ALA policy, the Council rescinded all of the Dallas resolution except for Articles 4 and 5. In addition, the Council amended the IFC's resolution, confirming the ALA's support of all those against whom governmental power has been employed. The Resolution on Governmental Intimidation, approved by the ALA Council on February 2, 1973, read as follows:

> WHEREAS, The principle of intellectual freedom protects the rights of free expression of ideas, even those which are in opposition to the policies and actions of government itself; and
>
> WHEREAS, The support of that principle is guaranteed by the First Amendment, thus insuring constitutional protection of individual or collective dissent; and
>
> WHEREAS, Government, at whatever level, national, state, or local, must remain ever vigilant to the protection of that principle; and
>
> WHEREAS, Government, although properly empowered to promulgate, administer, or adjudicate law, has no right to use illicitly its legally constituted powers to coerce, intimidate, or harass the individual or the citizenry from enunciating dissent; and
>
> WHEREAS, The illegitimate uses of legitimate governmental powers have become increasingly a matter of public record, among them being the misuse of the Grand Jury and other investigative

procedures, the threat to deny licenses to telecommunications media, the indictment of citizens on charges not relevant to their presumed offenses, and the repressive classification, and hence denial, of documentary material to the very public taxed for its accumulation; and

WHEREAS, These illicit uses not only constitute an abrogation of the right to exercise the principle of freedom of expression but also, and perhaps more dangerously, prefigure a society no longer hospitable to dissent;

NOW THEREFORE BE IT RESOLVED, That the American Library Association, cognizant that in the scales of justice the strength of individual liberty may outweigh the force of power, express its unswerving opposition to any use of governmental prerogative which leads to the intimidation of the individual or the citizenry from the exercise of the constitutionally protected right of free expression; and

BE IT FURTHER RESOLVED, That the American Library Association encourage its members to resist such improper uses of governmental power; and

FURTHER, That the American Library Association support those against whom such governmental power has been employed.

During the review of the ALA intellectual freedom policies and statements which followed Council's adoption in 1980 of the revision of the *Library Bill of Rights,* the Intellectual Freedom Committee determined that two problems existed with the "Resolution on Governmental Intimidation." The first was the matter of format. It was a resolution and included a series of "whereas clauses," which were helpful in explaining the "policy" section but were not theoretically a part of the policy. The second problem related to the policy section itself, which the Committee believed should stand alone without the necessity of explanatory phrases. As in all cases when examples are used, these tend to date the policy to the period of time in which it was originally created. They also tend to dilute the clarity and force of the policy statement.

The Committee agreed that any policy on governmental intimidation should strongly oppose this activity and that, in addition, the policy should indicate ALA support of those who resist governmental intimidation. In presenting the amended policy to the ALA Council, the Intellectual Freedom Committee decided that the 1973 version would be maintained in full in the historical file and that it would be made available as necessary. The amended policy on governmental intimidation was adopted by the ALA Council on July 1, 1981.

5

Resolution on Access to the Use of Libraries and Information by Individuals with Physical or Mental Impairment: Policy Statement

WHEREAS, The Intellectual Freedom Committee is concerned with freedom of access; and

WHEREAS, The *Library Bill of Rights* states that "books and other library resources should be provided for the interests, information and enlightenment of all people of the community the library serves" and "a person's right to use a library should not be denied or abridged . . ."; and

WHEREAS, Federal and state constitutional and statutory laws forbid public institutions from discriminating against handicapped individuals, i.e., persons who have a physical or mental impairment; and

WHEREAS, Court opinions have clearly interpreted said laws as proscribing discrimination against persons who have acquired immune deficiency syndrome ("AIDS"), AIDS-related complex ("ARC"), or who test positive for the human immunodeficiency virus ("HIV"); and

WHEREAS, The American Medical Association and the United States Department of Health and Human Services have opined that while the human immunodeficiency virus that causes AIDS is a contagious disease, it cannot be transmitted by casual contact;

Now, THEREFORE BE IT RESOLVED, That the *Library Bill of Rights* of the American Library Association, which insures access to library facilities, materials and services by all people of the community, includes individuals with physical or mental impairments; and

BE IT FURTHER RESOLVED, That the American Library Association deplores discrimination against and denial or abridgment of library and information access to persons of all ages who have acquired immune deficiency syndrome ("AIDS"), AIDS-related complex ("ARC"), or who test positive for the human immunodeficiency virus ("HIV").

Adopted January 13, 1988, by the ALA Council.

Resolution on Access to the Use of Libraries and Information by Individuals with Physical or Mental Impairment

Immediately before the 1988 Midwinter Meeting in San Antonio, the Intellectual Freedom Committee received a request for a statement of ALA's position concerning access to libraries and information by those with physical and mental impairments, particularly persons with the AIDS virus.

The occasion for this request was the barring of a child in Lake City, Tennessee, from attendance at the public school because the child had AIDS. Public librarians in the area perceived a need for their boards to adopt a clear policy about the access rights of persons with AIDS. In the search for existing policy statements, the Intellectual Freedom Committee was contacted, but no such statements were found.

Recognizing the need for definitive language affirming the access rights of all physically and mentally impaired persons and in light of a rising hysteria over AIDS, the IFC took to the ALA Council the following: "Resolution on Access to the Use of Libraries and Information by Individuals with Physical or Mental Impairment." It was adopted by the Council on January 13, 1988.

6

Guidelines for the Development and Implementation of Policies, Regulations and Procedures Affecting Access to Library Materials, Services and Facilities

Publicly supported libraries exist within the context of a body of law derived from the United States Constitution and appropriate state constitutions, defined by statute, and implemented by regulations, policies and procedures established by their governing bodies and administrations. These regulations, policies and procedures establish the mission of the library, define its functions, services and operations and ascertain the rights and responsibilities of the clientele served by the library.

Publicly supported library service is based upon the First Amendment right of free expression. The publicly supported library provides free and equal access to information for all people of the community it serves. Thus, publicly supported libraries are governmental agencies designated as limited public forums for access to information. Libraries that make meeting rooms, exhibit spaces and/or bulletin boards available for public use are also designated as limited public forums for the exchange of information.

Many libraries adopt administrative policies and procedures regulating the organization and use of library materials, services and facilities. These policies and procedures affect access and may have the effect of restricting, denying or creating barriers to access to the library as a public forum, including the library's resources, facilities and services. Library policies and procedures that impinge upon First Amendment rights are subject to a higher standard of review than may be required in the policies of other public services and facilities.

Policies, procedures or regulations that may result in denying, restricting or creating physical or economic barriers to access to the library's public forum must be based on a compelling government interest. However, library governing authorities may place reasonable and narrowly drawn restrictions on the time, place or manner of access to library resources, services or facilities, provided that such restrictions are not based upon arbitrary distinctions between individuals or classes of individuals.

The American Library Association has adopted the *Library Bill of Rights* and Interpretations of the *Library Bill of Rights* to provide library governing authorities, librarians and other library staff and library users with guidelines on how constitutional principles apply to libraries in the United States of America.

The American Library Association's Intellectual Freedom Committee recommends that publicly supported libraries use the following guidelines, based on constitutional principles, to develop policies, regulations and procedures.

Guidelines

All library policies, regulations and procedures should be carefully examined to determine if they may result in denying, restricting or creating barriers to access. If they may result in such restrictions, they:

1. should be developed and implemented within the legal framework that applies to the library. This includes: the United States Constitution, including the First and Fourteenth Amendments, due process and equal treatment under the law; the applicable state constitution; federal and state civil rights legislation; all other applicable federal, state and local legislation; and applicable case law;
2. should cite statutes or ordinances upon which the authority to make that policy is based, when appropriate;

3. should be developed and implemented within the framework of the *Library Bill of Rights* and its Interpretations;

4. should be based upon the library's mission and objectives;

5. should only impose restrictions on the access to, or use of library resources, services or facilities when those restrictions are necessary to achieve the library's mission and objectives;

6. should narrowly tailor prohibitions or restrictions, in the rare instances when they are required, so they are not more restrictive than needed to serve their objectives;

7. should attempt to balance competing interests and avoid favoring the majority at the expense of individual rights, or allowing individual users' rights to interfere materially with the majority's rights to free and equal access to library resources, services and facilities;

8. should avoid arbitrary distinctions between individuals or classes of users, and should not have the effect of denying or abridging a person's right to use library resources, services, or facilities based upon arbitrary distinctions such as origin, age, background or views;

   In the *Library Bill of Rights* and all of its Interpretations, it is intended that: "origin" encompasses all the characteristics of individuals that are inherent in the circumstances of their birth; "age" encompasses all the characteristics of individuals that are inherent in their levels of development and maturity; "background" encompasses all the characteristics of individuals that are a result of their life experiences; and "views" encompasses all the opinions and beliefs held and expressed by individuals;

9. should not target specific users or groups of users based upon an assumption or expectation that such users might engage in behavior that will materially interfere with the achievement of substantial library objectives;

10. must be clearly stated so that a reasonably intelligent person will have fair warning of what is expected;

11. must provide a means of appeal;

12. must be reviewed regularly by the library's governing authority and by its legal counsel;

13. must be communicated clearly and made available in an effective manner to all library users;

14. must be enforced evenhandedly, and not in a manner intended to benefit or disfavor any person or group in an arbitrary or capricious manner;

    Libraries should develop an ongoing staff training program designed to foster the understanding of the legal framework and principles underlying library policies and to assist staff in gaining the skill and ability to respond to potentially difficult circumstances in a timely, direct and open manner. This program should include training to develop empathy and understanding of the social and economic problems of some library users;

15. should, if reasonably possible, provide adequate alternative means of access to information for those whose behavior results in the denial or restriction of access to any library resource, service or facility.

Adopted June 28, 1994, by the ALA Intellectual Freedom Committee.

Guidelines for the Development and Implementation of Policies, Regulations and Procedures Affecting Access to Library Materials, Services and Facilities

A s part of the review of all of the Interpretations of the *Library Bill of Rights*, begun in 1989 in response to a request by the Minority Concerns Committee that the policy reflect equity of access without regard to language or economic status, the Intellectual Freedom Committee took up the Interpretation entitled "Administrative Policies and Procedures Affecting Access to Library Resources and Services." In 1991, that Interpretation was revised substantially and retitled "Regulations, Policies and Procedures Affecting Access to Library Resources and Services." The newly revised Interpretation responded to issues raised in two 1991 court cases which had important implications for libraries. The policy also addressed intellectual freedom concerns raised by challenges to materials that were inappropriately handled where the challenges had originated within libraries by librarians, library administration, or library staff.

The two court cases referenced in the Interpretation were *Rust* v. *Sullivan*[1] and *Kreimer* v. *Morristown*.[2] In *Rust* v. *Sullivan*, the United States Supreme Court decision upheld Department of Health and Human Services regulations prohibiting recipients of Title X funds (primarily, family planning clinics) from providing information about abortion or any abortion counseling whatsoever to their clients. In a close 5–4 decision, the Court held that the prohibition was a permissible government choice, favoring some activities over others. In a stinging dissent, Justice Blackmun pointed out that, for the first time, the Court had sanctioned outright viewpoint-based discrimination in a federally funded program. In other words, the Supreme Court had said that it was permissible for the federal government selectively to fund a speech promoting one point of view while prohibiting the mention of the opposing position.

The decision was significant for libraries because, although libraries take no position on the underlying issue, they do provide materials and information from all points of view on topics of current and historical interest, including abortion. Librarians realized that, if medical professionals working in facilities supported by federal funds could be "gagged," so could libraries that received public money. The *Rust* decision was issued in an atmosphere of severe fiscal conservancy, when many public libraries already had experienced massive funding cuts. The potential of those cuts to be linked to ideological, viewpoint-based restrictions on library collections was clear.

The other significant court decision addressed in the 1991 revision of the Interpretation was *Kreimer v. Morristown,* a case that came from the United States District Court in New Jersey. Richard Kreimer, a homeless man, challenged rules and regulations of the Morristown, New Jersey, Public Library, on the grounds that they, on their face, discriminated against homeless and economically disadvantaged patrons.[3] Library officials, in turn, contended that Mr. Kreimer had annoyed other patrons, exuded a body odor so offensive as to interfere with other patrons' use of the library, stared at people, and followed children around the stacks. According to the Court's decision, the library admitted that some of the regulations had specifically been designed to bar Mr. Kreimer from the institution.

The district court found that the library's regulations prohibiting patrons from staring or annoying other patrons were overbroad and vague and, therefore, unconstitutional. The court recognized and firmly supported the right and the responsibility of public libraries to make rules governing their use and governing patron behavior, but the court also firmly upheld the First Amendment right to receive information in publicly funded libraries. The court held that, in the interest of all patrons, library rules should be specific, necessary, and neutral, and not susceptible of discriminatory application. In addition, they must not be so vague that their application is subject to the whims of individual library staff members.

The *Morristown* decision firmly upheld First Amendment rights to receive information in libraries and provided a powerful argument supporting libraries' resistance to censorship. At the same time, the judge recognized the necessity of specific, necessary, and neutral rules governing patron behavior to ensure equal access for all.

The Morristown Library appealed the district court's decision to the United States Court of Appeals for the Third Circuit. That court reversed the lower court's decision, finding that the Morristown Library's rules were constitutional on their face. However, the court also found that rules that could result in the expulsion of a person from a public library do implicate First Amendment rights and must be analyzed under First Amendment principles—in addition, the court held that public libraries are limited public fora for access to information. This is a highly significant holding—placing public libraries squarely within the First Amendment realm and recognizing, for the first time by any court, that libraries have a unique position in the fulfillment of the First Amendment right to receive information.

The Intellectual Freedom Committee believed it would be beneficial to produce a policy statement of the American Library Association that placed ALA's intellectual freedom policy squarely within the realm of First Amendment law. Such placement would counter accusations by opposition pressure groups that the American Library Association's policies were simply ALA's opinion and not in any way binding in effect. Whereas it is true that no library is compelled to adopt ALA's policies, publicly supported libraries are subject to First Amendment legal principles. The newly revised Interpretation made this explicit by quoting language from both the *Rust* and *Morristown* decisions.

The document adopted by Council at the 1991 Annual Conference included quotes from the district court's opinion in the *Morristown* case, which was subsequently reversed by the Third Circuit, necessitating a review for possible revision. The process of revising the Interpretation began at the Annual Conference in 1993. At the 1994 Midwinter Meeting in Los Angeles, it became apparent that the Interpretation attempted to address very broad areas of library operation, which could conceivably be addressed in many different library policies; revision was proving difficult. Given the difficulty the IFC had had in attempting revision, the Committee concluded that it might be more appropriate and successful to revise the Interpretation into a set of guidelines. A draft of "Guidelines for the Development of Policies, Regulations and Procedures Affecting Access to Library Materials, Services and Facilities" was produced at the Midwinter Meeting and circulated to ALA units for comment following that meeting. At the 1994 Annual Conference in Miami Beach, the Committee revised and renamed the document, and formally adopted it. "Guidelines for the Development and Implementation of Policies, Regulations and Procedures Affecting Access to Library Materials, Services and Facilities" was presented to Council for its information, together with a recommendation that the Interpretation of the *Library Bill of Rights* entitled "Regulations and Procedures Affecting Access to Library Materials, Services and Facilities" be rescinded. Council acted on the IFC's recommendation, rescinding the Interpretation. The Guidelines were made available to libraries contemplating new or revised policies.

The Guidelines were intended to provide signposts for libraries as they develop policies, procedures, and regulations governing many areas of library operation, encouraging libraries to consider at the outset the First Amendment implications of their policies, as well as the potential applicability of state constitutional principles and federal, state, and local law. In addition, the Guidelines suggest that policies address considerations such as due process and equity of access, and that they ensure nondiscrimination between classes of library patrons.

NOTES

1. *Rust* v. *Sullivan*, 59 U.S.L.W. 4451, 111 S.Ct. 1759 (1991).
2. *Richard R. Kreimer* v. *Bureau of Police for the Town of Morristown, et al.*, 765 F.Supp 181 (D.N.J. 1991), rev'd and remanded, 958 F.2d 1242 (3rd Cir. 1992).
3. For more on the *Morristown* case, see part V, section 4, "Public Libraries as Limited Public Fora for Access to Information."

7

Guidelines for the Development of Policies and Procedures regarding User Behavior and Library Usage

L ibraries are faced with problems of user behavior that must be addressed to insure the effective delivery of service and full access to facilities. Library governing bodies must approach the regulation of user behavior within the framework of the ALA "Code of Ethics," the *Library Bill of Rights* and the law, including local and state statutes, constitutional standards under the First and Fourteenth Amendments, due process and equal treatment under the law.

Publicly supported library service is based upon the First Amendment right of free expression. Publicly supported libraries are recognized as limited public forums for access to information. At least one federal court of appeals has recognized a First Amendment right to receive information in a public library. Library policies and procedures that could impinge upon such rights are subject to a higher standard of review than may be required in the policies of other public services and facilities.

There is a significant government interest in maintaining a library environment that is conducive to all users' exercise of their constitutionally protected right to receive information. This significant interest authorizes publicly supported libraries to maintain a safe and healthy environment in which library users and staff can be free from harassment, intimidation, and threats to their safety and

180

well-being. Libraries should provide appropriate safeguards against such behavior and enforce policies and procedures addressing that behavior when it occurs.

In order to protect all library users' right of access to library facilities, to ensure the safety of users and staff, and to protect library resources and facilities from damage, the library's governing authority may impose reasonable restrictions on the time, place, or manner of library access.

Guidelines

The American Library Association's Intellectual Freedom Committee recommends that publicly supported libraries use the following guidelines, based upon constitutional principles, to develop policies and procedures governing the use of library facilities:

1. Libraries are advised to rely upon existing legislation and law enforcement mechanisms as the primary means of controlling behavior that involves public safety, criminal behavior, or other issues covered by existing local, state, or federal statutes. In many instances, this legal framework may be sufficient to provide the library with the necessary tools to maintain order.

2. If the library's governing body chooses to write its own policies and procedures regarding user behavior or access to library facilities, services, and resources, the policies should cite statutes or ordinances upon which the authority to make those policies is based.

3. Library policies and procedures governing the use of library facilities should be carefully examined to insure that they are not in violation of the *Library Bill of Rights.*

4. Reasonable and narrowly drawn policies and procedures designed to prohibit interference with use of the facilities and services by others, or to prohibit activities inconsistent with achievement of substantial library objectives, are acceptable.

5. Such policies and the attendant implementing procedures should be reviewed regularly by the library's legal counsel for compliance with federal and state constitutional requirements, federal and state civil rights legislation, all other applicable federal and state legislation, and applicable case law.

6. Every effort should be made to respond to potentially difficult circumstances of user behavior in a timely, direct, and open manner. Common sense, reason and sensitivity should be used to resolve issues in a constructive and positive manner without escalation.

7. Libraries should develop an ongoing staff training program based upon their user behavior policy. This program should include training to develop empathy and understanding of the social and economic problems of some library users.

8. Policies and regulations that impose restrictions on library access:

a. should apply only to those activities that materially interfere with the public's right of access to library facilities, the safety of users and staff, and the protection of library resources and facilities;

b. should narrowly tailor prohibitions or restrictions so that they are not more restrictive than needed to serve their objectives;

c. should attempt to balance competing interests and avoid favoring the majority at the expense of individual rights, or allowing individual users' rights to supersede those of the majority of library users;

d. should be based upon actual behavior and not upon arbitrary distinctions between individuals or classes of individuals. Policies should not target specific users or groups of users based upon an assumption or expectation that such users might engage in behaviors that could disrupt library service;

e. should not restrict access to the library by persons who merely inspire the anger or annoyance of others. Policies based upon appearance or behavior that is merely annoying or which merely generates negative subjective reactions from others, do not meet the necessary standard unless the behavior would interfere with access by an objectively reasonable person to library facilities and services. Such policies should employ a reasonable, objective standard based on the behavior itself;

f. must provide a clear description of the behavior that is prohibited so that a reasonably intelligent person will have fair warning and must be continuously and clearly communicated in an effective manner to all library users;

g. to the extent possible, should not leave those affected without adequate alternative means of access to information in the library;

h. must be enforced evenhandedly, and not in a manner intended to benefit or disfavor any person or group in an arbitrary or capricious manner.

The user behaviors addressed in these Guidelines are the result of a wide variety of individual and societal conditions. Libraries should take advantage of the expertise of local social service agencies, advocacy groups, mental health professionals, law enforcement officials, and other community resources to develop community strategies for addressing the needs of a diverse population.

Adopted January 24, 1993, by the Intellectual Freedom Committee.

Guidelines for the Development of Policies and Procedures regarding User Behavior and Library Usage

In the wake of the 1991 District Court decision in *Kreimer* v. *Morristown*,[1] a case involving a challenge to regulations implemented by the Morristown, New Jersey, Public Library, the Intellectual Freedom Committee recognized a need for guidance in the development of library policies governing patron behavior. At the 1991 Annual Conference in Atlanta, the Committee established a task force to draft guidelines. The task force was charged with seeking expert legal advice in developing suggestions to assist local libraries in reviewing or drafting policies to deal with problem patrons that would meet constitutional standards. From the very beginning, the Intellectual Freedom Committee recognized that it would be impossible to present a set of model regulations, because the legal considerations governing actual behavior in differing jurisdictions vary. Instead, the Committee took the approach of providing a constitutional framework and encouraging libraries to consider carefully local statutory law, which might apply to particular patron-behavior situations.

The task force, chaired by then Public Library Association IFC chair Candace Morgan, presented a draft at the 1992 Midwinter Meeting in San Antonio. In presenting the draft to the Committee, Morgan explained that it was based almost entirely on advice obtained from ALA and Freedom to Read Foundation legal counsel firm Jenner and Block. The Committee also sponsored an open hearing at that Midwinter Meeting to receive additional comment on the draft from librarians. Despite explanations of why it would be unwise and probably impossible to provide a model set of rules, many librarians who testified and offered comments requested more specificity. Following the hearing, the task force met and agreed that, although it would be difficult to promulgate specific regulations within the context of widely varying local and state law, the task force could address the need for specificity by highlighting the necessity to refer to that local law. The task force also decided to address, in a similar, general way, health and safety regulations, equal access concerns, civil rights and due process, and so forth. Reference to staff training also was added. Another open forum was held at the 1992 Annual Conference in San Francisco to receive additional comment on a revised draft addressing these issues.

Throughout the development of the Guidelines, the library community continued to discuss the *Kreimer* v. *Morristown* case. The Intellectual Freedom Committee and the task force to develop the Guidelines took great pains to inform the library community that the Guidelines were not meant as a specific response to the *Morristown* case. The subject of the task force's hearings was not the *Morristown* case but the draft Guidelines, which went far beyond the specifics of that dispute. The task force stressed that it was attempting to provide a constitutional framework in which libraries could proceed in the development of their own regulations regarding user behavior of all types, not just the conduct addressed by the rules of the Morristown library that were challenged in the litigation.

However, because questions and misunderstandings persisted about the legal issues involved, Judge H. Lee Sarokin, the federal district court judge who rendered the original opinion in the *Kreimer* v. *Morristown* case, appeared at the 1992 Annual Conference in San Francisco to speak generally about those legal issues. The reception he received from some librarians in the audience, many of whom had not read his opinion and did not understand the legal status of the case, could only be described as openly hostile. Librarians from New Jersey continued to focus on the alleged behavior of one library patron, Richard Kreimer, and were patently uninterested in the broader legal issues the judge addressed.

Following Judge Sarokin's appearance, the task force once again revised the draft Guidelines. The intent was to make the Guidelines as broad and general as possible so that local libraries would have a framework in which to formulate their own rules with reference to both local law and constitutional principles. The task force stressed that the Guidelines did not, and were not intended to, constitute an ALA response to the *Morristown* decision. The IFC voted to approve the revised draft and to circulate it once again for additional comment.

After final editorial revisions in light of additional comments, the IFC adopted the final version of the "Guidelines for the Development of Policies and Procedures regarding User Behavior and Library Usage" and presented it for information to the ALA Council at the 1993 Midwinter Meeting in Denver.

NOTE

1. 765 F.Supp. 181 (D.N.J. 1991); rev'd in part and remanded, 958 F.2d 1242 (3rd Cir. 1992). For more on the *Morristown* case, see part V, section 4: "Public Libraries as Limited Public Fora for Access to Information."

8

Dealing with Concerns about
Library Resources:
Procedural Statement

As with any public service, libraries receive complaints and expressions of concern. One of the librarian's responsibilities is to handle these complaints in a respectful and fair manner. The complaints that librarians often worry about most are those dealing with library resources or free access policies. The key to successfully handling these complaints is to be sure the library staff and the governing authorities are all knowledgeable about the complaint procedures and their implementation. As normal operating procedure each library should:

1. Maintain a materials selection policy. It should be in written form and approved by the appropriate governing authority. It should apply to all library materials equally.

2. Maintain a library service policy. This should cover registration policies, programming, and services in the library that involve access issues.

3. Maintain a clearly defined method for handling complaints. The complaint must be filed in writing and the complainant must be properly identified before action is taken. A decision should be deferred until fully considered by appropriate administrative authority. [A sample form may be found in part III, "Procedures for

Handling Complaints," figure 4.] The process should be followed, whether the complaint originates internally or externally.

4. Maintain in-service training. Conduct periodic in-service training to acquaint staff, administration, and the governing authority with the materials selection policy and library service policy, and procedures for handling complaints.

5. Maintain lines of communication with civic, religious, educational, and political bodies of the community. Library board and staff participation in local civic organizations and presentations to these organizations should emphasize the library's selection process and intellectual freedom principles.

6. Maintain a vigorous public information program on behalf of intellectual freedom. Newspapers, radio, and television should be informed of policies governing resource selection and use, and of any special activities pertaining to intellectual freedom.

7. Maintain familiarity with any local municipal and state legislation pertaining to intellectual freedom and First Amendment rights.

Following these practices will not preclude receiving complaints from pressure groups or individuals but should provide a base from which to operate when these concerns are expressed. When a complaint is made, follow one or more of the steps listed below:

a. Listen calmly and courteously to the complaint. Remember the person has a right to express a concern. Use of good communication skills helps many people understand the need for diversity in library collections and the use of library resources. In the event the person is not satisfied, advise the complainant of the library policy and procedures for handling library resource statements of concern. If a person does fill out a form about their concern, make sure a prompt written reply related to the concern is sent.

b. It is essential to notify the administration and/or the governing authority (library board, etc.) of the complaint and assure them that the library's procedures are being followed. Present full, written information giving the nature of the complaint and identifying the source.

c. When appropriate, seek the support of the local media. Freedom to read and freedom of the press go hand in hand.

d. When appropriate, inform local civic organizations of the facts and enlist their support. Meet negative pressure with positive pressure.

e. Assert the principles of the *Library Bill of Rights* as a professional responsibility. Laws governing obscenity, subversive material and other questionable matter are subject to interpretation by courts. Library materials found to meet the standards set in the materials selection policy should not be removed from public access until after an adversary hearing resulting in a final judicial determination.

f. Contact the ALA Office for Intellectual Freedom and your state intellectual freedom committee to inform them of the complaint and enlist their support and the assistance of other agencies.

The principles and procedures discussed above apply to all kinds of resource related complaints or attempts to censor and are supported by groups such as the National Education Association, the American Civil Liberties Union and the National Council of Teachers of English, as well as the American Library Association. While the practices provide positive means for preparing for and meeting pressure group complaints, they serve the more general purpose of supporting the *Library Bill of Rights,* particularly Article III, which states that: "Libraries should challenge censorship in the fulfillment of the responsibility to provide information and enlightenment."

Revised January 12, 1983, by the Intellectual Freedom Committee.

Dealing with Concerns
about Library Resources

The *Library Bill of Rights* and its Interpretations are all broad statements of policy. Their purpose is to clarify application of the
basic principles of intellectual freedom to libraries. As statements of
policy, they offer general guidance for the resolution of practical
problems, but they are not in and of themselves practical or procedural documents. Yet in the course of applying the principles of the
Library Bill of Rights, librarians frequently encounter pressures and
concerns from those who, consciously or not, may seek to distort the
library into an instrument of their own beliefs. "Dealing with Concerns about Library Resources" outlines basic procedural and practical measures for responding to such pressure.

"Dealing with Concerns about Library Resources" is a procedural document. Its goal being to assist librarians in implementing
ALA's intellectual freedom policies, it is not itself a policy statement.
Its roots, however, lie in a previous Interpretation of the *Library Bill
of Rights,* titled "How Libraries and Schools Can Resist Censorship,"
first adopted in 1962 but rescinded by the ALA Council at the request of the IFC in 1981.

The early 1960s saw increased censorship attacks on libraries
and strenuous assaults on the freedom to read; "witch hunts" in
Georgia, censorship of some best-sellers, and heated controversy
over Henry Miller's *Tropic of Cancer* were prominent during the

period. In response to this situation, a group of librarians and publishers met in Washington, D.C., on January 5, 1962, to draft a statement on censorship. The committee was composed of David H. Clift, executive director of the American Library Association; Dan Lacy, managing director of the American Book Publishers Council; Margaret Dudley, executive secretary of the National Book Committee; Emerson Greenaway, chair of the ALA Legislative Committee; and Archie McNeal, chair of the ALA Intellectual Freedom Committee. The statement this group wrote, titled "How Libraries and Schools Can Resist Censorship," gave support and step-by-step guidelines whereby a library can thwart the censor.

In introducing the statement to the ALA Council, McNeal urged its support, especially in light of the countrywide attempts at censorship. "How Libraries and Schools Can Resist Censorship" was approved unanimously by the ALA Council on February 1, 1962. The statement was endorsed by the Adult Education Association Executive Committee, the American Book Publishers Council, the American Civil Liberties Union, the National Book Committee, the National Council of Teachers of English, the National Education Association Commission on Professional Rights and Responsibilities, and the National Education Association Department of Class Room Teachers.

At the 1972 Midwinter Meeting of the Intellectual Freedom Committee, the original statement on resisting censorship was altered to include all types of libraries, not just school and public libraries; and "library materials" was substituted for "books." The new document, "How Libraries Can Resist Censorship," was adopted by the ALA Council on January 28, 1972:

> Libraries of all sizes and types continue to be targets of pressure from groups and individuals who wish to use the library as an instrument of their own tastes and views. The problem differs somewhat between the public library, with a responsibility to present as wide a spectrum of materials as its budget can afford, and the school or academic library, whose collection is designed to support the educational objectives of the institution. Both, however, involve the freedom of the library to meet its professional responsibilities to the whole community.
>
> To combat censorship efforts from groups and individuals, every library should take certain measures to clarify policies and

191

establish community relations. While these steps should be taken regardless of any attack or prospect of attack, they will provide a firm and clearly defined position if selection policies are challenged. As normal operating procedure, each library should:

1. Maintain a definite materials selection policy. It should be in written form and approved by the appropriate regents or other governing authority. It should apply to all library materials equally.
2. Maintain a clearly defined method for handling complaints. Basic requirements should be that the complaint be filed in writing and the complainant be properly identified before his request is considered. Action should be deferred until full consideration by appropriate administrative authority.
3. Maintain lines of communication with civic, religious, educational, and political bodies of the community. Participation in local civic organizations and in community affairs is desirable. Because the library and the school are key centers of the community, the librarian should be known publicly as a community leader.
4. Maintain a vigorous public relations program on behalf of intellectual freedom. Newspapers, radio, and television should be informed of policies governing materials selection and use, and of any special activities pertaining to intellectual freedom.

Adherence to the practices listed above will not preclude confrontations with pressure groups or individuals but may provide a base from which to counter efforts to place restraints on the library. If a confrontation does occur, librarians should remember the following:

1. Remain calm. Don't confuse noise with substance. Require the deliberate handling of the complaint under previously established rules. Treat the group or individual who complains with dignity, courtesy, and good humor. Given the facts, most citizens will support the responsible exercise of professional freedom by teachers and librarians, and will insist on protecting their own freedom to read.

2. Take immediate steps to assure that the full facts surrounding a complaint are known to the administration and the governing authority. The school librarian–media specialist should go through the principal to the superintendent and the school board; the public librarian, to the board of trustees or to the appropriate governing authority of the community; the college or university librarian, to the president and through him to the board of trustees. Present full, written information giving the nature of the complaint and identifying the source.

3. Seek the support of the local press when appropriate. The freedom to read and freedom of the press go hand in hand.

4. Inform local civic organizations of the facts and enlist their support when appropriate. Meet negative pressure with positive pressure.

5. In most cases, defend the principle of the freedom to read and the professional responsibility of teachers and librarians. Only rarely is it necessary to defend the individual item. Laws governing obscenity, subversive material, and other questionable matter are subject to interpretation by courts. Responsibility for removal of any library materials from public access rests with this established process.

6. Inform the ALA Office for Intellectual Freedom and other appropriate national and state organizations concerned with intellectual freedom of the nature of the problem. Even though censorship must be fought at the local level, there is value in the support and assistance of agencies outside the area which have no personal involvement. They can often cite parallel cases and suggest methods of meeting an attack.

The foregoing principles and procedures apply to all kinds of censorship attacks and are supported by groups such as the National Education Association, the American Civil Liberties Union, and the National Council of Teachers of English, as well as the American Library Association. Whereas the practices provide positive means for preparing for and meeting pressure group complaints, they serve the more general purpose of supporting the *Library Bill of Rights*, particularly Article III, which states that "censorship should be challenged by libraries in the maintenance of their responsibility to provide public information and enlightenment." Adherence to this principle is especially necessary when the library is under pressure.

During 1980–81, following the 1980 revision of the *Library Bill of Rights*, the Intellectual Freedom Committee reviewed "How Libraries Can Resist Censorship" and found that the bulk of the document was simply a procedural elaboration and repetitive of other policies. Stripped to its essentials, its main utility was as a concise statement of practical measures libraries can and should take in preparing for and responding to potentially censorious complaints and pressures. At the 1981 Annual Conference, the IFC voted to request ALA Council to rescind the former Interpretation, which the Council did. Later that year, "Dealing with Complaints about Resources," based in part on the former Interpretation and on discussions by the IFC, was published as a procedural statement. At the 1983 Midwinter Meeting in San Antonio, the statement was again revised by the Committee and retitled "Dealing with Concerns about Library Resources." This document is the basis for part III of this manual, Before the Censor Comes: Essential Preparations.

PART III

Before the Censor Comes: Essential Preparations

1

Before the Censor Comes: Essential Preparations

Many challenges to intellectual freedom go unchecked or are mishandled simply because preparations for an effective defense have not been made. An "intellectual freedom toolbox" must be stocked and available for use not just at the moment the librarian is confronted by the would-be censor but for building and maintaining a strong foundation of support in the community before the censor comes. Tools must be polished and ready for use at a moment's notice: they must be in writing and a part of the library's procedures manual.

Why written procedures? First, they encourage stability and continuity in the library's operations. Library staff members may come and go, but the procedures manual—kept up-to-date, of course—will help ensure smooth transitions when organization or staff changes occur. Second, ambiguity and confusion are far less likely to result if a library's procedures are set down in writing.

Additional and convincing reasons for maintaining written procedures include the following:

1. They show everyone that the library is running a business-like operation.

2. They inform everyone about the library's intent, goals, and aspirations.

3. They give credence to library actions; people respect what is in writing, even though they may not agree with everything in the library's procedures manual.

4. They are impersonal; they make whimsical administration difficult.

5. They give the public a means to evaluate library performance; publicly pronounced policy statements prove that the library is willing to be held accountable for its decisions.

6. They contribute to the library's efficiency; many routine decisions can be incorporated into written procedures.

7. They help disarm potential censors; unfounded accusations seldom prevail when the library's operations are based on clear-cut and timely written procedures that reflect thorough research, sound judgment, and careful planning.

The library's governing body adopts broad policies that are implemented through more specific written procedures, which may or may not be adopted by the board. Regardless of whether or not the governing body adopts them, four procedures, at least, are vital for the good of the library and the defense of intellectual freedom: materials selection criteria, a complaints procedure, procedures that protect user confidentiality, and public relations procedures.

In the following sections, these four most essential preparations are described in depth, and practical guidelines are provided. These guidelines derive from and expand upon the basic outline of procedures offered in the document "Dealing with Concerns about Library Resources"(see part II, section 8), which should be reviewed in conjunction with the following chapters. Such preparations are important on a day-to-day basis. If they also have the endorsement of the library's governing body, they provide an even firmer foundation for supporting intellectual freedom in the event of a censorship dispute.

2

Development of a
Materials Selection Policy

The primary purpose of a materials selection or collection development policy is to promote the development of a collection based on institutional goals and user needs. A secondary purpose is defending the principles of intellectual freedom.

The basis of a sound selection program is a materials selection statement, identifying specific criteria to be met for materials being added to the collection. Although a majority of professional librarians believe a materials selection statement is desirable, in too many instances the belief does not become reality. Librarians have given many reasons for not writing such a statement, but often two unmentioned ones are the most important: lack of knowledge about how to prepare one and lack of confidence in one's abilities to do so. Regardless of past failures and present difficulties, there is an absolute need for the firm foundation that a selection statement provides.

In virtually every case, it will be the librarian's task to prepare the materials selection statement. Although approval or official adoption of the statement rests with the institution's legally responsible governing body, it is the librarian who has the expertise and practical knowledge of the day-to-day activities of the library necessary for the development of useful and comprehensive selection and collection development criteria.

A materials selection statement must relate to concrete practices. It should provide guidelines for strengthening and adding to the library's collection. Furthermore, if the statement is to fulfill its secondary purpose, that of defending intellectual freedom, it must be a viable, working document that relates to the specific, day-to-day operations of the library or library system of which it is a part. In the case of very large libraries or even medium-sized institutions with highly sophisticated holdings, the librarian may prefer to prepare both an overarching policy or mission statement describing the philosophy of collection development that will guide selection decisions, and a separate list of specific procedures that staff will follow in carrying out the policy. Thus, the materials selection statement should reflect institutional policies, whereas a separate procedures manual should deal with the day-to-day applications of those policies.

A strong collection and intellectual freedom go hand in hand. It is less likely that problems will remain unresolved if the collection reflects the logical, coherent, and explicit statement from which it grows. In developing a materials selection statement, four basic factors must be considered: (1) service policy, (2) environmental characteristics, (3) collection specifications, and (4) current selection needs.

Service Policy

A service policy will provide practical operational guidelines to govern future collection development in accordance with the needs of the library's users and the goals of the library. In order to establish a service policy, it is necessary to determine what groups the library is striving to serve and what purposes it is attempting to achieve. To do so will entail a study of user-group characteristics and institutional objectives. Guidelines for such a study follow (fig. 1).

FIGURE 1
Guidelines for Establishing Service Policy

___

I. **User groups.** A materials selection statement must reflect the needs of the people the library will serve in trying to fulfill its objectives. To establish guidelines for collection development and related library activities, it is necessary to gather detailed information on various user groups.

A questionnaire to establish basic data can be prepared and completed by each staff member working with the public, or such information can be compiled on the basis of institutional statistics and records. After the library staff has been surveyed, users can be given questionnaires regarding their purposes in using the library, their library activities, and the like. It should be noted that certain sections of the prepared form can be used to determine the desired state of affairs as well.

A. Population characteristics

1. Age
2. Education
3. Employment level
4. Others

B. Size of each user group
C. Primary purpose of each group in using the library
D. Kinds of material used in accomplishing these purposes
E. Kinds of activities engaged in during the accomplishment of these purposes

II. **Institutional objectives.** The materials selection statement should define the library's goals and reason for existing. Institutional goals can be determined from at least two sources:

A. Statements of objectives are ideally available in a public document designed to inform all concerned persons.

1. General need(s) the library is designated to fulfill
2. Activities or standards most valued
3. Distinction in some field of endeavor

B. Public documents and records, in lieu of a statement of objectives, may outline the institution's objectives and supplement statements of objectives.

1. Annual reports of the institution
2. Charter of the institution
3. Published history of the institution
4. Records of the governing body
5. Budget (Because preparation of a budget usually demands a resolution of difficult questions of priorities in order to allocate scarce resources, this item should not be overlooked.)

Environmental Characteristics

The librarian should determine all aspects of the environment surrounding the institution that could possibly influence the development of the library collection and the library's related activities. A few such environmental factors and their implications follow (fig. 2):

Environmental factors	Provisions affected
Relative geographical isolation	Materials related to the cultural and recreational needs of users
Economic structure	Materials related to specific educational needs
Presence or absence of library resources external to the institution	Degree of self-sufficiency or completeness of materials
Presence or absence of postsecondary learning institutions	Scholarly and technical works
Relationship to local industries	Technical reports and business materials
Relationship to local professional and cultural groups	Specialized subcollections

FIGURE 2
Factors That Influence Development of the Library Collection

Collection Specifications

Specifications should be established for each subject area or area of concern. (The data gathered to determine service policy and environmental characteristics will show, in large measure, what the library requires.) For this section of the selection statement, each subject area should be carefully reviewed in order to determine the types of materials to be acquired in each and the depth in which materials are to be sought. Such a review is especially important in smaller libraries where funds are severely limited and the needs of the users potentially great. If possible, the following data should be collected for each area:

Number of library materials currently held

Total number of relevant materials available

Percent of total materials held

Distribution of current holdings by publication date

In addition, holdings should be rated by subject area in terms of specific user purposes:

Recreation

Self-help

Continuing education

Business

Finally, a desired acquisition level should be specified for each area.

The section of the selection statement dealing with collection specifications will no doubt be the largest and most detailed of all. It will specify the criteria to be used in selecting and reevaluating materials in terms of (1) types of materials (books, periodicals, newspapers, government publications, maps, records, films, etc.); (2) users' special needs by virtue of occupation, cultural interest, language, etc.; and (3) users' age groups. This section will also specify policies to be used in handling such matters as gifts and special bequests.

Current Selection Needs

Current selection needs can be determined by the difference between the present collection and the collection specifications. In deciding what is currently needed, the desired state of affairs that may have been detailed under service policy should also be consulted. Once current needs are determined, other considerations come into play. Most prominent among these is the library's budget. Regardless of the amount of money available, the selection statement should indicate in as clear a manner as possible which materials are to be bought and which are not.

Components of a Selection Policy

After full consideration of the aforementioned four factors—service policy, environmental characteristics, collection specifications, and current selection needs—the next step is to prepare a final draft of the selection (or collection development) statement itself for submission to the library's governing body. Taking into account the factors discussed above, the statement should relate to and include all materials and services offered by the library.

A good policy statement will first discuss the library's objectives in acquiring materials and maintaining services. It will state in succinct terms what the library is trying to accomplish in its program of services and the specific objectives in given areas of service.

The policy should derive from the library's mission statement. It is helpful if the role of the library in society (or in the parent institution) is spelled out in the policy and related to the objectives of selection, collection development, and maintenance. The overarching goal may be expressed in the broadest terms. For example, a policy for a public library should include reference to the traditional function of the library in the marketplace of ideas. It could include language like the following:

> The library serves a traditional role as a public forum for access
> to the full range of recorded information within the marketplace
> of ideas. Collection development shall be content neutral so that
> the library represents significant viewpoints on subjects of inter-
> est and does not favor any particular viewpoint.

A school library may declare that its main objective is to make available to faculty and students a collection of materials that will enrich and support the curriculum and meet the educational needs of the students and faculty served. Such a statement may then be divided into more specific objectives, such as to provide background materials to supplement classroom instruction, to provide access to classics of American and world literature, or to provide a broad range of materials on current issues of controversy to help students develop critical analytic skills.

The policy should precisely define responsibility for selection of all types of library materials. It should name, by professional position, those persons responsible in each area of selection. Although selection of materials will, of course, involve many people other than professionally trained librarians, ultimate responsibility should be delegated by the library's governing body to the professional staff. A public library's statement of responsibility might read thus:

> The elected Library Board shall delegate to the Head Librarian the authority and responsibility for selection of all print and nonprint materials. Responsibilities for actual selection shall rest with appropriate professionally trained personnel who shall discharge this obligation consistent with the Board's adopted selection criteria and procedures.

Depending upon the size and purpose of the library, the statement might continue by elaborating on any specialized selection responsibilities, the role of user input, and the like.

In terms of subject matter covered, the policy should include criteria, and the application of criteria, relevant to the library's stated objectives. These should include artistic or literary excellence, appropriateness to level of user, authenticity, interest, cost, and circumstances of use. Technical criteria, such as clarity of sound in audio materials, can be included as well. To guide the professional staff with responsibility for selection, criteria should be spelled out as specifically as possible. Bibliographies, reviewing journals, and other selection aids to be consulted should be listed. Special criteria to be applied in exceptional cases should be clearly stated. So, for example, a public library that regularly purchases all books on the *New York Times* best-seller list, even if these titles do not always meet other criteria, should state this clearly in the policy. There should be a section explaining how the library will treat donated materials and that such materials will be subject to the same selection criteria as materials the library purchases.

The policy should directly address problems associated with the acquisition of controversial materials. The document should include a statement on intellectual freedom and its importance to librarianship and an affirmation of the *Library Bill of Rights*. Some libraries also include the text of the First Amendment to the U.S. Constitution. A statement on intellectual freedom might read: "The library subscribes in principle to the statements of policy on library philosophy as expressed in the American Library Association *Library Bill of Rights,* a copy of which is appended to and made an integral part of this policy." The statement can also include the text of *The Freedom to Read* and the ALA "Policy on Confidentiality of Library Records," which states that circulation records and other records identifying the names of library users are considered confidential in nature.

The library's selection procedures should be described step-by-step from initial screening to final selection. The procedures should provide for coordination among departments and professional staff, for handling recommendations from library users, and for review of existing material. Any special procedures pertinent to collection development should be spelled out precisely in the materials selection statement. Some items to consider for treatment in the statement are sponsored materials, expensive or fragile materials, ephemeral materials, relations with jobbers and salespersons, distribution of free materials, and handling of special collections. The document should review procedures for collection maintenance.

Finally, occasional objections to materials will be made despite the quality of the selection process. The procedure for review of challenged materials in response to concerns of library users should be stated clearly (see also part III, section 3). The procedure should establish a fair framework for registering complaints, while defending the principles of intellectual freedom, the library user's right of access, and professional responsibility and integrity. Each specific step to be taken when a request for reconsideration is made, and all possible avenues of appeal, should be listed.

The final format and organization of the materials selection statement will depend, of course, on the particularities of the library concerned. One possible table of contents, however, might be outlined like this (fig. 3):

PART 1: Selection of Library Materials

I. Statement of Policy

II. Objectives of Selection

III. Responsibility for Selection

    A. Delegation of Responsibility to Professional Staff
    B. Particular Responsibilities of Staff Members

IV. Selection Criteria

    A. General Selection Criteria
    B. Specific Selection Criteria

V. Policy on Controversial Materials

    A. General Statement
    B. *Library Bill of Rights*
    C. *Freedom to Read*

PART 2: Procedures for Selection of Library Materials

I. Procedures for Implementation

    A. Selection Aids
    B. Outside Recommendation Procedures
    C. Gifts
    D. Special Collections and Concerns

II. Collection Maintenance: Evaluation and Review of Existing Materials

III. Procedures for Dealing with Challenged Materials

    A. Request for Review
    B. The Review Committee
    C. Resolution and Appeal

FIGURE 3
Materials Selection Considerations

It hardly need be said that preparation of a complete statement requires work—a great amount of it. And the work must be done before the censorship problem arises. Unfortunately, there are no shortcuts. The materials in this manual, including the texts of current ALA intellectual freedom policies, will be of some assistance. For school libraries, the American Association of School Librarians distributes a document entitled "Policies and Procedures for Selection of Instructional Materials." OIF distributes a "Workbook for Selection Policy Writing," with specific suggestions and examples of how to write a school library policy, the basic principles of which are also helpful in formulating policies for other libraries. The OIF and many state intellectual freedom committees have also collected sample selection statements that can serve as examples. It is, however, impossible simply to borrow a statement based on another institution's goals and needs: the statement must be a working document, a handbook for daily activities reflecting the specific needs of those who are to use it.

3

Procedures for Handling Complaints

A ll librarians must be aware that at some time there will be complaints about library service—and sometimes these complaints will center around a particular book, magazine, or other item which the library distributes. What should one do when a complaint of this kind is made?* As in handling any type of complaint about library operations, a courteous and calm approach is essential. Above all, complainants must know that their objections will be given serious consideration and that interest in the library is welcome. Complainants should be listened to courteously and invited to file a complaint in writing, if the problem cannot be resolved through informal discussion. If the complaint comes by letter, it should be acknowledged promptly. In either case, the complainant should be offered a prepared questionnaire in order that a formal complaint may be submitted. In addition, the rationale for having a formal complaint procedure should be explained.

A prepared form is not just an additional record to keep. There are a number of advantages in having a complaint procedure. First, knowing that a response is ready and that there is a procedure to be followed, the librarian will be relieved of much of the initial panic

---

* See also "Dealing with Concerns about Library Resources" in part II, section 8.

that inevitably strikes when confronted by an outspoken and perhaps irate library patron. Also important, the complaint form asks complainants to state their objections in logical, unemotional terms, thereby assisting the librarian in evaluating the merits of the objections. In addition, the form benefits the complainant. When citizens with complaints are asked to follow an established procedure for lodging their objections, they feel assured they are being properly heard and that their objections will be considered.

The accompanying sample complaint form, titled Request for Reconsideration of Library Resources (fig. 4), was adopted by the Intellectual Freedom Committee and most recently revised in 1995. Libraries and librarians should feel free to use it as a model, although alternative forms may certainly be devised to reflect the specifics of a given library situation.

As soon as the complaint has been filed, the objections should be reviewed. The review should consist of specific steps, although the number will vary somewhat according to the individual library involved. Simultaneous with the review, the governing body (that is, board of trustees, school board, etc.) should be routinely notified that a formal complaint has been made.

First, the person or committee that selected the item, or an ad hoc committee, should evaluate the original reasons for the purchase. The objections should be considered in terms of the library's materials selection statement, the principles of the *Library Bill of Rights,* and the opinions of the various reviewing sources used in materials selection. If the materials selection statement is sufficiently detailed to function as a guide for selection decisions, it should not be difficult to make a logical, strong response to the objections.

Second, the objections and the response should be forwarded to the acquisitions librarian who has final responsibility for selecting materials and who, in turn, should review the response and either add relevant comments or return the response to the individual or committee for further clarification. At this point, then, either the acquisitions librarian or the selection committee can make a written response to the complainant.

It is critical that the review process be as objective as possible. If the challenged item does not meet the library's own criteria for selection (assuming, of course, that these criteria themselves are consistent with the principles of intellectual freedom), the library

Request for Reconsideration
of Library Resources

[This is where you identify who in your own structure has authorized use of this form—director, Board of Trustees, Board of Education, etc.—and to whom to return the form.]

Example: The school board of Mainstream County, U.S.A., has delegated the responsibility for selection and evaluation of library/educational resources to the school library media specialist/curriculum committee, and has established reconsideration procedures to address concerns about those resources. Completion of this form is the first step in those procedures. If you wish to request reconsideration of school or library resources, please return the completed form to the Coordinator of Library Media Resources, Mainstream School Dist., 1 Mainstream Plaza, Anytown, U.S.A.

Name_____ Date_____

Address_____

City_____ State_____ Zip Code_____ Phone_____

Do you represent yourself?_____ your organization?_____

1. Resource on which you are commenting:

   __Book   __Textbook   __Video   __Display
   __Magazine   __Library Program   __Audio Recording
   __Newspaper   __Electronic information/network (please specify)
   __Other _____

   Title_____

   Author/Producer_____

2. What brought this resource to your attention?_____

3. Have you examined the entire resource?_____

4. What concerns you about the resource? (Use other side or additional pages if necessary.)
   _____

5. Are there resource(s) you suggest to provide additional information and/or other viewpoints on this topic?
   _____

Revised by the American Library Association
Intellectual Freedom Committee
June 27, 1995

FIGURE 4
Sample Complaint Form

must be ready to acknowledge that the material is indeed unsuitable and withdraw it from the collection. If, on the other hand, as is most often the case, the material does meet the selection criteria and is deemed suitable for the collection, it is the responsibility of the library staff to respond to the complaint clearly and precisely. This response should also inform the complainant how to pursue the matter further. If the complainant is not satisfied, then the head administrator of the library (the person to whom the governing body has given authority) can serve as the person to whom an initial appeal is made. The complainant should be contacted promptly, given an explanation of the library's decision, and advised that further discussions are welcome.

If the complainant still feels that the problem has been dealt with inadequately, the complainant may make a final appeal (within the structure of the library) to the governing body of the institution. This body will take approriate action—for example, conduct a public hearing—according to the established procedures for such appeals. It must be emphasized, however, that requests for action from the governing body should not be routine; such requests are best avoided by an adequate initial response to the complaint.

At each step of this process, the utmost courtesy toward and respect for the complainant should be maintained. There is no reason for a librarian to become defensive or jealous of professional privilege when a complaint is made. Not only is this counterproductive, but it runs counter to library efforts to encourage user involvement. Most complainants are sincere in their concerns and frequently can be prevailed upon to see the censorious implications of their actions. It should be recognized that many library users are intimidated by the librarian's authority and expertise, and for many patrons the decision to complain may be an act of admirable personal courage and a reaffirmation of their democratic right to involvement, from which all may benefit.

The review procedure, including the written questionnaire, should be designed not only as a defense against potential censors but also as a means to facilitate constructive dialogue. Although these procedures do offer the library a defense against arbitrary attacks, they should never be permitted to degenerate into a bureaucratic smoke screen. In a word, the library should welcome constructive input even as it maintains firm barriers to censorship.

Conducting a Challenge Hearing

Challenges to materials only occasionally reach the stage of a full-blown administrative hearing; often they are resolved at an earlier step in the challenge resolution process. When a hearing is necessary, however, certain important do's and don'ts should be observed. A number of battles have been lost because the challenge hearing has been poorly organized. Even though procedures have been followed to the letter up to this point, the handling of the challenge hearing may be the weak link in the process.

The challenge process begins when someone objects to materials in a library collection. At this point, providing (1) an explanation of selection procedures, (2) a copy of the selection policy, or (3) a copy of the reconsideration or complaint form will often resolve the concern. A complainant sometimes may not return the reconsideration form, because he or she sees the logic of the selection process that emphasizes intellectual freedom and due process. The complainant tends to be satisfied in registering a concern and knowing the library is taking the concern seriously.

There are some, however, who will wish to follow through on the procedures established in the selection policy approved by the governing authority for handling complaints. To activate the reconsideration procedure, a complaint should be in writing. In fact, the written and approved selection policy should state that, to best serve the interests of all concerned, anonymous or unwritten complaints are not honored; action occurs only when the reconsideration or complaint form has been returned. When a written complaint is filed, the reconsideration committee, usually composed of representatives of all library users and the librarian (often, all are library staff—the actual composition of the committee is up to the individual institution), is formed. The committee should then undertake the following:

1. Read, view, or listen to the challenged material in its entirety;
2. Review the selection process and the criteria for selection;
3. Check reviews and recommended lists to determine recommendations by the experts and critics;
4. Meet to discuss the challenge; and
5. Make a recommendation to the administrator on removal, retention, or replacement.

Before the Hearing

After a formal, written request for reconsideration has been submitted and reviewed, and a recommendation for retention or removal has been made, the complainant should be notified of the committee's decision. At the same time, the procedure for appealing the decision also should be provided. The appeal may involve a hearing by a school board, a board of trustees, or a city or county board of commissioners or council. (The selection policy should clearly identify the chain of command.) The appeal also must be in writing in order for the chair of the governing authority to place it on the agenda for the next meeting. The librarian should follow up on this step to make certain the presiding officer is aware of the policies and procedures, including open meetings laws and the agenda, that should be followed. Normally, the board conducts a challenge hearing, which provides the forum for the complainant to air his or her objections to the title in the collection and the recommendation of the reconsideration committee.

A hearing on challenged material is serious and often lengthy. Such a hearing may be the only item on the agenda; indeed, best results are most often achieved this way.

Decide in advance on a length of time for the entire hearing. Have a definite beginning and ending time. Guard against overlong meetings when decisions may be made by small groups in the late hours. This has spelled disaster in some instances.

Never attempt to stage a hearing quietly. The entire community should be aware of the meeting and what has transpired up to this point. The hearing should be announced well in advance. Publicity is very important to ensure good attendance at the meeting. Make the time and place very clear. Indicate in an announcement or news release that an open hearing is being held and that the public is invited. Try to obtain full coverage by the local press, radio, and television. Prepare a news release for each of these groups to make certain they have the facts correct. Deliver to them copies of the media center's or library's selection policies, along with a copy of the *Library Bill of Rights*. These policies, of course, should include procedures for handling complaints.

Seek help and advice from your state intellectual freedom committee, local and state colleges and universities, educational groups, teachers' professional organizations and coalitions, and the ALA Office for Intellectual Freedom (OIF). If requested, the OIF will activate the Intellectual Freedom Action Network (see part VI, section 1, p. 344) and ask members in your area to offer help or attend hearings. In addition, many nonlibrary groups have committees on intellectual freedom, freedom of speech, and/or academic freedom. Even when representatives from these groups are not present at the hearing, solicited resolutions in written form sometimes help in supporting your philosophy.

Find people who will be willing to speak in support of the freedom to read, view, and listen. This pool of speakers should be notified well in advance of the hearing. In fact, many librarians have lists of persons they have informed previously and who are library supporters. The best spokespersons in hearings tend to be attorneys, ministers, people from the news media, educators, and, of course, librarians. Response to persons from the local community is usually more favorable than to people brought in from outside. Student speakers are also effective. They speak from the heart and have no vested interest other than maintaining their freedom of choice guaranteed by the Constitution.

Attempt to estimate in advance the size of the gathering for the hearing. Make certain the meeting place is large enough to prevent postponing the meeting or changing locations at the last minute. A late site change may result in losing part of the group attending.

Long before a hearing, members of the advisory board, the reconsideration committee, and governing board should have become well schooled in intellectual freedom principles and procedures. It is the responsibility of the librarian to accomplish this, and it will ensure board support when a challenge hearing is necessary. All those selected to testify should be reminded that they are defending a principle more than an individual title. The actual title in question should play a secondary role. It is very difficult to disagree with the freedom to read, view, and listen in a democratic society.

The Hearing

As people arrive for the hearing, they should be given a copy of the selection policy. The policy should include the following elements, among others: a statement of the philosophy of materials selection, a statement asserting that the governing board has the final responsibility for selection of materials, a statement detailing the delegation of this responsibility to the professional library personnel, criteria for selection of materials, and a section on procedures for handling challenged materials. If the *Library Bill of Rights* is not a formal part of the policy, it should be duplicated and distributed as well.

One or more persons should be stationed at the entrance to sign in people wishing to speak. Request that they identify the side on which they will be speaking. If at all possible, attempt to ensure that there will be a balanced number of speakers on both sides.

Begin the hearing on time. The chair of the governing board should preside, as at any other business meeting. After calling the meeting to order, he or she should review the procedures to be followed at the meeting and the process followed up to this point for reconsideration of the material. The board should announce at the beginning of the hearing that it will issue its decision at the next regularly scheduled meeting, and that the meeting is simply to hear all sides of the issue. Speakers should be allowed to speak in the order they signed in. Limit each speaker to a specific amount of time (e.g., three or four minutes) and appoint a timekeeper in advance. No participant should be allowed to speak a second time until everyone registered has been heard once. It is extremely important to adhere strictly both to the time limits and to the order of the speakers.

Through the whole process, it is crucial to follow the traditional advice of remaining calm. Remember to practice what you preach and ensure due process. Listen carefully and courteously to everyone. By using good communication skills, you will help people understand your logic in ensuring diversity in library collections.

After the Hearing

The board should announce its decision publicly at its next regularly scheduled meeting. The agenda should include an item showing that the board will announce its decision (but not the decision itself). The usual notices and publication of the agenda will alert the public; news releases may also be used to ensure coverage and attendance at the meeting if desired. Whatever the board's decision, the principles of the *Library Bill of Rights* should be reiterated, and the agreement of the decision with those principles should be explained. A very brief statement of the reason for the decision should also be made (e.g., "We have concluded that the material meets our selection criteria, and will be retained without restriction").

The library's governing authority must be kept current on all events and incidents. Librarians also should examine personal philosophies of intellectual freedom on a regular basis to renew their committment to the principles that form the bedrock of the profession. Counteract negative pressure with positive pressure, such as emphasizing intellectual freedom rather than the perils of censorship.

By following this advice, the library board will be able to conduct a successful challenge hearing and improve the library's image in the process.

4

Developing a
Confidentiality Policy

R ecent years have seen an increase in the number and frequency
of challenges to the confidentiality of library records across the
United States, and a new dimension has been added to confidentiality concerns. Throughout the 1980s, the Office for Intellectual Freedom (OIF) received queries from individual librarians who had been
pressured by the FBI or local law enforcement agencies for information about library users, or who were afraid of being held liable
for a patron's acts after providing information on such topics as
bomb construction, weapons, or satanism. Some of these librarians
were tempted to maintain special files on patrons who seemed "suspicious" or who made "unusual" requests. These queries revealed a
lack of confidence in confidentiality procedures or a misunderstand-
ing of the important links among confidentiality, intellectual freedom, and librarians' professional and legal obligations to uphold
the privacy rights of patrons.

Why Is Confidentiality Crucial
to Freedom of Inquiry?

Inquiries about patron reading habits raise serious questions for
librarians and patrons. For example, are you what you read? Would

you want others to base decisions affecting your life on their opinion of the books you read, the music you listen to, the information you access over the Internet or other electronic networks or database services, or the films you view? How would library use change if patrons thought their reading records and other information about their lives would be open for scrutiny? How widely would people read knowing their choices might prejudice others against them? If libraries are to survive as centers for the free and uninhibited access to information so necessary to a democratic society, librarians must vigilantly guard their patrons' privacy and freedom of inquiry.

To support librarians in their role as defenders of the right to read, in 1971 the IFC proposed, and the ALA Council adopted, the "Policy on Confidentiality of Library Records" (revised in 1975). This important addition to the IFC's expanding inventory of tools for defending intellectual freedom was initiated in response to U.S. Treasury Department efforts to identify potentially "subversive" individuals based on their choice of reading material. Looking for the names of those who had borrowed or read books about the construction of explosives, treasury agents conducted inquiries in libraries in Ohio, California, Georgia, and Wisconsin. Librarians sounded the alarm over these apparent "fishing expeditions," and the department ceased its inquiries—but not before some librarians had handed over their records.

Firmly committed to the freedom to read as a necessary corollary to freedom of expression, the IFC encouraged librarians to resist such open-ended government inquiries. One cannot exercise the right to read if the possible consequences include damage to one's reputation, ostracism from the community or workplace, or criminal penalties. Choice requires both a varied selection and the assurance that one's choice is not monitored. In the case of criminal investigations or other government inquiries, it is especially critical that a librarian preserve the patron's confidentiality because the consequences of releasing information about the individual(s) under investigation may be dire and the potential for abuse of information about a person's reading habits great.

A case in Decatur, Texas, dramatically illustrates this danger. Early in 1990, the Wise County District Attorney's office, investigating a child-abandonment case, subpoenaed the records of the Decatur Public Library, requesting the names, addresses, and telephone numbers of all individuals who had checked out books on childbirth within the previous nine months, the titles they borrowed, and the dates the materials were checked out and returned. The police had no evidence indicating that the person who abandoned the child might have borrowed library books or otherwise used the library. Lacking any other leads, police were simply conducting a "fishing expedition."

The director of the Decatur Public Library refused to release the records. Instead, she chose to respond, with the help of the city attorney, by filing a motion to quash the subpoena on behalf of the library's patrons. On May 9, 1990, Texas District Court Judge John R. Lindsey ruled in favor of the library and quashed the subpoena.[1] The library director in this case was successful in defending her patrons, but imagine the consequences if she had failed: all patrons who had borrowed books on childbirth might have been subjected to police interrogation based solely upon their choice of reading materials. Thanks to this librarian's courageous implementation of the library confidentiality policy, patrons were not subject to such unjust and humiliating proceedings.

Threats to confidentiality arise within the library from loosely managed information or circulation systems, library staff or board members who are unaware of their responsibilities under existing confidentiality policy or state law, or from lack of any policy at all on the issue. Librarians or their staff may be asked for confidential information by patrons, journalists, students, or professors who wish to check on the reading habits of their students, or parents of young children who must pay overdue fines or who wish to monitor their children's reading preferences. As more libraries become automated and computerize their patron information files, and as more libraries add access to the Internet, other electronic networks, database services, and e-mail services to the array of resources they offer their patrons, threats to privacy may arise from abusers of the system. Known as crackers, these pranksters and vandals enter the system without authorization and attempt to spy on other users or sabotage the system as a whole, using software of their own design or by exploiting loopholes in the system, sometimes causing major system breakdowns.

Finally, many of the most difficult and complicated challenges come from local or federal law enforcement officials investigating criminal activities, or from feuding litigants in civil cases. Although these situations are relatively infrequent, they can be intimidating if a librarian, staff, and governing board are inadequately prepared to respond.

In 1989, responding to an increase in external threats and the clear need for further education on intellectual freedom and confidentiality for all librarians, the ALA Intellectual Freedom Committee (IFC) initiated *Confidentiality in Libraries: An Intellectual Freedom Modular Education Program.* Concurrently, the ALA Council requested a new and more specific policy to address the problem of confidentiality in the context of law enforcement inquiries, a trend sparked by the FBI Library Awareness Program and emulated by law enforcement agencies at all levels across the country—from county sheriffs to urban detectives. The IFC developed a new policy, and Council adopted it at the June 1991 Annual Meeting (see "Policy concerning Confidentiality of Personally Identifiable Information about Library Users," part II, section 3).

Confidentiality and the Law

Although librarians' main concern has been the potential chilling effect a violation of confidentiality could have on the exercise of First Amendment rights, a growing body of law exists that protects individual privacy rights and the confidentiality of library records, raising concerns of librarian liability when confidentiality is breached. The right to privacy is not among the rights enumerated in the Bill of Rights, but legal scholars and U.S. Supreme Court interpretations of the Constitution have found an implied right of privacy or zones of privacy surrounding the First Amendment freedom of expression.[2] Justice Douglas stated that "the First Amendment has a penumbra where privacy is protected from governmental intrusion": the Fifth Amendment privilege against self-incrimination, the Fourteenth Amendment provision for due process and, above all, the Fourth Amendment protection against unreasonable search and seizure.

The Supreme Court, in two decisions, laid the foundation for recognizing a right to privacy in one's choice of reading materials and explained that freedom of expression includes the right to read. In *Lamont v. Postmaster General,*[3] the Court affirmed the right of an individual to receive controversial political materials through the

U.S. mail. Later, in *Stanley* v. *Georgia*,[4] the Court made explicit the right of individual privacy in controversial reading material, holding that an individual may read as he or she chooses—even material alleged to be obscene, as was the case in *Stanley*—within the privacy of his or her home. In 1990, however, this right was limited in *Osborne* v. *Ohio*,[5] when the Supreme Court upheld an Ohio law banning the possession of child pornography, arguing for a narrow interpretation of *Stanley*, and stating that "the interests underlying child pornography prohibitions far exceed the interests justifying the Georgia law at issue in *Stanley*. Every court to address the issue has so concluded."[6]

Early Supreme Court interpretations of the Fourth Amendment sought to protect private property against government intrusion. This protection was expanded by later Court decisions, in cases such as *NAACP* v. *Alabama*[7] and *Griswold* v. *Connecticut*,[8] to protect a person and personal information, as opposed to a particular place or property. In the *NAACP* case, the Court recognized the "chilling effect on First Amendment rights of unauthorized disclosure of member lists." A 1967 ruling in *Katz* v. *United States*[9] took this recognition further, setting forth a standard for constitutionally protected zones of privacy. In this case, the individual's expectation of privacy was weighed against the government's interest in searching or invading that privacy. Based on *Katz* and preceding cases, the Court has interpreted the Fourth Amendment and the Bill of Rights as a whole to protect an individual's property, communications, personality, politics, and thoughts.

Although some Supreme Court decisions had favored the right to privacy, there remained a need for more explicit protections for individuals in an age of computer-based information systems. Seeking to address this need, Congress passed the Privacy Act of 1974,[10] prohibiting the maintenance of secret data files, ensuring the right of individuals to know what files are kept and what information they contain, and outlining a process by which individuals can correct false or misleading information found in records maintained about them.

The Act was amended in 1988[11] to prevent the establishment of a national data bank, merging information on individuals maintained in systems of records by other federal agencies; the direct linking of computerized systems of records; the computer matching of records not otherwise authorized by law; and the disclosure of records for computer matching except to a federal, state, or local government agency. This attempt to legislate a right to privacy has had mixed success in the courts and has suffered some setbacks. To compensate for its inadequacies, nearly all states now recognize the right to privacy in their statutory law.

State Law Protection of Library Records

Forty-five states and the District of Columbia also have laws that provide for the confidentiality of library records.[12] This protection usually takes one of two basic forms: affirmative protection of a patron's privacy rights; or, exceptions to open public records or state freedom of information acts, exempting library records from public scrutiny. Direct protection is preferable, of course, because this format often provides for punitive action and redress if the law is broken; an exemption from an open public records act is not so easily enforced. Laws that do not specifically forbid revealing the information contained in library records are subject to varying interpretations and manipulation that might allow law enforcement agents easier access to privileged information.

It is imperative for librarians to know their legal rights and responsibilities and to create or revise confidentiality policies to conform with the law. Without taking these steps, the librarian may risk civil liability for harm suffered by a patron because the individual's library records were revealed to law enforcement agents, government officials, or others. Librarians also may be subjected to the penalties provided in state laws in the event that confidential records are revealed.

What Is a Librarian to Do?

Although questions of confidentiality can be complicated and have potentially serious consequences, they are exceedingly manageable and may be responded to in a way that protects both librarians and patrons. As all politics are local, so too are most attempts at censorship local in origin. Victories for the First Amendment are won (or lost) case by case and usually without fanfare through the conviction and dedication (or lack thereof) of individuals who stand up for the freedom of expression, regardless of the alleged offensiveness of content or the good cause of the person requesting or demanding confidential information. This means that every librarian must understand the importance of maintaining confidentiality and be prepared to educate people with a wide range of interests and expertise about the role of confidentiality in protecting the intellectual freedom of all library users.

This critical responsibility is best managed by choosing to be proactive and take the initiative, rather than waiting for a crisis to develop. Protecting confidentiality requires a rapid and well-orchestrated defense, beginning with a library policy on confidentiality.

Writing a Policy

The basis in policy and law for the protection of confidentiality can be found in the following documents:

1. *Library Bill of Rights* and its Interpretations
2. American Library Association "Code of Ethics"
3. ALA "Policy on Confidentiality of Library Records"
4. ALA "Policy concerning Confidentiality of Personally Identifiable Information about Library Users"
5. First, Fourth, Fifth, and Fourteenth Amendments to the United States Constitution
6. Privacy Act of 1974, amended
7. State confidentiality of library records laws

An effective policy should include the following sections:

Objective: Who or what is to be protected? From whom or what? Why is the policy necessary?

Responsibility: Who is responsible for implementing the policy? Who will enforce it? Who has a right to know? A need to know?

Criteria: Which information will be protected? How will this be determined?

Procedures: What steps are to be taken by staff in identifying situations where the policy applies? How will the policy be implemented in response to such situations? How will

224

the policy be adopted, amended, repealed? How will it be incorporated into the training of new staff, and what specific steps must staff follow under the policy? What provisions will there be for making the policy known to patrons and the public at large?

Circumstances, if any, under which records will be released.

Librarians will find it useful to append supporting documents (chosen from those in the foregoing list) to their policy. With these resources close at hand, librarians can prove formidable opponents for anyone who seeks access to confidential information.

Adopting a Policy

A policy stands a much better chance of being adopted if key board members have participated in the policy's development. This may involve consultation by phone or even a special meeting to explain the need for policy and seek board members' insights. This step, although perhaps cumbersome or inconvenient, will help smooth the way for board adoption of the final document.

Before the meeting at which the policy will be considered, copies of the draft, along with the agenda and other enclosures, should be sent to all board members. Enlisting supportive board members to "lobby" amongst their colleagues in advance is a valuable aid to the process.

Enlisting the most persuasive and supportive board member to present the policy to the entire board may prove useful. In addition, library directors may want to invite the library's counsel to be present and support the policy from a legal perspective. If opposition to the policy is anticipated, the presenter should be ready to use data on other libraries in the state or region that already have confidentiality policies and on "real-life" examples of horrendous situations that can and do arise in the absence of such a policy.

Implementing a Policy

Once the policy has been successfully adopted by the governing board, the real work begins. Every member of the staff should be responsible for knowing the policy and his or her role in its implementation. This is important, even, and especially for those who have no direct role to play. When initial attempts to obtain information through proper channels have been unsuccessful, determined and harried law enforcement officials, invasive journalists, and irate patrons have been known to try prying the information they seek from staff members who appear more easily intimidated than their supervisors.

The new policy should be incorporated into all training manuals and procedure books, especially those sections that involve the use of patron information: circulation, registration, and information services. The technology the library uses should be carefully assessed for weak points that could cause breaches of user confidentiality.

The governing board and legal counsel also must be familiar with the policy and the roles they will be expected to play when the library is faced with a challenge to the confidentiality of patron information. If board members and counsel have been involved in the policy process from the beginning, this aspect of the task will take care of itself.

NOTES

1. *The Decatur Public Library* v. *The District Attorney's Office of Wise County,* Case No. 90-05-192, letter opinion dated May 9, 1990.
2. *Griswold* v. *Connecticut,* 381 U.S. 479, 483 (1965).
3. *Lamont* v. *U.S. Postmaster General,* 381 U.S. 301 (1965).
4. *Stanley* v. *Georgia,* 394 U.S. 557 (1969).
5. *Clyde Osborne* v. *Ohio,* 109 L.Ed. 2d (1990).
6. Id., 108.
7. *NAACP* v. *Alabama,* 357 U.S. 449 (1958).
8. *Griswold* v. *Connecticut,* 381 U.S. 479 (1965).
9. *Katz* v. *United States,* 389 U.S. 347 (1967).
10. 5 U.S.C. #552(a).
11. "Computer Matching and Privacy Protection Act of 1988," P.L. 100-503. 5 U.S.C. #552(a).
12. As of this writing, only five states are without legislative protection of the confidentiality of library records: Hawaii, Kentucky, Mississippi, Ohio and Utah. Kentucky has an opinion from its attorney general, affirming the right of privacy in regard to library patron records.

5

Public Relations: Promoting Intellectual Freedom

Promoting library services and promoting intellectual freedom mean reaching out to the public. But such promotion is a two-way street. To be an effective advocate of intellectual freedom, just as to be an effective promoter of library services, one must first know the people one seeks to reach. Promotion efforts begin by identifying library users. What are their needs? What "competition" do libraries face? It is important to remember that each library exists to serve all of its users.

With respect to intellectual freedom, it is essential to know what attitudes and forces exist in a given community or state and how these relate to national trends. Those working for intellectual freedom must do their homework. Who are the people with influence? What are their views? Which political, social, religious, business, and labor groups are potential allies? Which are potential supporters of censorship? What are their principal concerns? The Office for Intellectual Freedom has developed an intellectual freedom modular education program, *Confidentiality in Libraries*, which provides participatory exercises and guided lessons designed to elicit this type of information in an ordered way, using confidentiality of information about library patrons as the operative example (the program, however, was designed so that all the exercises are easily adapted to insert other examples of intellectual freedom issues). The modular education program teaches basic intellectual freedom principles and specific skills to protect the freedom to read in libraries. Its five modules address the areas of policy writing, technology and confidentiality, libraries and the law, using the legislative process, and public and media relations.[1]

State intellectual freedom committees can use the modular education program to keep themselves and librarians in their state informed of the activities and ideas of potentially censorious organizations and individuals, both local and nationwide. The more that is known about the philosophies and beliefs held by potential censors, as well as their organizational goals and concerns, the better prepared librarians will be to engage censors in meaningful dialogue when the time comes to do so.

In gathering information on potential censors, however, there is the danger of opposing censorship with the tactics of the censors themselves. The American Library Association opposes all practices that involve the prejudgment and labeling of groups and individuals as censors—libraries do not blacklist. Those involved in the defense of intellectual freedom should work hard to avoid developing an adversary relationship with individuals or groups who have been involved in censorship activity. It is much more productive to work toward developing relationships based on mutual respect. The more librarians and their supporters understand about the feelings and beliefs of would-be censors, the easier it will be to relate to them as individuals with serious concerns. Building an image of receptivity, openness, fairness, and friendliness toward the entire community can only enhance the standing of libraries and the concept of intellectual freedom.

In 1994, the Office for Intellectual Freedom established the Intellectual Freedom Action Network, an ad hoc group of volunteers who have identified themselves as willing to come forward in support of intellectual freedom in controversies in their localities. Action Network members may be called upon to attend board meetings, write letters to the editor, or simply lend moral support to librarians addressing censorship challenges. New volunteers are welcome.[2]

Working with the Media

Promotion of intellectual freedom through the mass media must be understood within the context of the overall commitment of the libraries to public relations. State intellectual freedom committees should thus coordinate all media work with the state library association public relations committee. Media treatment of questions relevant to intellectual freedom in libraries has its particularities, however, which should be thoroughly understood.

In general, members of the mass media are among the best potential allies in the promotion of intellectual freedom. Much has already been done to make the national media aware of censorship problems. Just about every major television network, every major newspaper, and many national magazines have carried feature stories on challenges to the public's right of access to certain materials in libraries. Usually, the more nationally oriented the media, the more likely they are to be sympathetic. Such sympathy, however, does not mean that the case for intellectual freedom must not be presented as forcefully and as skillfully as possible at all times.

The media seek out conflict. Hence, they are far more likely to cover a censorship story when there are data to prove a marked increase or change in direction of censorship pressures, when a case is pending in the courts, or when there is a local incident. At moments of controversy, members of state committees and local librarians may find media attention thrust upon them, but such attention will be extensive and better focused if regular contact is maintained at all times with appropriate media figures.

The media are always looking for local people who can be quoted with authority regarding specific issues, including intellectual freedom. Where appropriate, members of state intellectual freedom committees can make themselves known to the media as such a resource, or they may inform the media of the presence in the community or state of other authorities, including figures of national reputation. To do this, write the feature and city editors of local newspapers and send along pertinent background. A brief letter could simply say "Intellectual freedom issues are much in the news, and if you are interested in a local point of view, I would be happy to help." Provide a short biography. The same approach can be used with radio and television programs by writing the producer of these shows.

One also need not wait to be called by reporters or television producers. Some techniques for getting coverage include the following:

Letters to the editor. Don't write long letters; stick to the point; and write well. A letter has a better chance of getting printed if it is related to something the paper has featured.

Guest columnist. Many newspapers provide for guest columnists on certain days of the week.

Columns and editorials. Many newspapers carry locally originated columns, and nearly all run editorials. Writing a potentially sympathetic columnist with an idea, or a phone call to determine who writes the editorials and a conversation about the subject, might prove fruitful. The Office for Intellectual Freedom coordinates the First Freedom Op-ed Service, an independent project of ALA's Intellectual Freedom Committee and the Freedom to Read Foundation Board of Trustees. The service targets smaller, local weekly newspapers, offering op-ed pieces written by First Amendment experts discussing intellectual freedom and related issues. Watch for First Freedom Op-ed Service pieces in local papers and build on them when they appear. If they have not been picked up in local newspapers, ask that the editorial page editor include them.[3]

Talk shows. Listen to the various stations in your area and make a list of those with talk shows. Call the station and get the name of the producer and either write or call about doing a show on intellectual freedom. Be prepared to offer both a rationale for the show (perhaps a local "hook") and to suggest potential guests, including perhaps someone from the "other side."

Situations will arise when those working for intellectual freedom will be the focus of a story or will be sought for an interview. When a local incident occurs, members of the state intellectual freedom committee may be asked to comment. Or comment may be sought on a situation that has occurred elsewhere—an incident, a court decision, or a reported increase in censorship pressures. Individual librarians faced with censorship challenges may also have media attention thrust upon them; they very likely will seek advice on handling the situation from the state committee.

Regardless of the circumstances, the following general advice will be useful to those contacted by the media:

Try to get all the information possible about the story or program. Don't be afraid to ask questions.

Make sure to have the facts at hand. Avoid giving quotes or comments without first thinking through the situation. It is permissible to get the questions from a reporter and answer them at a later time, especially if the reporter has simply telephoned.

Don't offer personal opinions unless you are convinced they can really advance your cause. Stick to facts and the explication of basic principles. Be prepared to quote the *Library Bill of Rights* and other ALA policies.

Try not to become embroiled in particulars. Move the discussion to larger issues—the true impact of censorship and the importance of intellectual freedom.

Don't assume that those you are speaking to know the background of the continuing challenge to intellectual freedom. Be prepared to go over basic principles and issues, starting with the First Amendment itself.

Don't make long speeches. Reduce your arguments to one or two pithy sentences.

Control your emotions. Angry people don't win arguments. Try to identify with your audience and speak to their concerns.

Try to think of all the questions you might be asked and prepare convincing responses in advance. A meeting with a writer or reporter, or an appearance on radio or television, no matter how brief, needs preparation.

NOTES

1. For more information on the modular education program, call the Office for Intellectual Freedom at (312) 280-4223.
2. For more information on the Intellectual Freedom Action Network, see "What ALA Can Do to Help Librarians . . . ," p. 344–345, or call the Office for Intellectual Freedom at (312) 280-4221.
3. Copies of First Freedom Op-ed pieces are available from the Office for Intellectual Freedom, American Library Association, 50 East Huron Street, Chicago, IL 60611; call (312) 280-4225.

5.1

Public Relations: Crisis Communications

Jeanne Thorsen

In crisis situations, the glare of the television camera, the tone of the radio interview, and the shock of reading oneself quoted in print can be quite piercing. Planning media responses, stating points clearly, and maintaining poise can help libraries come out on top during hot-seat, bright-lights, name-in-the-headlines times.

Crisis Communication: Preparing for the Unpredictable

How can the Gerber Products Company and Johnson and Johnson serve as role models for libraries? These companies successfully handled news media during crisis-level situations in ways that provided key information and restored confidence in the companies and their products.

When poisoned Tylenol capsules caused a series of deaths and reports of broken glass in baby food sparked negative publicity, these companies' public relations and media experts turned to their

---

Jeanne Thorsen is manager of community relations at the King County Library System in Washington State.

communications plans, which laid out general objectives, strategies, and tactical approaches. These plans served as the foundation for response, enabling the companies to address the issues and, in time, to regain customer confidence.

Although intellectual freedom controversies are not life threatening, they do cause unrest and require a fast, professional response. The time to prepare is now—before the television cameras descend upon the library because of a title on the shelf, a work of art in the collection, a speaker in the meeting room, or some other situation.

Planning for the unexpected crisis and practicing responses can, to some extent, influence the way a controversy is covered in the media. The emphasis here is "working with" the media. Although these challenging situations may feel like attacks, it's important to avoid the instinct to react in a defensive or adversarial way. Media attention provides an excellent opportunity to tell the library's story.

Skillful planning, organized communication, a responsive attitude, and quotable statements will help present the library's position effectively, by quickly and clearly explaining the organization's viewpoint on the issues. Presenting clear and concise statements that show the involvement and support of top management can turn the tide of public opinion.

Understanding the Media

The most effective form of communication—the best way to tell the story—is via the mass media. Beyond the "upcoming events" calendar level, media coverage falls into two general categories: features and news. The two often are approached from different perspectives. Features tell a story in some detail, frequently from a positive viewpoint. As a rule, features are not controversial, not urgent, can be planned and developed carefully and run when there's time or space for them.

News is what people talk about. It's what sells newspapers and draws audiences to radio and television. Newsrooms are hectic, busy places, and reporters often cover a handful of stories each day. Controversies present opportunities for news, and reporters have one job: to get a story. It's not their job to tell the story the library or its opposition wants to tell—reporters are looking for both conflict and balance. Opposing points of view, implications, novelties, different perspectives, and good quotes add to the interest of the piece.

Setting the Stage

Establishing good working relationships with the media on a day-to-day basis makes media relations smooth during a crisis situation. It is important to know the newspapers, the reporters, and their points of view, and to understand the differences between radio and television stations, the views of their talk show hosts, and who their audiences are. Contacts that provide information on stories under normal, everyday circumstances gain status as good sources. News or features on noncontroversial subjects bring welcome attention and publicity, and help local media know the library and its representatives—and where to find them.

It is crucial for the library to have its policies in order and to be clear about its role in promoting diversity of the collection and presenting various perspectives and points of view. Frequent opportunities to communicate with the public help tell the library's story all year long.

Strategic Communications Planning

The crisis is not the issue—the issue is how well the library responds to the crisis. In most cases, a controversy doesn't come as a surprise. A key part of the planning process is to identify broad potential issues that are newsworthy—acquisition of questionable materials, use of the meeting room by controversial groups, and so forth—and to establish general strategies for dealing with these issues ahead of time, before the crisis develops. A communications plan helps avoid the known pitfalls and handle the unknown ones.

Preparing a plan is a process of forethought that both helps to identify the real issues at stake, separating them from rhetoric, and establishes procedures for response to controversy. Then, when the crisis hits, there is time to focus efforts on clearly stating and responding to the issues.

Steps to an Effective Communications Strategy

Here's how to plan ahead so media relations work smoothly during times of crisis.

> *Designate a team to develop a strategy.* Get up to speed quickly and make prompt decisions about key responses and messages.
> *Talk it out.* Think of all the things that can go wrong and how to prevent or handle them. This is where the team is especially helpful: first, to get the best thinking and cooperation from other departments; and then, to sift all the information into statements for the media.
> *Don't be afraid to ask for help.* Call in a public relations or media consulting firm to coach the team. The consultant will play devil's advocate, helping to review and renew philosophies, hone responses, and determine the message. The narrower the message, the more effective it is. This can be a solidifying time—all members of the team will clearly know the library's position.
> *Name someone to put together the information and materials.* You will need official position statements, policy documents, copies of media coverage, home phone numbers for key contacts, and more. The person assigned to this project can also serve as the primary reference source when new questions are raised and keep the communications team supplied with the latest information.
> *Establish a communications chain of command.* The organization must speak with a single voice to keep its message from being fragmented. The media wants to talk to someone who has knowledge and is able to tell them what is going on at the decision-making level, so the spokesperson should probably be the director or a board member.
> *Be sure to rehearse.* The spokesperson must be comfortable with the library's position and message—a stiff, bureaucratic response doesn't play well on the evening news. Know the opposition and its arguments. Then use every point as an opportunity to address the library's agenda. Throw the hardest questions at the spokesperson to sharpen responses. Show no mercy—no one else will.

Determine who takes which calls. When the phones are ringing off the hook, it helps to separate the calls. Designate one person to take the media calls and have someone else handle calls from the public.

Be flexible. Things change. The communications plan is designed to handle the probable situations. Something else will develop—count on its requiring a quick response. Update responses as new information is available.

Keep the staff and other interested parties informed. They have pride in the organization, have concerns about the library in the media spotlight, and want to be up-to-date and in the know. These important library ambassadors need to understand the situation and how to respond when patrons ask them for information on what is in the news.

Set aside less crucial issues. When a controversial situation arises, deal with it first. Business won't be back to normal for a while, so be prepared to rearrange priorities.

Track coverage and plan for feedback. Follow news stories, route clippings, and tapes.

Talking to Reporters

Reporters need relevant, accurate information that meets their deadline in sound bite–sized chunks. The goal is to provide information in concise statements that clarify and support the library's position. Ask for information that puts the story in context (who else is being interviewed? when will the story appear? what's the angle? what questions will be discussed?). This can be helpful to reporters—and can help tailor a better response for the library. Keep in mind a few simple guidelines:

Be timely. If the first response is "no comment" or "unable to reach," the reporter will write the story anyway—without the library's side—and may cast the library in an unflattering role. If there is bad news, it's best to release it first—before the reporters hear it from the opposition.

Tell the story in language that everyone understands. Avoid technical terms or jargon.

Sometimes the best answer to a question is "I don't know." For example, if the board is meeting later that evening to make a decision, speculation on the outcome is dangerous and unnecessary. Arrange to call the reporter back when information is available. If questions asked require greater expertise, arrange time to gather facts and statements, or recruit someone to speak and call the reporter back at an agreed-upon time. Always offer to be available to answer or clarify points for the reporter while the story is being written.

Have solid quotes and sound bites ready. Use no more than three brief, easy-to-understand statements, memorized and presented in order of importance. Repeat the message over and over; this puts pressure on the reporter to use it at least once in the story.

What's a "sound bite?" It's a short quote that is easily used and remembered. Having good, short statements ready can help avoid creating unfortunate sound bites by mistake. Here are some memorable ones, for better or worse: "I am not a crook!" "Read my lips. . . . No new taxes." "I have a dream." "We have nothing to fear but fear itself." "Ask not what your country can do for you; ask what you can do for your country."

Decide how to release information or updates. Treat reporters fairly and equally.

Watch out for manipulative questions. Don't assume that because reporters believe in the First Amendment they will tell the story the library wants told. The reporter's job is to get a story about the issue—the library spokesperson's job is to tell the library's story.

Beware of "Would you say . . .?" and "What if . . .?" Such leading questions, as well as naive ones such as: "I don't know much about this controversy, can you help me out?" suggest that the reporter may be unprepared, error prone, lazy—or smart. Such questions can result in the library's name being attached to a reporter's statement.

Stay on the record. Reporters know that people tend to babble on when greeted by a silence, and chatter at the end of the interview can lead to unplanned, and often regrettable, comments.

Think about what is going on. While the interview is happening, consider the viewer's or the reader's perspective. Represent the interests of the library, colleagues, and the public. Don't say anything that shouldn't be broadcast or seen in print.

If something more must be said, reinforce earlier points. Once information is out of the mouth of a spokesperson, control over it is lost.

Think about headlines. The headline writer is not the person who writes the story. Headlines are written by someone who skims the story—under tremendous deadline pressure—to come up with something catchy that fits into an allotted space. The goal of the headline is to get people to read, listen to, or watch the story—not to tell what's in the story. That's why a headline will say "Looking for Sex? Try the County Library"—instead of "Library Upholds Intellectual Freedom and Open Access Policies." This makes it even more important to give the reporter focused, interesting information and quotes that have a little zing. This is another reason for creating great "sound bites."

Embrace voice mail and put it to work. Reporters leave names, numbers, deadlines, and even a question or two. When calls are returned—ideally, very shortly after they are received—enough information will have been exchanged to ensure good preparation for the interview when reporter and spokesperson finally connect.

Watch out for stories that won't die. If a news organization creates a story about the library, it has a stake in the story and will try to keep it alive and use it as a news story, feature story, and perhaps an editorial. If someone else attacks the library's policy and creates a story, keep it alive long enough to get the library's point across. Don't help keep a story alive when it is better dead and gone: overreacting to a quote out of context or a slight misinterpretation keeps the issue in the spotlight.

A note on accuracy. The majority of news consumers won't care as much about the accuracy of a story as those close to it do. If something in a story is downright wrong, call the reporter or the editor immediately and discuss it politely in an informative and helpful manner.

Remember to Breathe

Recovering and returning to normal take time. The spotlight will fade eventually. When it does, replay events, reread newspaper articles, take a look at or listen to interviews, and evaluate plans and events. Be objective and talk about what worked well and what might work better next time. With experience and practice, those who speak on behalf of libraries can become more skilled in working with the media.

Be sure to thank the staff members who helped during this flurry of activity and community supporters who spoke up on behalf of the library. Their goodwill is priceless, and they'll appreciate the recognition. Depending on the situation, a thank you to a reporter or editor may also be in order.

Some Final Thoughts

Crisis media coverage comes just often enough to reveal that practice makes perfect—and rustiness in media relations shows. That can make a controversy seem like a disaster, when it's really an excellent opportunity to state a position, make a case, or tell a story. The best way to remain calm, clear, and focused in a crisis is to be ready before it comes. Have a plan of action and practice it. Then, when the *60 Minutes* crew comes to the door, their visit can be viewed with confidence, as a valuable opportunity to tell the library's story nationwide.

6

The Censor:
Motives and Tactics

The term *censor* often evokes the mental picture of an irrational, belligerent individual. Such a picture, however, is misleading. In most cases, the one to bring a complaint to the library is a concerned parent or a citizen sincerely interested in the future well-being of the community. Although complainants may not have a broad knowledge of literature or of the principles of freedom of expression, their motives in questioning a book or other library material are seldom unusual. Any number of reasons are given for recommending that certain material be removed from the library. Complainants may believe that the materials will corrupt children and adolescents, offend the sensitive or unwary reader, or undermine basic values and beliefs. Sometimes, for these reasons, they may argue that the materials are of no interest or value to the community.

Although an attempt to stereotype the censor would be unfair, one generalization can be made: regardless of specific motives, all would-be censors share one belief—that they can recognize "evil" and that other people must be protected from it. Censors do not necessarily believe their own morals should be protected, but they do feel compelled to save their fellows.

240

Why Censorship?

In general, there are four basic motivational factors that may lie behind a censor's actions. The four motivations are by no means mutually exclusive; indeed, they often merge, both in outward appearance and in the censor's mind.

Family values. In some cases, the censor may feel threatened by changes in the accepted, traditional way of life. Changes in attitudes toward the family and related customs are naturally reflected in library materials. Explicitly sexual works in particular are often viewed as obvious causes of repeated deviation from the norm. Because they challenge values, censors may want to protect children from exposure to works dealing frankly with sexual topics and themes.

Religion. The censor may also view explicitly sexual works and politically unorthodox ideas as attacks on religious faith. Antireligious works, or materials that the censor considers damaging to religious beliefs, cause concern about a society many see as becoming more and more hostile to religious training, and these works buttress beliefs about society's steady disintegration.

Political views. Changes in the political structure can be equally threatening. The censor may view a work that advocates radical change as subversive. (The fact that such works have been seen as attacking basic values is confirmed by the number of attempts to label library materials with such broad terms as "communistic," "un-American," or "ungodly.") If these works also contain less than polite language, it will not be difficult for the censor to formulate an attack on the grounds of obscenity in addition to—and sometimes to cover up—objections on political grounds.

Minority rights. Of course, not all censors are interested in preserving traditional social order. The conservative censor has been joined by groups who want their own special group values recognized. For example, ethnic minorities and women struggling against long-established stereotypes are anxious to reject materials viewed as perpetuating those stereotypes. These groups too may use the devices of the censor.

Whatever the censor's motives, attempts to suppress certain library materials may also stem from a confused understanding of the role of the library and of the rights of other library users. The censor's concern about library materials is based upon a view of the library as an important social institution. But the censor may fail to see that the library fulfills its obligations to the community it serves by providing materials presenting all points of view and that it is not the function of the library to screen materials according to arbitrary standards of acceptability. Would-be censors may think that it is the role of the library to support certain values or causes—which are, of course, their values and their causes.

In the United States, under the First Amendment, no citizen and no librarian can properly assume the duty or right to restrict or suppress legally protected expressions of ideas. The censor may not understand that a request that certain works be labeled or restricted, if fulfilled, would lead to an abridgment of the rights of other library users.

The Censor in Action

A censorship incident usually begins with a library user's complaint about specific library materials. In general, the immediate aim of the complainant is to inform the library that the materials in question are unacceptable. In some cases, the complainant may asume that the library will immediately agree that the materials are not appropriate and should not be in the library.

The censor may want to state publicly that he has found "objectionable" materials in the library and may attend a meeting of the library board to announce his "discovery." Those sections of the work that are considered especially offensive may be read aloud or distributed in writing to the library board, the local press, and the public. The censor may also go one step further and organize an ad hoc censorship organization. Even if an ad hoc group is loosely organized, the censors could use it effectively to promote a statement of purposes among other community groups, to conduct a letter-to-the-editor campaign, and to circulate petitions. The organization could also influence public funding, the appointment of the library director, and the appointment or election of library board members.

Although most censorship incidents begin with an objection to a specific work, if the censors are unsuccessful in getting the item banned, they may turn their efforts to library policy. If they cannot bring about a change in the library's policy on materials selection and distribution, they may then ask that the library establish a closed shelf or adopt a policy of restricted access.

Opposing the Censor

Well in advance of the appearance of the censor, a materials selection program, a procedure for handling complaints, and a public relations program will, of course, have been established. After the censor comes, censorship of library materials can be resisted by informing a number of key support sources: (1) community leaders and community organizations who would support the position of the library, (2) local news media whose editorial support would be valuable, (3) other librarians in the community and state whose support could then be available if needed, (4) the publisher of the challenged work who may have on file all its reviews and also may be interested in the legal questions raised by such practices as labeling and restricted access, (5) all library staff members and the governing board, (6) library's legal counsel, (7) the state library association's intellectual freedom committee, and (8) ALA's Office for Intellectual Freedom.

A censorship attempt presents the library with a good opportunity to explain the philosophy of intellectual freedom that underlies library service in the United States. For example, the library should prepare an article for local newspapers, explaining the role of the library and its commitment to the *Library Bill of Rights*. The article can emphasize the importance of the freedom to read as established by the First Amendment.

It is important to keep in mind that not every attempt to resist censorship will be successful; in many instances, developments will take a discouraging turn. However, it is certain that if the library is not prepared to offer any resistance, no battle will be won. And every battle won will contribute to establishing the library as an institution for free citizens in an open society.

7

Pressure Groups: Politics, Religion, and Censorship in Libraries

Carol Nielsen

In the past thirty years, the United States has become a more pluralistic society. Affirming differences rather than encouraging
homogenization has become the trend in business, academia, and
government. The "melting pot" concept that was used as an explanation of the greatness and the power of the United States has
been retired in favor of a "smorgasbord" or "salad bowl" metaphor.
An affirmation of ancestral roots and differing cultures and traditions is considered not only good but necessary, particularly in education. Native Americans, who in the past have been marginalized,
are now presented in textbooks with new understanding. African
Americans have a more prominent voice in shaping cultural norms.
Puerto Rican, Mexican, Cuban, and Central American cultures have
enriched many sections of this country and are now dominant in
areas where Spanish speakers are the majority. Defining what is
"truly American" is more complex in a society where differences are
acknowledged and celebrated.

Not all persons embrace these changes or are comfortable with
them. A growing sector of American society considers such plural-

Carol Nielsen is the information and research coordinator, Office of Research and Sponsored Programs, Northwestern University.

ism dangerous. Some believe that our founding fathers did not intend for us to become a country of such diversity. Others believe that we were mandated to be a "Christian" nation and that this focus is being lost in a cacophony of competing cultural styles. Coalitions have been formed that combine conservative politics and fundamentalist religion to fight for a "traditional" view of American society and "family" values. These groups engage in active campaigns, through the mass media, the school system, the publishing industry, and materials found in libraries, to combat the expression of points of view they perceive as threatening to their values.

At the same time, individuals and organizations have become more sensitive to diversity and a celebration of differences. Racial, national, and ethnic identities have become strong motivating factors for making new laws and for embracing new societal norms; ironically, they also have become reasons for demands for censorship—the so-called "political correctness" phenomenon. It therefore must be kept in mind that censorship comes from all points along the political and social spectrum. While religious conservatives may seek removal of materials on the grounds that they are blasphemous or un-Christian, women, gays, African Americans, Asians, Latinos, and other cultural and ethnic groups may seek removal of materials on the grounds that they perpetuate outdated and offensive stereotypes and fail to promote social justice.

Although it is true that demands for censorship know no political or cultural bounds, it is also true that in the 1980s and 1990s, the overwhelming majority of complaints about school and library materials have come from conservative religious (mainly Christian) perspectives. At the same time, there has been tremendous organizational growth among conservative religious groups, sometimes referred to in the press as the "religious right," "Christian fundamentalists," or the "radical right." No analogous phenomenon has occurred on the "left," despite media attention to the excesses of "political correctness" on college campuses. There is simply no "liberal" or "left wing" group that can claim the combination of financial backing, huge membership, and sophisticated national and state chapter political organization with an agenda that includes the censorship of information that now exists on the side of the "religious right." Thus, librarians who must be vigilant against censorship, regardless of the point of view of the censor, must also

245

familiarize themselves with self-described "Christian conservative" pressure groups. In the 1980s and even more so in the 1990s, these pressure groups have received more coverage in the media, more attention by political candidates, and more consideration in the minds of some Americans.

Why is membership in such pressure groups increasing? Fear of the unknown, a feeling of lack of control over one's life, and a longing for a mythical "simpler time" may all be factors. These are coupled with a strong yet simplistic view of Christianity: that the Bible should be interpreted literally and that its lessons are not metaphors but laws.

These new pressure groups have developed a political agenda based on the notion that matters of religious belief, or at least personal morality, can be legislated, creating a troublesome and potentially dangerous mix of religious dogma and political ideology. The groups are often unabashed about drawing strong distinctions between themselves and other religious people, even claiming outright that their type of Christianity is the only true or correct Christianity—a claim many Christians dispute. Thus, these groups have engendered divisiveness not only in politics but between "mainstream," traditionally liberal Protestant denominations and newer, independent, fundamentalist-evangelical congregations, which disavow any connection with mainline churches. Some of these fundamentalist believers claim that Catholicism too is outside the realm of "true" Christianity, while other conservative religious pressure groups have forged alliances with conservative Catholics to accomplish political goals.

As the ills of our society seem to become more pronounced, and new problems are introduced, some of the newly organized fundamentalist groups feel a need to control the reading and dissemination of information. Such control is needed not only for their own families but also for families in the broader community, whom they regard as having lost their way and in need of the guidance of those who possess spiritual and moral certainty about the right way to live.

In the past, many censorship cases involved the concerns of an individual parent whose child had been assigned a book at school the parent believed was objectionable. The book may have included sex scenes or "foul" language. In other instances, a child may have checked out a book about sex from the public library to which a parent objected on the grounds that the book was not age appropriate. Demands to remove the materials often were solved by respecting an individual parent's right to guide their own child, offering alternatives to that parent without infringing on the rights of others by labeling materials, setting up age-segregated collections, or removing materials that dealt with subjects offensive to some.

Now, however, library collections and textbook content have become ideological battlegrounds. The overall effect of organized religious pressure on local school policies has been, in some instances, a "chilling effect." Schools and textbook publishers are taking a more tentative and careful path—avoiding materials that might inflame a segment of the population and keeping to the middle ground in the hopes of universal acceptability.[1]

Librarians have always promoted the concept that citizens can make enlightened decisions if they have adequate information. Librarians generally believe that maintaining a diverse collection of library materials is good professional practice and should be above reproach. Yet, when faced with the religious conservatism of those whose interpretations of the Bible are literal, no material presenting ethical debate outside the context of the Bible or presenting worldviews not consistent with a creationist paradigm will satisfy.

Who Are the Pressure Groups?

Pat Robertson—Christian Coalition

Founded in 1989 by televangelist Pat Robertson, the Christian Coalition has two self-stated primary goals: (1) to take control of the Republican Party by working from the grass roots up, and (2) electing "Christian candidates" to public office. The Coalition distributed more than forty million voter guides for the 1994 elections. Running as "stealth" candidates (an appellation that resulted from the exhortation of Coalition Executive Director Ralph Reed, Jr., to supporters to "fly under the radar"), Christian Coalition–backed candidates have been elected to school and library boards without communities' knowing their affiliation. This tactic has now been abandoned by the Christian Coalition, and members and supporters of this organization are more open about their background.

Christian Coalition officials claim a $20 million budget, a membership roster of 1.4 million, and 1,100 grassroots chapters. In 1995, emboldened by the results of the 1994 congressional elections (which it claims to have influenced), the Christian Coalition presented Congress with the "Contract with America's Families," a list of ten "suggestions" to Congress for "pro-family" legislation.

Dr. James Dobson—Focus on the Family

Training evangelical Christians to become more active in the political process, through "Community Impact Seminars," is one of the top priorities of Focus on the Family. Founded in 1977 by psychologist Dr. James Dobson after the success of his first publication, *Dare to Discipline*, Focus on the Family advocates corporal punishment as part of its religiously oriented family values organization. Dr. Dobson's radio addresses are heard on more than one thousand stations nationwide.

Focus on the Family has grown into a multimillion-dollar enterprise, with a very successful publishing operation selling video and audiotapes on child rearing (particularly on how to raise conservative, chaste teenagers) and magazines targeting traditional families, single parents, teachers, and teenagers with its Christian message. Focus on the Family's activist publication, *Citizen*, exhorts members and subscribers to support or oppose legislation according to its perceived effect on traditional families and to work in local communities to limit access to sexual materials and textbooks it deems inappropriate. Would-be textbook and library book censors often use Focus on the Family materials when challenging a title.

Paul Weyrich—The Free Congress Foundation

Weyrich was the first president of the Heritage Foundation and is the driving force behind National Empowerment Television (NET), a conservative cable television network. The Free Congress Foundation focuses on a "family values" agenda and message.

248

Beverly LaHaye—Concerned Women for America

Membership numbers for Concerned Women for America (CWA) have been put at six hundred thousand, making it one of the largest women's groups in the United States. CWA works at a grassroots level, expressing views on a family values agenda that is antifeminist, antiabortion, abstinence-only sex education, and antigay.

A chapter of CWA in Oxford, Mississippi, successfully sued the local library, challenging its meeting room policy, which excluded religious groups. The suit stemmed from the denial of a request by the local chapter to use the auditorium of the library for a meeting that would include prayer and politics. The Fifth Circuit Court of Appeals ruled that because the library had allowed a broad range of other organizations to use the auditorium, it had established itself as a limited public forum. It therefore could not exclude groups on the basis of the content of their speech.

Robert Simonds—National Association for Christian Educators/Citizens for Excellence in Education

The Reverend Robert Simonds is director of Citizens for Excellence in Education (CEE). In a front-page article in the *Wall Street Journal* on July 15, 1992, Simonds announced his intention to "re-Christianize" American public education. The group also strongly supports school voucher legislation. CEE targets local school board elections, working to elect candidates sympathetic to CEE's values.

Phyllis Schlafly—Eagle Forum

Opposition to the Equal Rights Amendment was the original focus of the Eagle Forum, but the group has gone on to oppose any activities that are "profeminist" or "antifamily," including sex education that is not abstinence-only based, abortion rights, and federal support for day care and family leave. The group opposes any public school program it perceives as "outcome-based" education. Phyllis Schlafly is particularly clear in her dislike of the "radical feminist agenda," which, according to her publications, includes women working and pay equity for women. One of the Eagle Forum's more recent projects is called Eagle Forum Collegians. Its goal is to create chapters of the organization on college campuses.

Pressure Group Perspectives

In their publications and public statements about their goals and aspirations, these religious-political pressure groups use language couched in terms of warfare. They are waging war on what they see as the immorality of America; they are fighting for what they believe is right, and they consider themselves under siege.

The following list, although not complete, provides a general overview of the types of ideas and issues that are addressed by the pressure groups:

Sexuality. Basic sex education in the schools, expanded media coverage about AIDS, the idea that homosexuals are "ungodly" and sinful, and objections about pornography, sex, and sexuality are core concerns for pressure groups. Restricting the availability to minors of information about sex is often the goal of pressure group–generated controversies in libraries.

Abortion. These pressure groups view abortion as murder. Some have indicated at least tacit acceptance of violent assaults on medical staff who perform abortions. Some libraries have become caught in the middle of the pro-life–pro-choice debate when proponents of one side or the other accuse the library of failing to represent their point of view in library displays, on bulletin boards (where pro-life groups sometimes request that extremely graphic posters be placed), in exhibit spaces, and in the collection itself. A few libraries have received donations of pro-life materials, including videos, with assertive follow-up to pressure the library to add the materials to the collection, whether or not they meet selection criteria.

Family values. To conservative religious pressure groups and their supporters, the family is the center of the rules, values, and lifestyles of individuals. Feminism and the rise of the women's rights movement is wrong because a woman's place is in the home supporting her husband, who is the "head" of the household, according to biblical law. Children are to honor their parents, not disagree, and not rebel or question the traditional ways. Deviations from this "norm" by others are considered "un-Christian" and threatening to family values.

Government. The conservative religious pressure groups believe that government must be reorganized to support Christian values and themes. They believe, and often publish materials contending, that the founding fathers intended this to be a Christian nation and that Christian principles must be the primary foundation of our laws.

Evolution. The belief that evolution is just a theory that has not been scientifically proven and that the biblical view of creation is the correct view motivates pressure groups to continue their long-standing crusade to remove the teaching of evolution from science curricula and to add information about creationism to science texts.

Secular humanism. The so-called religion of secular humanism is a worldview that allegedly (and wrongly, in the pressure groups' view) promotes humans as rational beings who can make decisions based on information. As a result, people can control their fate, a concept that denies the authority of God, according to the beliefs of these pressure groups. Conservative religious pressure groups disagree with the ideas of secular humanism because they see humanity as controlled by God, and it is God's plan that is operative. Concepts of self-esteem and of one's ability to have an impact on one's fate through learning, exposure to new ideas, or embracing different cultures is seen as a form of blasphemy.

Secular humanism has been defined by various religious conservatives as "an incorrect view of mankind, placing the created at the center of all things, rather than the Creator."

By arguing that secular humanism is endorsed by the government in court decisions, laws, and school curricula, the conservative Christian groups claim that secular humanism constitutes an official state religion, in violation of the Establishment Clause of the First Amendment. This argument serves as the linchpin for many corollary arguments against sex education, the teaching of evolution in public schools, drug abuse prevention programs that train students to make their own decisions based on information (rather than a direct right-and-wrong approach), the women's movement, environmentalism, popular music, and even the mere presence of books that depict mythology, folktales, fantasy, or witches in school library collections. If secular humanism is the official government religion, goes the logic, then countless disturbing moral trends are implicitly endorsed by the government—in violation of the Constitution's "wall of separation" between church and state.[2]

Ironically, these groups simultaneously argue that the founders never intended that there be a "wall of separation" between church and state, and frequently argue that the United States was intended to be a "Christian" nation, citing established churches in the colonies and writings of colonial leaders as evidence; yet these groups are the first to claim the protection of the Establishment Clause when ideas with which they disagree are taught in schools.

In some respects, the pressure groups are railing against ideas that first came forward during the Age of Enlightenment. The concept of humans as rational beings, with the power to make decisions and the power to influence what happens to them, emerged in the seventeenth century after the rise of the Protestant Reformation, when many great thinkers explored a more humanistic and rational approach to philosophy than ever before. The founding documents of our nation are commonly understood to be Enlightenment documents, written from the perspective of educated, aristocratic supporters of Enlightenment ideas. Yet, the pressure groups have even begun to publish pamphlets and books taking issue with this generally accepted interpretation, contending that the Constitution and Bill of Rights were to be applied in a "Christian" nation and do not work effectively, and in fact create chaos, otherwise.

Tactics Employed by Pressure Groups

The pressure groups employ a number of methods and tactics to deliver their message and to have an impact on political issues.

One of the most disturbing methods used successfully until it was widely reported is that of "stealth" campaigns. When local political races—for example, school board elections—are being held, the pressure groups find a sympathetic candidate or promote a candidate they know will agree to censorial tactics. The campaign literature of the candidate does not identify that person as being affiliated with such pressure groups.

Money is channeled into the candidacy. And because voter turnout in such elections has traditionally been very low, the pressure groups have learned that they need muster only 15 percent of registered voters to win a seat on school or library boards. Often, they are successful in reaching that goal by campaigning solely among local church congregations.[3]

Members of Congress also are evaluated on the "fit" of their political agenda with that of these pressure groups. When the "fit" is right, money is again channeled to support lobbying and legislation that such pressure groups find appropriate. The issue of prayer in the schools is an example, and another is the Christian Coalition's overt and highly visible "Contract with the American Family," offered to Congress as a legislative agenda that will win the votes of millions of conservative Christians.

It must be remembered, however, that in expressing their opinions and concerns, would-be censors are exercising the same rights as those who created and disseminated the material they are complaining about—the same rights, in fact, that librarians seek to protect when they confront censorship. The rights of both sides must be protected, or neither will survive. Pressure groups are aware of their First Amendment rights, even as they work to curtail the rights of others. Librarians should take care to ensure that their pro-intellectual freedom stance is understood to include the rights of conservative religious groups to express their opinions.

What Can Be Expected in the Future?

Well-organized, well-funded, and *vocal* are adjectives often used to describe the religious right. These same adjectives should describe the activities of those who wish to retain a tolerant and free society. Those who describe themselves as liberals, free thinkers, and supporters of the rights protected in the First Amendment must make their beliefs known in their communities. Children should be educated about their rights as citizens. Libraries must become information centers supplying background on all candidates and the electoral process. The library must be seen as a neutral place to find information from all points of view about issues, legislation, and community well-being. Librarians should remember that pressure groups represent only a sector of the religious public and that many people of faith disagree with the agenda and tactics of such groups, and support intellectual freedom in libraries. Librarians should work with teachers, clergy, families, and community leaders to educate the community to be advocates for intellectual freedom.

There are often high costs associated with fervent defense of the values of the First Amendment—emotional turmoil, legal fees, time, and occasionally even personal attacks, threats, and smear campaigns. Pressure groups have been effective in capitalizing on the concept that those defending the First Amendment are sinful, evil, or less than wholesome.

Unfortunately, some "liberal-minded" people have gained a dubious reputation for complacency and even smugness—and for their tendency to take liberty for granted and ignore the need to be constantly vigilant. Pressure groups know this and take advantage of it, particularly in local elections where the turnout has traditionally been dismally low, creating the opportunity for "stealth" candidates to win election with very low percentages of the community voting. Librarians must be as well organized as the pressure groups— organization will pay off when libraries are faced with demands to remove books from the library collection or schools are faced with the demand to reevaluate textbooks. Librarians should use their reason, education, and understanding of the Constitution to promote free speech and freedom of the press.

Libraries are caught up in the rapidly changing cultural and political dynamic of American society. We cannot return to a simpler time, but we can ensure that social changes take place in an atmosphere of openness, where the inevitable debate is (at least potentially) a fully informed one, where various points of view are available, accessible, and equitably presented for the public's consideration. The children of this country are the hope for the future. Libraries that demonstrate, in their daily operation and their public statements, the value of intellectual freedom help to ensure the preservation of a free society by educating those children to be tolerant of the expression of nonconforming ideas and to respect the right to disagree.

NOTES

1. For more on this phenomenon, see Joan DelFattore, *What Johnny Shouldn't Read: Textbook Censorship in America* (New Haven, Conn.: Yale University Press, 1992).

2. David Bollier, *Liberty and Justice for Some: Defending a Free Society from the Radical Right's Holy War on Democracy* (Washington, D.C.: People for the American Way, 1982), 97.

3. Greg Goldin, "The Fifteen Percent Solution: How the Christian Right Is Building from Below to Take Over from Above," *The Village Voice* (April 6, 1993), 19.

PART IV

Intellectual Freedom:
An All-Embracing Concept

1

Intellectual Freedom: An All-Embracing Concept

When an institution is supported by public funds, taxpayers naturally believe they have the right, if not the obligation, to influence the operations of that institution. Where the selection and availability of library materials are concerned, this belief is especially prevalent, regardless of the kind of library or library activity involved. Unfortunately, there is little public understanding of the principles of intellectual freedom in this context and of the First Amendment's protection for, and libraries' responsibility to make available, unpopular and controversial materials. Supreme Court Justice Hugo Black once said, "The layman's constitutional view is that what he likes is constitutional and that which he doesn't like is unconstitutional." Add to this the simplistic understanding of democracy as "majority rule," and publicly supported libraries of all types find themselves subject to the accusation that in making available a broad range of materials, they are unresponsive to their taxpayer supporters.

The First Amendment does not say, "Congress shall make no law . . . abridging the freedom of speech . . . for everyone who agrees with me." The Bill of Rights exists to carve out individual liberties that are to be held inviolate from government and majoritarian intrusion. The First Amendment protects the right of dissent, the right to voice unpopular and even offensive opinions. It protects the "voice crying in the wilderness" every bit as much as it protects the most popular novel or video.

Freedom of expression and the corollary right to have access to the expression of others are principles that permeate and define library service. Too often, however, librarians and others engaged in one particular kind of library or library activity believe that their situation is so unique as not to have any relationship to intellectual freedom at all.

The following articles, written by experienced authorities on the philosophy and operation of the most common types of publicly supported libraries—public, school, academic, federal, and state—illustrate that intellectual freedom does indeed affect all types of libraries and library activities. These articles also outline librarians' professional responsibilities with regard to the modifications a particular library environment may impose on the nature and functioning of the all-embracing concept, intellectual freedom.

2

Public Libraries and Intellectual Freedom

Gordon M. Conable

*If this nation is to be wise as well as strong, if we are to achieve
our destiny, then we need more new ideas for more wise men
reading more good books in more public libraries. These libraries
should be open to all—except the censor. We must know all the
facts and hear all the alternatives and listen to all the criticisms.
Let us welcome controversial books and controversial authors.
For the Bill of Rights is the guardian of our security as well as
our Library.*

—John F. Kennedy

A merican democracy is dependent upon a belief that the people
are capable of self-government. To secure our basic rights, we
believe that "governments are instituted among men deriving their
just powers from the consent of the governed." In this country, we
have taken this to mean "informed consent."

Gordon M. Conable is the director of the Monroe County Library System
in Monroe, Michigan. He served on the board of the Freedom to Read Foundation in 1988–95 and was president in 1992–95. He was chair of the ALA
Intellectual Freedom Committee in 1989–91 and served on the committee in
1987–91.

The concept of informed consent only has meaning if the full range of human ideas is accessible to the people. The proponents of the various points of view must be able to make their cases fully and openly, however popular or unpopular they may be, before the individual and collective judgment of their fellow citizens.

This principle is embodied in the First Amendment to the Constitution, which protects the free expression of ideas:

> Congress shall make no law respecting an establishment of religion, or prohibiting the free exercise thereof; or abridging the freedom of speech, or of the press; or the right of the people peaceably to assemble, and to petition the government for a redress of grievances.

By providing the information and resources necessary for open, free, and unrestricted dialogue on all issues of concern, the public library preserves these freedoms.

It is the genius of the American system that we base our liberty on the broadest protection of each individual's rights to free expression and on the corollary right to access the expression of others. It is the genius of the American public library to be an institution dedicated to promoting the exercise of these rights.

American public libraries flourish out of a commitment to the principle that knowledge and access to information empower the individual. Libraries embody the firm belief that information must not be the exclusive province of a privileged few and that it should be widely and freely available to all.

At the time the public library movement began, books and education were scarcer commodities than they are now. Today, the quantity of information that is generated and distributed is increasing exponentially. The issue of scarcity is superseded now by new problems of access. But the essential function of the public library is unchanged: to offer knowledge and information to the average citizen who cannot afford, with individual resources alone, to secure all the information necessary to meet his or her self-defined needs in a complex and challenging world. In this way, public libraries provide tangible commitment to free speech, self-government, and self-education by collecting, organizing, preserving, disseminating, and protecting everyone's rights of access to the richness of human expression in all its recorded forms. This responsibility goes further to justify the existence and support of public libraries than any of the many other roles and functions that public libraries fulfill within their communities.

Libraries are storehouses and access-distribution-and-retrieval centers for an exploding body of human knowledge and opinion. They serve as neutral ground for opposing positions. Human beings, after all, are very different from each other. Their differences sometimes motivate individuals to attack the messages that elucidate, represent, or advocate ideas that seem to threaten their own beliefs, way of life, sense of security, understanding of the world, or desires and aspirations. Thus, the contents of libraries may become targets for censors who seek to have particular items removed from the library collection, restricted as to access, expurgated, labeled, or otherwise censored. A public librarian cannot remain unconcerned but must understand the nature of censorship, the motives of censors, and what yielding to them means.

Such attacks are often well intentioned; they are also frequently emotionally charged. They may represent the personal distress of an individual coming in contact with material that he or she is unprepared to deal with or finds frightening. Fear—often expressed as concern about harm that could be caused to children through exposure to certain books, films, videotapes, recordings, or ideas—motivates many complaints. Such a response is quite natural and human; parents are expected to protect their offspring. The concern may be real, but the requested response—the censorship of library materials—is an inappropriate means of dealing with perceived danger to children. Calm discussion will frequently provide the opportunity to reassure concerned parents, support the parents' role in guiding their own children's—and only their own children's—reading, and assist them in finding library materials that meet their own family needs.

It is appropriate for parents to guide their children's reading, television viewing, and exposure to media as they see fit. The public library can assist in this process by providing reader's advisory services, book lists, and other related services in a positive, proactive manner. What the library should not do is act in loco parentis— in the place of the parents—either by limiting access to materials or services solely on the basis of the user's age or by attempting to enforce parentally dictated controls.

The librarian must be able to respond sensitively to any complaints about collection materials without compromising the rights of others or the integrity of the library collection and its policies.

Supreme Court Justice Louis D. Brandeis spoke directly to the stakes involved: "Fear of serious injury cannot alone justify suppression of free speech and assembly. Men feared witches and burned women. It is the function of speech to free men from the bondage of irrational fears." Others have feared ideas and burned books. It is the function of libraries and librarians to protect ideas and books and access to them.

Some attacks on libraries or their collections represent the calculated political agenda of sophisticated, well-organized individuals or groups who see the issue of material in the library as a means of advancing other social or political interests within a broader framework. These are rarer than the spontaneous outrage of the individual reader, but they can be more difficult to handle.

Regardless of the motive or the specific target of the censor, the function of the library and the task of the librarian are the same. It is our duty to stand firm against such pressure. This is our trust and this is our purpose. With common sense, honesty, and an open approach based upon accountability and not defensiveness, reason and not ideology, many complaints about books can be handled without either escalating them into major public controversies or giving in to pressure.

When the occasional controversy does erupt, the process can provide a healthy demonstration of democracy and free speech in action. It should be approached in this manner, and the library should utilize the experience as a means of making its point about the importance of the underlying issues of free expression. This can provide a wellspring of community support and goodwill that can last long after the shouting has died.

Reviewing the astonishing range of materials that have come under attack in public libraries in recent years, it is impossible to predict or anticipate which items may arouse anyone's wrath. Chaucer, the Bible, and generally acknowledged classics have come under the would-be censor's fire, but so have innumerable works of less literary merit, less recognized authority, and less successful authorship. The librarian must be willing and able to defend them all, for to sacrifice the trivial, the controversial, or the distasteful means sacrificing the ability to defend anything.

Supreme Court Justice Hugo Black put it like this: "It is my belief that there are 'absolutes' in our Bill of Rights, and that they were put there on purpose by men who knew what words meant and meant their prohibitions to be 'absolutes.'" The First Amendment must apply to everyone or it will protect no one.

Living up to the public trust embodied in professional standards relating to intellectual freedom requires courage, creativity, humor, determination, wit, patience, and commitment. Those who would shirk these standards should seek other employment.

Joanne Goldsmith has said:

> The librarian who quietly removes a book from the shelf because of a noisy complaint is more guilty of restricting intellectual freedom than the complainant. The librarian has responsibility to a tradition, a body of law, and to the procedures established and approved for dealing with complaints. Worse, once the librarian has surrendered on a single occasion, he or she is the first target in future assaults. Extremism feeds on success. It is made bolder and more demanding by victory.

The issues with which public libraries must deal relating to intellectual freedom are varied and complex. In addition to the defense of challenged materials, the range of related issues includes, among others, the following:

Fees. The imposition of service charges may provide a significant economic barrier to information access. As libraries embrace automation, electronic media, and connectivity, the temptation to impose fees may increase, but it should be resisted.

Formats. Many libraries and librarians are committed to and effective in defending nonillustrated, printed material. Philosophical assumptions, cost, or ambivalence based upon other factors may lead to practices in the handling of video, sound recordings, film, or other nonprint formats that violate basic intellectual freedom standards.

Facilities. Libraries that provide public meeting rooms and display or exhibit facilities may be subject to pressure if the subject matter of meetings, exhibits, or displays is deemed controversial or offensive.

Political agendas. Supporters of particular causes may seek to have opposing points of view excluded from the library or may charge the library with bias or censorship if their viewpoint is underrepresented. The library that actively seeks representative material from across the full political spectrum, and actively solicits user suggestions and responds to them with purchases, not only serves its function better but also develops reservoirs of goodwill that help negate charges of bias in collection development.

User confidentiality and privacy. Failure to protect the rights of library users to utilize library materials and services privately can limit the practical exercise of First Amendment rights. Incursions of this sort—which are illegal in many jurisdictions—have been attempted by the FBI, police agencies, marketing firms, religious missionaries, the press, and others. Protecting confidentiality in an automated, networked environment provides new challenges for libraries. Security becomes an issue not only to ensure the integrity of the library's own databases and computer operating systems but also to protect users' privacy rights.

Public libraries operate in a public arena. The legal structures that establish and finance library service, the reasonable requirements for public accountability, and the realities of the political process provide the context in which libraries must carry out their mission. This context may appear to add to the pressures that librarians face in opposing censorship. If properly understood, however, these factors provide significant tools for librarians in defending their collections and services from the censor's attacks. Law, the rights and protections of public employees (which in many ways surpass those offered to private employees), and the protection that comes from an open process and public debate can all work to the librarian's advantage in exercising his or her ethical responsibilities.

Censorship pressure can come from both sources external to the library and sources within the library itself. The external sources include the following:

Parents. Either singularly or in groups, parents may seek the removal of materials from a library's collection. Their concerns often center around materials that deal with sex in an explicit or realistic way, but they may also attack books dealing with witchcraft and the occult, and books that differ from their vision of the traditional family structure. In recent years, there has been an increase in challenges to picture books.

Religious groups. Either individual members of a religious group or the group as a whole may attack material. Moral issues, sexual issues, the role of women, "demonic" or "satanic" material, or the presentation of religion in a manner perceived to be negative are all common reasons for challenges.

Political groups. These people may charge a library with political bias on the basis of perceived imbalance within the collection, or they may charge that material representing their political viewpoint is being systematically excluded by librarians with differing political views. Material describing communist societies still comes under fire.

Protected minority groups. Material that is considered racist, presents specific ethnic groups in stereotyped ways, or inaccurately treats the culture or history of minority groups frequently comes under fire. Similar attacks on sexist or other stereotyped materials are also common.

Patriotic groups. These groups may protest materials criticizing the government or national traditions—or materials that outline alternative interpretations of American life and history.

Emotionally unstable individuals. Some individuals who are emotionally unstable may focus on any of the above causes as outlets for their frustration. It is important, however, to determine whether the underlying cause is a real intellectual confrontation of differing ideas and philosophies or an emotionally upset person who is striking out against the public library as a convenient target.

It is important to note that people who complain about materials are not themselves censors, unless they are in a position actually to limit access to material or censor it by their own actions. Complaints and protests are not censorship, and those who object to material in libraries are exercising their own free-speech rights. It is those very rights that librarians defend when they protect challenged material. Censorship only occurs when libraries and librarians respond to complaints about, and challenges to, collection materials by removing or restricting books or other items. Such actions, carried out by librarians or by their governing bodies or institutions, are the censorship, and it is the public officials or employees who engage in such activities that are the censors, not the original protesters.

Censorship from inside the institution may include the following sources:

Trustees or governing bodies. Because such groups are the policy-making bodies, they may build censoring devices into policy. If the board demands the removal of a book because of local pressure, it has established a precedent severely limiting the materials that may be included in a collection. On the other hand, with the support of the board, the librarian can stand up to any would-be censor.

Library staff. One of the most difficult kinds of censorship to combat is that imposed by the library's own staff. Staff members are frequently in a position to censor materials either overtly or covertly, by direct action or by omission. Professional ethics constrain library staff to be wary of the temptation to impose their personal viewpoints and beliefs on library collections. Library staff may be offended by material the same way as anyone else. If material remains unordered, uncataloged, or uncirculated, or is expurgated or stolen simply because certain staff members object to it, censorship has occurred.

Management. If top administrators shy away from controversial issues, they set the tone for the rest of the staff, and this may have a chilling effect on library acquisitions. They may also establish procedures or recommend policies for board adoption that limit access to materials on the basis of age, sequester controversial materials in locked cases or rooms, or take other steps that negate accessibility.

Selection policies. A library's selection policy can be misused to restrict intellectual freedom. Policies that are inclusive, that are based upon the First Amendment, and that successfully balance the issue of collection diversity and demand buying are much stronger than those that narrowly limit collection scope on the basis of purely subjective factors such as "quality" or "popularity," which require outside endorsement in the form of reviews or recommended lists to justify every acquisition, or which are written in a way to justify the exclusion of controversial material from the collection.

Circulation, access, and interlibrary loan policies. Some libraries still limit children's borrowing of materials from the adult collection or limit their access to certain informational formats and sources such as the Internet, videotapes, or other audiovisual materials. Along the same lines, ILL services are sometimes denied to children, or children's materials may be excluded from bibliographic databases that are searched to obtain materials from other libraries. Such barriers are a form of censorship and violate professional standards.

Public libraries need to remember that with proper groundwork, preparation, and training, censorship attacks from without can be withstood and that individuals and groups exist in the community who will defend the library. Thoughtful determination and self-awareness are required to confront censorship issues from within.

The active advocacy of intellectual freedom is a challenge that all librarians accept when they join the profession. It lies at the heart of the public's trust, and it is the librarian's highest duty.

3

School Library Media Centers and Intellectual Freedom

Dianne McAfee Hopkins

A s the first library that many children and young adults are introduced to and use on a continuing basis, school library media programs play a vital role in promoting intellectual freedom. Intellectual freedom issues arise in many broad areas of school library administration and operation. School library media specialists should consider the intellectual freedom implications of their role as a resource specialist; how they provide intellectual and physical access for students; how their collection development policies address intellectual freedom; procedures for handling challenges to school library resources and services, including student access to the Internet; professional practice; and how they might appropriately promote intellectual freedom as an aspect of a free and democratic society.

Access

As views on schools and schooling evolve, so does the role of the school library media specialist in pre-K–12 education. The notion of

Dianne McAfee Hopkins is an associate professor at the School of Library and Information Studies, University of Wisconsin–Madison. She served on the ALA Intellectual Freedom Committee, 1991–95.

textbooks as the only major resource used in teaching has been replaced in many learning environments with a resource-based teaching approach. In resource-based teaching, a recognition of individual student learning styles, as well as student variation in background, ability, and interests, results in a multifaceted, multiple-resource approach to learning.[1] The school library media specialist promotes access to a wide variety of resources, including materials in the school's library media center, as well as nearby schools, public libraries, academic libraries, and networks.

In the school, the library media specialist works closely with classroom teachers to make school library media center (LMC) resources an integral part of daily instruction. In so doing, intellectual freedom is promoted for students.

Today, resources available in school LMCs have expanded beyond books and basic audiovisual materials in many schools to include CD-ROM products and electronic information. The library media specialist's role in the promotion of intellectual freedom, in this context, includes that of telecommunications resource specialist. This role takes on added importance in light of two recent studies: the U.S. Office of Technology Assessment, a bipartisan research agency of the U.S. Congress, prepared the report "Teachers and Technology: Making the Connection." The report found limited teacher knowledge, preparation, and use of technology in the curriculum (as reported in the April 12, 1995, issue of *Education Week*). In addition, the March 31, 1995, issue of the *Chronicle of Higher Education* reported the findings of a new survey by the American Electronics Association's National Information Infrastructure Task Force. The survey found that tomorrow's college students are likely to have had limited experience with computer technology unless they have been working with school library media specialists, whose telecommunications technology access and expertise exceed that of teachers.

Thus, today, the presence of a professionally staffed, appropriately budgeted, and physically accessible school LMC takes on increased importance. All pre-K–12 students, regardless of age or grade level, have information needs that can be met through the library media center. All classroom teachers can benefit from collaborative planning and teamwork with the library media specialist.

Students' right to access to information includes the right to develop skills necessary to locate and obtain materials and to examine critically and interpret the information that they find. Library media specialists should examine the nature of information skills instruction. They need to work with administrators and teachers to ensure the integration of information skills into the instructional curriculum, the full use of resources available at the school, and the inclusion of electronic materials for maximizing student learning.

Policies and Procedures

Collection Development Policy

Public school districts are governed by school boards that are legally responsible for the materials available to students. They delegate selection of materials to certified library media specialists and administrators under whom the library media specialist works. A well-thought-out, written collection development policy, approved by the school board, establishes the climate in which, and the criteria by which, library media collections are developed. The policy may encompass all instructional materials used in the district. The collection development policy should be formulated through the efforts of many who provide leadership and active participation in the LMC program: school library media specialists, teachers, administrators, students, and community members. The policy should promote intellectual freedom through a recognition of the value of information in a variety of formats. Materials should reflect the cultural diversity and pluralistic nature of contemporary American society. The policy should include the American Library Association's *Library Bill of Rights* and other appropriate intellectual freedom statements from professional associations such as the Association for Educational Communications and Technology, International Reading Association, National Council of Teachers of English, and the National Council for the Social Studies.

The procedures for the evaluation and selection of materials are central to the development of the library media center collection. Procedures employed by library media specialists include wide use of professional, reputable, selection resources (in combination, where possible, with firsthand examination of materials), and consultation with school faculty members to ascertain their instructional needs and involve them in the selection and review of materials. The strengths and weaknesses of the existing collection, access to other resources, and educational goals at the district and school level also are important considerations in the evaluation and selection of library media center collections.

Library media specialists should give careful attention to the section of the collection development policy dealing with the procedures for the reconsideration of materials. Such procedures must be clearly written and thoughtfully considered with a view toward promoting intellectual freedom on behalf of students and teachers. It is critical that the established procedures be followed systematically in dealing with each question, whether the question originates within the staff inside the district or within the local community. School library media center collections focus on a direct relationship to the school's instructional curriculum. However, collections should also reflect student needs and interests. These include the recreational interests of students and may include the fiction collection of the library media center, in particular. The collection development policy, therefore, should reflect a recognition of students' personal, information, recreational reading, listening, and viewing needs, and should take into account their varying skills, interests, abilities, and backgrounds.

Once developed, the collection development policy should be used regularly as the basis for the evaluation and selection of materials. It should be reviewed and revised at least every three years. School policies and guidelines should also evaluate the electronic resources available to teachers and students through the library media center.

Procedures

Professional practice, in terms of rules and regulations that govern student access to school library media centers, should be scrutinized to ascertain the promotion of intellectual freedom. The overriding question is whether rules encourage or inhibit intellectual freedom for students. Specific questions to be asked include: Where electronic resources are available, are all students given the opportunity to use them? Are certain groups of students unfairly favored in the use of electronic resources? Is student confidentiality respected? Are lists of students with overdue materials or other library infractions posted for all to see? Are students unfairly denied access to library resources because of rule infringement such as overdue materials? Is access to the library media center restricted to rigidly scheduled classes? Are rules governing access to the LMC by students in study halls appropriate? Are students permitted and encouraged to use the LMC before school, during lunch, after school, and at other times during the school day? Are students discouraged from using nonprint materials?

In addition to rules and regulations, professional practice in the selection and evaluation of materials requires examination from the standpoint of intellectual freedom. Library media specialists must ensure that access to information is promoted, not only in the English language but, where appropriate, in the languages that accommodate students for whom English is a second language.

The criteria for selection of library media center materials, as set forth in the board-approved collection development policy, should be followed in the selection of materials. Decisions about selection or reevaluation should not be based on perceived notions about the controversial nature of materials.

In summary, access to information for children and young adults must include an examination of their opportunities for intellectual and on-site physical access. The presence of an LMC alone is not sufficient to guarantee intellectual freedom for students.

Challenges

Materials challenged in school library media centers are primarily printed resources such as books and magazines. Because of the expanded use of library media materials in instruction through resource-based teaching, there is a greater possibility that these resources may be challenged, not only because of their availability in the LMC, but because of their use in instruction (e.g., optional or required reading, whole-language instruction). Some individuals may seek to ascertain whether their personal, value-laden objectives are met in trade books. Some ask, for example, that these materials always provide positive role models or show agreement with their particular family values. Challenges may be brought about any book, including award winners or those that have received notable distinctions.

Questions about school library media materials can be expected, based on individual as well as organized group concerns. Calls for censorship may come from any source, whether conservative or liberal. While many may view with alarm any question that arises, every question is not necessarily an effort to censor. Parents of students have the right to query public school officials regarding the materials that are made available for student use. Providing an understanding of the selection process and the principles upon which libraries exist may go far in answering questions that may be asked. Letting a questioner know that a concern is respectfully received is another way to respond constructively.

Most surveys of challenges to school library media materials find that parents are the initiators in a majority of challenges. However, internal challenges from school staff are also reported. A recent national study of middle, junior, and senior high school LMC challenges found that teachers and principals initiated challenges 20 percent of the time.[2] A more recent senior high school Wisconsin state-level study by Hopkins conducted during the 1994–95 school year found that teachers and principals initiated challenges 31.8 percent of the time. Much professional literature focuses on responding to challenges that are initiated by persons outside the school, but attention is also appropriate for internal challenges within the school. Although fewer in number than many other challenges, the most difficult challenges with which a library media specialist may deal are those from the school principal. Challenges from school principals noted in the national study as reported by library media specialists were analyzed and revealed the following:[3]

1. challenges from principals were overwhelmingly oral;
2. the materials selection policy's reconsideration section was not adhered to in a majority of cases;
3. challenged material was most often removed or restricted, (i.e., 75 percent of the time).

The analysis also revealed that when principals initiated challenges, school library media specialists were less likely to inform others of the challenge. Thus, they were unlikely to receive support that might have helped them communicate more fully about the questioned materials.

The difference in the school library media specialist's response to challenges initiated by principals is even more striking when factors are identified that affect whether challenged materials are retained, restricted, or removed. Overall, six general factors were found to influence whether challenges to LMC materials were retained, restricted, or removed:

> the existence of a school board–approved district materials selection policy and the degree to which it was used when LMC materials were challenged;
>
> the school environment, including the influence and power of the school principal and the support of classroom teachers;
>
> the community environment, through support received outside the school district in which a challenge occurred;
>
> the initiator of the challenge;
>
> selected characteristics of the library media specialists, including their responses to dogmatism and the internal or external locus of control;
>
> complaint background, including whether there was active support for retention or removal of materials, and whether the challenge was oral or written.

The national study found that library media specialists who seek consistent implementation of the materials selection policy, seek support during the challenge process, and require that challenges to library materials are written have a higher rate of success in retaining challenged materials.

Reasons for Challenges

The national study of challenges to middle, junior, and senior high schools, and the more recent state-level Wisconsin study, also examined reasons for challenges to materials. Areas that formed the basis for challenges were consistent with most previous K–12 studies. The primary continuing reason for complaints, as reported by library media specialists experiencing challenges, was a concern about sexuality. Other primary reasons were concerns about profanity, morality, and obscenity. Because challenges to materials may also reflect societal issues, the nation's ambivalence about sexual intimacy and sexual orientation (particularly gay and lesbian) is reflected among the few publicized challenges of recent years (most challenges to school LMC materials are not known outside the school or district). Other expressed concerns over the years have included witchcraft, the occult, immaturity of possible student users, nudity, violence, and material said to be inconsistent with family values. In addition, the noteworthy objective of many school districts to reflect fully the nation's diversity through multicultural literature and a broad depiction of the nation's families has been met with criticism by some who deem this an effort to denigrate their cultural or religious values. Henry Reichman (1993) discusses many of the reasons offered for challenging materials in schools.

In recent years, an expressed basis for challenges from conservative groups, especially religious right groups, has been the belief that public school students are being indoctrinated in the "religions" of secular humanism, New Age, and globalism. *Secular humanism* is a difficult term to define. It suggests a Christianless force operating in the public schools. Called a religion by some conservative groups, secular humanism is depicted as being responsible for the destruction of God-based family values.

In a similar way, the view of New Age as a religion is also difficult to define, although its focus includes the belief that there are efforts to control the world through a one-world religion and a one-world government. The focus of groups that claim that the "religions" of secular humanism, New Age, and globalism are being promoted in the public schools is broad and encompasses the total school environment, including the curriculum, textbooks, and library media center materials. Few challenges are reported by library media specialists as being initiated by conservative groups, but during the challenge process, conservative groups may offer support to those whose challenges to materials are based on fundamentalist principles.

Electronic access to information, especially to the Internet, offers still another area for potential challenges. Unlike materials physically located in the LMC, the Internet, by its very nature, carries the potential for exposing students to information that may be controversial or possibly deemed unsuitable for students. Here, the communication of the school with its students and parents is important, in addition to the development of appropriate guidelines and policies.

Finally, library automation carries the potential of challenges of a different nature. How does the library media specialist respond to calls for printouts of all holdings or holdings in selected subject areas that are deemed inappropriate for students? How does the library media specialist respond to calls for printouts of material checked out by specific students? How does the library media specialist respond to calls for computerized restricted check-out for individual students or entire grades, such as all primary grade students? Serious consideration of the appropriate use of library automation in maintaining an atmosphere supportive of intellectual freedom is a necessity.

Promotion of Intellectual Freedom

Intellectual freedom must be promoted within the school as well as in the community. Selection of library media center materials, although coordinated by the library media specialist, should actively involve teachers, administrators, and students. Discussions and in-service programs about the philosophy of libraries in general, the purpose and objectives of the library media center, and the criteria used in selection should be ongoing, not only for new faculty but for all faculty, as well as school staff (e.g., school secretaries, support staff). These programs should include building-level, as well as district-level, staff. School board members also should actively participate. In addition, up-to-date information on a continuing basis is valuable to the community.

School leaders, including library media specialists, must be aggressive in regularly communicating information about the district's educational objectives and the purposes of school library media programs, as well as in introducing information about selected materials themselves. The communication can be accomplished through such means as school newsletters, community newspapers and other information media, and parent workshops or presentations on topics such as realism in children's and young adult literature.

Communication must be facilitated both inside and outside the district.

Intellectual freedom is also promoted by example. School board members, administrators, teachers, and library media specialists should demonstrate their support for intellectual freedom. Negative examples include (1) immediate removal of materials when a complaint or challenge first occurs regardless of the policy; (2) full discussion of a complaint in a school board meeting when complaining individuals have not followed established procedures or when such discussion is not on the agenda; (3) precensorship, which is the decision not to select material for the collection because of its perceived potential for controversy; (4) elimination of potentially controversial materials in the collection under the guise of ongoing evaluation; and (5) limiting access to a collection by imposing barriers such as restricted shelving or parental-permission requirements because the material is thought to be potentially controversial. Whether such acts are conducted openly or in secret, the climate for open access and availability of information directly affects the students who are served.

Conclusion

Intellectual freedom, when viewed in the broad context of access, has many focuses. It includes the following:

> the selection of materials that will meet the instructional, recreational, and informational needs of students;
> the school library media specialist's leadership as a resource specialist who collaborates with the classroom teacher in fully integrating library media resources in instruction, whether print, audiovisual, or electronic;
> the student's intellectual access to materials through information skills instruction;
> interpretation of the policies to those who might challenge the resources that are available.

Intellectual freedom in schools demands the commitment of library media specialists who do the following:

actively support intellectual freedom committees, coalitions, and
association at all levels (i.e., local, state, regional, national);

promote an understanding of the value of information to the
young, which includes diverse viewpoints and relevance
to today's world;

communicate the importance of intellectual freedom in an ongoing manner to principals, teachers, and other school staff;

practice the selection of materials on the basis of sound educational criteria unbiased by personal, political, social, or
religious views;

invite the active participation of teachers in the selection of
materials;

promote the use of the collection development policy for the
selection or reconsideration of materials;

seek support when a challenge to library media center materials occurs;

take every challenge, whether oral or written, seriously;

introduce all aspects of library resources to the community,
including those dealing with the Internet;

empower students to gain further access to information beyond
the walls of the school library media center through interlibrary loans and computer networks, thereby nurturing
independent, lifelong learning;

promote student learning about the First Amendment and intellectual freedom and what it means to them.[4]

Intellectual freedom requires that all who are responsible for the
education of the young—school board members, administrators,
teachers, and library media specialists—work together continuously
to ensure that First Amendment rights and intellectual freedom are
a reality for children and young adults.

NOTES

1. David V. Loertscher, *Taxonomies of the School Library Media Program*
   (Englewood, Colo.: Libraries Unlimited, 1988).
2. Dianne McAfee Hopkins, *Factors Influencing the Outcome of Challenges to
   Materials in Secondary School Libraries: Report of a National Study.* Pre-

pared under Grant #RO39A9004-89, U.S. Department of Education, Office of Educational Research and Improvement, Library Programs (Madison: University of Wisconsin, School of Library and Information Studies, 1991).

3. Dianne McAfee Hopkins, "Challenges to Library Materials from Principals in U.S. Secondary Schools—A 'Victory' of Sorts," *School Libraries Worldwide* 1, no. 2 (July 1995).

4. Excellent resources to promote student learning about the First Amendment, intellectual freedom, and what it means to them are available from the First Amendment Congress, University of Denver, 2301 Gaylord St., Denver, CO 80208.

ADDITIONAL RESOURCES

American Association of School Librarians and Association for Educational Communications and Technology. *Information Power.* Chicago: American Library Assn., 1988.

Hopkins, Dianne McAfee. "A Conceptual Model of Factors Influencing the Outcome of Challenges to Library Materials in Secondary School Settings." *Library Quarterly* 63, no. 1 (Jan. 1993): 40–72.

———. "Put It in Writing: What You Should Know about Challenges to School Library Materials." *School Library Journal* 39, no. 1 (Jan. 1993): 26–30.

Kaplan, George R. "Shotgun Wedding: Notes on Public Education's Encounter with the New Christian Right." *Phi Delta Kappan* 75, no. 9 (May 1994): K1–K12.

Kruse, Ginny Moore. "No Single Season: Multicultural Literature for Children." *Wilson Library Bulletin* 66 (Feb. 1992): 30–33, 122.

Loertscher, David V. *Taxonomies of the School Library Media Program.* Englewood, Colo.: Libraries Unlimited, 1988.

McDonald, Frances M. "Information Access for Youth: Issues and Concerns." *Library Trends* 37, no. 1 (Summer 1988): 28–42.

"On Line." *Chronicle of Higher Education* 41, no. 29 (March 31, 1995): A19.

Reichman, Henry. *Censorship and Selection: Issues and Answers for Schools.* Rev. ed. Chicago: American Library Assn. and American Assn. of School Administrators, 1993.

Scales, Pat. "Remarks by Pat Scales." *Newsletter on Intellectual Freedom* XL, no. 6 (Nov. 1991): 223–225.

———. "Teaching the First Amendment." *Book Links* 5, no. 1 (Sept. 1995).

West, Peter. "O.T.A. Decries Lack of Focus on Teachers." *Education Week* 14, no. 29 (April 12, 1995): 1, 11.

Online Resources

Several existing gopher sites contain compilations of "acceptable use" Internet policies developed by K–12 schools, universities, library groups, civil libertarians, and others:

> gopher riceinfo.rice.edu
>> choose "information by subject area"
>> choose "education"
>> find "acceptable and unacceptable uses of Net Resources (K–12)"

> gopher ericir.syr.edu
>> choose "Internet guides and directories"
>> find "acceptable use policies/agreements for K–12"

> gopher eff.org
>> choose CAF (computers and academic freedom) archive
>> find "computer policies and critiques"
>> find also a "pointer" to other sites containing similar information

The foregoing sites may be updated or altered from time to time, and other such sites may now exist or come to be; however, the sites listed should provide a good overview of school Internet policies and some of the issues and concerns addressed by and related to such policies.

Selected Library Bill of Rights Interpretations

Access to Library Resources and Services Regardless of Gender or Sexual Orientation

Access to Resources and Services in the School Library Media Program

Challenged Materials

Diversity in Collection Development

Evaluating Library Collections

Expurgation of Library Materials

Free Access to Libraries for Minors

Restricted Access to Library Materials

Statement on Labeling

Also Relevant

Policy on Confidentiality of Library Records

Policy concerning Confidentiality of Personally Identifiable Information about Library Users

Acknowledgments

Appreciation is expressed to the following individuals for sharing perspectives with me on intellectual freedom and youth: Ginny Moore Kruse, director, Cooperative Children's Book Center, School of Education, University of Wisconsin–Madison and trustee, Freedom to Read Foundation, 1992–96; Fran McDonald, professor, Library Media Education Program, Mankato State University and past president, Minnesota Coalition against Censorship; and Pat R. Scales, library media specialist, Greenville, South Carolina, Middle School and member, ALA Intellectual Freedom Committee, 1994–96.

4

Academic Libraries and Intellectual Freedom

Paul B. Cors

Since the function of the academic library is to support the teaching and research programs of the college or university of which it forms a part, the degree to which the library enjoys intellectual freedom will be largely determined by the parent institution's commitment to academic freedom. If the institution is firmly committed to freedom of inquiry in all areas of knowledge, and this commitment has been made formal policy by its governing body, the library should be able to defend itself successfully against external censorship attempts. Although it is true that academic libraries are much less frequently the censors' targets than school and public libraries are (one would like to believe that this is because the principle of academic freedom enjoys general acceptance, but it may in fact be that academic libraries are not seen as sufficiently influential to merit the censors' attention), this should not cause academic librarians to become complacent; censorship controversies can and will arise, and the library's first line of defense must be the commitment of the college or university itself to academic freedom.

Paul B. Cors is a catalog librarian at the University of Wyoming Library, Laramie.

The library, of course, accepts an equally strong obligation to be certain that neither its formal policies nor the conscious or unconscious biases of its staff violate the intellectual freedom of its constituency. Regrettably, there appears to be good reason to believe that in academic libraries, as in all others, the greatest dangers to intellectual freedom are more often internal than external. Even if the parent institution is not wholly committed to academic freedom, the library should still attempt to practice intellectual freedom principles to the extent that it can. Although it must be conceded that the library in a college operated by a religious organization, for example, may have to function within doctrinal limits imposed by that organization, the library still has an obligation to provide the most diversified collection possible within those limits; it also has an obligation to inform both its patrons and employees of exactly what those limits are.

Every academic library needs to have a written collection development policy incorporating the principles of the *Library Bill of Rights*. This policy should be drafted by the library staff, preferably in cooperation with the faculty library committee if such a group exists, and ratified by the appropriate administrative body of the institution. One common problem can be prevented if the policy states clearly to what extent the library will acquire materials of general interest, including recreational reading, for student use. Copies of the policy should be freely available to students and faculty.

Academic library collections are predominantly determined by the program of the parent institution, but most larger academic libraries accept an archival role and collect materials that document a broad spectrum of human beliefs and activities. This will inevitably result in the acquisition of out-of-the-mainstream works presenting concepts that most people find offensive, even abhorrent, or irrational. Such materials are certain to draw complaints, and libraries will have to be able to make it understood that documenting malice and error is not equivalent to validating either. It will not be easy, for example, to defend the presence of blatantly racist or sexist works in the collection, but libraries should point out that such beliefs cannot be effectively countered by ignoring their existence.

The collection development policy should include a clearly outlined procedure for handling complaints about the presence—or absence—of specific titles or subject areas. All staff members should be thoroughly familiar with both policy and procedure. Standard library complaint forms may need to be adapted for use in academic libraries to include provisions for requests to add materials as well as remove them, since experience suggests that students' complaints are usually of the former type.

The library's cataloging-processing manual should specify that the organization of the collection must not be used as a tool of censorship. If the collection is basically "open stack," definitions of material to be housed in restricted access areas must be carefully drawn.[1]

Recognizing the many historical reasons for restricting access, the revised policy limits acceptable reasons to only those necessary to protect library materials, "for reasons of physical preservation including protection from theft or mutilation," adding the caveat that "[a]ny such policies must be carefully formulated and administered with extreme attention to the principles of intellectual freedom."

Restrictions resulting from donor agreements or contracts for special collections also must be narrowly tailored to respect intellectual freedom. The policy concludes, stating that, "[p]ermanent exclusions are not acceptable. The overriding impetus must be to work for free and unfettered access to all documentary heritage." Classifications and subject headings should accurately reflect content (which may mean that decisions to use standard subject headings lists without modification will have to be questioned), and all material in the collection should be listed in the public records of the library.[2]

Unlike public libraries, it is in the area of services—not collections—that academic libraries are more likely to fall short in their devotion to intellectual freedom. In part, this is a result of conditions that the library cannot alter: the academic community is a socially stratified one, and this stratification will affect the library. Nevertheless, one of the basic principles of the *Library Bill of Rights* is equality of access, and the library should strive to follow that principle. It is necessary, therefore, that certain traditional policies followed by many—if not most—academic libraries be reexamined. It is of little merit to develop an excellent collection and then place insurmountable obstacles in the path of those who wish to use that collection.

The primary constituency of the academic library is the students, faculty, and staff of the parent college or university. While most academic libraries provide some service beyond the campus (through interlibrary loan, if nothing else), such service, unless mandated by the charter of a public institution or agreed to by contract, is always a courtesy, not a right; academic libraries do not violate intellectual freedom if off-campus patrons are not given equal treatment with the libraries' prime constituency. Fairness, however, demands that the policies in this area be clearly enunciated and administered evenhandedly.

Circulation policies should be uniform for all patrons and should aim at providing adequate time for the use of material without allowing anyone to monopolize an item at the expense of others. Restrictions on the circulation of materials such as reference books, current journals, or rare books to ensure equitable access or for preservation, in order that access not be lost due to deterioration of materials, are not inherently in violation of intellectual freedom, provided that they apply equally to all. Reference staffs should respond to all requests for assistance with equal diligence, making no distinction based on the "importance" of the patron.

A most difficult question is posed by interlibrary loan. The present general practice of denying this service to undergraduates is incompatible with the *Library Bill of Rights*. The rationale for this limitation is not altogether indefensible, because faculty and graduate research often does require access to a wider range of materials than undergraduates normally need or any one library can supply. However, libraries should attempt to find some means of meeting the genuine interlibrary loan needs of undergraduates.

A similar problem is limited access to stacks, although again the reasons for the practice have some validity. Still, policies that provide some users with more direct access to the collection than others do not conform to the *Library Bill of Rights*. Security measures, designed to protect collections from theft, should be applied equally to all patrons, regardless of their status within the academic community.

The widespread replacement of printed information sources with online or compact disc databases can present some special problems. These tools commonly require special training to be used effectively, and academic libraries often require fees for their use; both circumstances may create barriers to access. The library must be prepared to provide adequate training for users and may do everything possible to provide services without additional cost to the users. The ALA asserts, in section 50.4 of the ALA Policy Manual, that "the charging of fees and levies for information services, including those services utilizing the latest information technology, is discriminatory in publicly supported institutions providing library and information services." Although it may be unrealistic to expect that all fees for database searching be eliminated, all libraries must strive to limit fees and find alternative means to pay for advanced technology.

Any other specialized services that the library provides (for example, photocopying or document delivery) should be available equally to everybody in its primary constituency.

The academic library has the same obligation to respect the privacy of its users as do other types of libraries. Circulation and interlibrary loan files, reference and database searching requests, journal routing lists and other records containing personally identifiable information about library users are confidential. Many states have laws governing the confidentiality of library records, which may apply to publicly supported academic libraries. Access to personally identifiable information about library users should be limited to those staff members who must use these records to perform their jobs.

Library records are sometimes sought by professors as evidence of the completion of reserve-reading assignments or of plagiarism; in such cases, the person making the request for records often views such access as a convenience and has not given any thought to the fact that such access is not only prohibited by library policy and possibly state law but, as a practical matter, is not really necessary. Library staff should inform professors about confidentiality policy and state law where it applies, and should remind professors of the practical reality that records showing that a student has borrowed materials prove nothing about whether the student has actually read them. Library staff could also suggest less intrusive means of investigation, such as giving a test or quiz covering reserve reading or borrowing the material suspected as the source for a plagiarized paper to compare it with the potentially offending passage. In neither case are library records needed, nor would they necessarily prove anything.

Library records should not be released even for an administrative or judicial hearing absent a court order. If such an order is issued, safeguards must be in place to ensure that the minimum number of people necessary see the records and that they still be maintained as confidential outside the narrow boundaries of the investigation or proceeding. Due process must be rigorously observed. Finally, library staff also must be aware that gossip about library users' interests is not acceptable, however harmless it may seem. The integrity of the institution is at stake even with such seemingly frivolous threats to library user confidentiality.

New technologies greatly complicate the issue of confidentiality, and their impact must be carefully considered. Files maintained online, especially in a central computer facility that is used for other purposes by many campus units, may be deliberately or inadvertently invaded without the library's knowledge, so it is essential to maintain the best security system possible. Given the well-publicized cases of computer hackers' gaining access to inadequately protected databases and the large body of skilled computer users on most college campuses, the security requirements of an academic library should be carefully established and rigorously fulfilled. Obsolete records such as completed circulation transactions should be purged from the file immediately; any permanent records needed for statistical purposes should not include the names of individuals.

The internal administrative procedures of the library, including its personnel policies, should foster a spirit of intellectual freedom among all staff members. Whether this is best done informally or through a structured program of in-service training will depend upon the size and character of the staff. In either case, it is especially important to include some instruction in the principles of intellectual freedom in the training given to student assistants, other temporary employees, and volunteers, who in most cases are not planning on a library career and are unlikely to be aware of the ethical commitments of the profession. They must also be assured that they will be fully supported by their supervisors when they put these principles into practice.

Finally, the more clearly the library administration exemplifies its own commitment to intellectual freedom, the more likely intellectual freedom will become the foundation for all library programs.

NOTES

1. The ALA policy, "Restricted Access to Library Materials," as revised at the 1991 Annual Conference, is quite clear on this point:

   > Libraries are a traditional forum for the open exchange of information. Attempts to restrict access to library materials violate the basic tenets of the *Library Bill of Rights.*

2. Classification of materials must not include judgments on the content of materials. As stated in the revised (1990) "Statement on Labeling":

   > A variety of private organizations promulgate rating systems and/or review materials as a means of advising either their members or the general public concerning their opinions of the contents and suitability or appropriate age for use of certain books, films, recordings, or other materials. For the library to adopt or enforce any of these private systems, to attach such ratings to library materials, to include them in bibliographic records, library catalogs, or other finding aids, or otherwise to endorse them would violate the *Library Bill of Rights.*
   >
   > Publishers, industry groups, and distributors sometimes add ratings to material or include them as part of their packaging. Librarians should not endorse such practices. However, removing or obliterating such ratings—if placed there by or with permission of the copyright holder—could constitute expurgation, which is also unacceptable.

5

Federal Libraries and Intellectual Freedom

Bernadine Abbott Hoduski

The federal library community is composed of a variety of libraries comparable in type to those in the library community as a whole. Federal libraries range from the one-of-a-kind Library of Congress to small school libraries on Native American reservations and to specialized libraries serving executive agencies.

Federal libraries have censorship problems just like other libraries, but these are seldom brought to the attention of the library profession or the public. Many federal librarians feel there is no problem with censorship in government libraries. Others do not agree. Most of them do agree that positive steps should be taken to help prevent possible censorship situations.

Even though federal libraries differ in many respects, they do have some things in common: (1) they must function according to a number of federal laws and regulations; (2) their mission is usually dictated by the agency to which they belong; and (3) because they are supported by federal taxes, they are answerable, directly or

Bernadine Abbott Hoduski retired as professional staff member for Library and Distribution Services, Congress of the United States, Joint Committee on Printing, in 1995 and was the founder of the Government Documents Round Table of the American Library Association.

indirectly, to all U.S. citizens. Many federal libraries are contracted out to private vendors, so it is important that the federal official legally responsible for seeing that the library function as a federal entity be involved in developing the library's policies.

Federal libraries can prevent many problems, including censorship, by following some simple procedures:

1. With the assistance of the agency's lawyer, it should be determined which laws and regulations govern the agency and the library because regulations differ from one agency to the next.

2. An order describing the purpose, functions, and policies of the library should be written, thus officially establishing and protecting the existence of the library. This order should be signed and distributed by the secretary of a department or the administrator of an agency.

3. Librarians should take every opportunity to educate the secretary of a department, the agency administrator, the staff, and the public as to the policies of the library.

4. Federal libraries should cooperate with each other, comparing policies on materials selection, access to the collection, and other issues, including policies about information in electronic and audiovisual formats. Such comparisons can be used as examples in establishing policies and educating the agency's staff.

5. Library directors should determine whether and how the Freedom of Information Act affects the library. Some federal libraries serve as the agency's public reading room in order to fulfill the requirements of the law, which states that the public must have reasonable access to documents issued by an agency. If the library is the official repository for agency documents, these have to be accessible to the public. If the library keeps classified and unclassified documents, some provision will have to be made to keep these separate. The library should also have an agreed-upon plan for providing documents once they are declassified. This should be done in consultation with the agency's attorney.

6. Library directors should determine what policies they should follow if they are a federal depository library. If the agency requires secrecy or denies access to the public, the library will be in direct conflict with the laws governing depository libraries. The agency

will have to explore ways of complying with both requirements or risk losing its status.

7. If possible, a library committee representing all elements of the agency should be established so that materials selection, access policies, and other practices will be fair to all. In turn, the library committee can help educate the rest of the agency employees and support library policies.

8. The library should have a written access policy not favoring one group in an agency over another. If the library circulates material to the public, it should do so for everyone, not just for a select few. Libraries may decide to lend through another library rather than to individuals. If so, this decision should be publicized. Some agencies have regulations that do not allow those outside the agency to use their libraries.

9. The library should maintain a written materials selection policy. Even though the subject area is often determined by the mission of the agency, the diversity of views in that subject area must be guarded. An obvious example of censorship would be refusal to buy publications critical of an agency.

10. Finally, the library should develop and implement a policy protecting the confidentiality of library users. Records associating individuals with the materials they borrow should never be released to others—whether requested by employers or colleagues—without the written consent of the individual in question.

Because federal libraries are important information links in the decision-making process of the U.S. government, and because citizen access to information about that process is crucial to the preservation of a free society, federal libraries must be protected from censorship.

6

State Library Agencies and Intellectual Freedom

Diana Young

The state library agency, as an institution, varies from state to state. Most state library agencies have responsibility for promoting library development and coordinating interlibrary cooperation. In some states, the agency is responsible for maintaining a collection, either to serve state government or to serve the residents of the state. Whatever the state library structure may be, it usually assumes the responsibility of fostering the free exchange of information and ideas. As part of that effort, some state libraries try, as North Carolina did (unsuccessfully), to encourage their state legislature to adopt the American Library Association's (ALA) *Library Bill of Rights*.

Whether or not intellectual freedom policy is adopted at the state level, the state library encourages local libraries to make local officials and boards aware of, and usually encourages them to adopt, the *Library Bill of Rights*, its Interpretation statements and other ALA policies or state standards well before there is a need to put them to the test. Local libraries are urged to follow their policies once in place. It sometimes happens that, for example, a local school

---

Diana Young is public library consultant for the North Carolina Department of Cultural Resources.

board is presented with a challenge but that its local superintendent didn't know of or follow its existing policy, perhaps even making public statements contrary to policy. Later, the board and superintendent both must find ways to explain why policy wasn't followed. State library agencies not only stress the importance of getting policies in place but also of alerting local government officials about their policies well before they have a problem. That way, when there is a challenge, everyone is prepared to respond in accordance with the library's board-adopted policies. This is especially important when dealing with censorship controversies.

John F. Kennedy said:

> We are not afraid to entrust the American people with unpleasant facts, foreign ideas, alien philosophies, and competitive values. For a nation that is afraid to let its people judge the truth and falsehood in an open market is a nation that is afraid of its people.

Kennedy's concept can be especially difficult to live by when the censor is at your door, or is friendly with a member of the library board or local newspaper, or is part of an organized group. The pressures imposed on libraries are very real. Recent examples include the following: an organized group's persistent attacks on several public libraries in North Carolina cost one director a job and resulted in the delay of a major library construction bond for several years because of objections to the books *Heather Has Two Mommies* and *Daddy's Roommate*; a Texas librarian lost her job after a dispute over the presence of Howard Stern's *Private Parts* in the library collection; and in Fairfax and Loudoun counties in Virginia, ongoing battles over minors' access to, and the presence of materials dealing with, the subject of homosexuality continue to plague the library systems.

State libraries help local libraries prepare to handle these challenges in many ways. First, all libraries are encouraged to have policies and procedures in place and adopted by library boards, delineating what to do and when to do it. Sample policies are often collected and made available, and libraries that have recently updated or developed new policies are encouraged to submit them to the state library. Where a state electronic network exists, these policies are often posted over the Internet for review by any library.

Second, many state libraries maintain a relationship with active and supportive intellectual freedom committees of their state's library association, which can provide assistance and a link to a statewide network of supporters of intellectual freedom willing to come forward in a crisis.

Serving as a catalyst, the state library agency must provide support and assistance in creating an environment that provides citizens with unrestricted access to information. State libraries work to assist library boards of trustees and/or library directors to focus all feasible methods of preparing for and handling the situation. Sometimes it simply means alerting them to channels for assistance (such as the ALA's Office for Intellectual Freedom), being a good listener, or helping to avoid panic. Librarians facing challenges help each other, and those who have survived a challenge freely offer their advice to those in the midst of one.

In working with library staffs and trustees, state agency staff should serve as change agents. Boards of trustees and library administrators should be encouraged to regularly examine library policies and programs to confirm that these support the fundamental tenets of intellectual freedom.

State libraries develop library standards or performance measures as a means by which libraries may be evaluated and held accountable. In developing such standards or measures, the state's libraries need to base them upon the philosophy that every individual should have equal access to information and that the citizens of the state should have access to library services as envisioned in the *Library Bill of Rights*. For example, in North Carolina's *Competencies for Youth Services Librarians* (State Library of North Carolina, 1988), developed by the state library's Youth Service Advisory Committee, the first section of the notebook indicates that children's and young adult services librarians should "demonstrate familiarity with the ALA *Freedom to Read* statement, the *Library Bill of Rights* (and Interpretation statements) as well as any other intellectual freedom policies and procedures adopted by their library boards."

In its leadership capacity, the state library agency must assume legislative leadership and coordination roles at both the state and federal levels. It is critical for the state library agency to monitor state and federal legislation and case law. Librarians, trustees, and other interested individuals need to be kept informed about legislative efforts and new court rulings that have an impact on intellectual freedom. In every state, there are a number of library advocacy groups—library associations, friends of libraries, trustee organizations—that work for the advancement of library services. State library agencies need to work closely with these organizations and be able to rally them when needed in the legislative arena. Additionally, state libraries often work closely with state library associations offering workshops or producing newsletters, journal articles, or sample policies that periodically focus on the topic of intellectual freedom.

As a component of state government, the state library agencies are in a unique position to influence state law and policy. State library administrators are informed about the philosophies of government leaders and are knowledgeable about the decision-making processes. Of particular importance is the state library agency's leadership role in guaranteeing the citizens' "right to know." First and foremost, the general public and government officials need to be kept aware of the importance of the free flow of government information. The state library agency needs to monitor the development and implementation of policy and procedure relating to the flow of both state and federal government information. If policies and procedures adverse to the free flow of information are promulgated, the state library agency needs to exert its leadership in changing them.

Technology has provided the means for states to develop sophisticated electronic networks. Since the operation of these networks is costly, there may be a tendency to question the need to make use of these resources at a library user's request, or the library may charge the user a fee for the service. Some libraries do not understand the intellectual freedom issues involved in networks and are only now becoming aware of the censorship and access issues that may arise. It is imperative that state library agencies strongly encourage libraries to provide equal access to all types of information resources for all library users regardless of socioeconomic status.

In many states, the state library agency maintains a collection that is used for government research or as a research library for state residents. It should serve as a model for the rest of the state. The collection should be developed from a selection policy that embodies the principles of the *Library Bill of Rights*. Additionally, the policies governing the use of the collection should be reflective of intellectual freedom principles.

The state library agency in any state plays a pivotal role in the development of library services. A significant part of that role is to ensure that citizens have the best possible access to information. This access will, in turn, help preserve our democratic society as we now know it and will allow citizens to participate fully in the society.

PART V

Intellectual Freedom and the Law

1

School Library Censorship and the Courts: Before Hazelwood

William D. North

During the 1970s, librarians, parents, teachers, and students, often supported by the Freedom to Read Foundation, began to challenge in court the censorious removal of books from school libraries. The results of such litigation efforts, by and large, were promising, although the courts, including the U.S. Supreme Court, offered conflicting interpretations of the issues presented, leaving the legal foundation to challenges of book removal uncertain. As of this writing, by far the most important case was *Board of Education, Island Trees (New York) Union Free School District 26* v. *Pico*, which was decided by the U.S. Supreme Court on June 25, 1982. But that decision, far from resolving the thorny legal questions raised by book removal, did little more than establish that these issues are unlikely to be resolved by the Supreme Court, at least as constituted in 1982, under any rationale commanding even a majority of the justices, let alone a consensus.

William D. North served as Freedom to Read Foundation general counsel, 1969–80; as vice president, 1980–81; and as president, 1981–84. This chapter is a revised version of an article, "Pico and the Challenge to Books in Schools," which appeared in the November 1982 *Newsletter on Intellectual Freedom*.

The *Pico* case, even though it did not produce a majority opinion, is, however, one of the most significant First Amendment decisions to be rendered by the Supreme Court since its obscenity decisions of June 1973. Like the obscenity decisions, *Pico* reflects the continuing and fundamental schism existing between two factions of the Court concerning the scope and application of the First Amendment.

The issue presented by *Pico* was whether "the First Amendment imposes limitations upon the exercise by a local school board of its discretion to remove library books from high school and junior high school libraries." The case involved the right of one junior high school and four high school students to challenge as unconstitutional the removal by the Island Trees Union Free School District board of all copies of nine books from the school libraries under the board's control. The board removed the books because they were, in the board's view, "anti-American, anti-Christian, anti-Semitic, and just plain filthy." The board justified the removal on the ground of its "duty, or moral obligation, to protect the children in our schools from this moral danger as surely as from physical and medical dangers."

Five of the books were removed despite the report of a Book Review Committee appointed by the board itself that recommended their retention under standards of "educational suitability," "good taste," "relevance," and appropriateness to age and grade level. The board gave no reasons for rejecting the recommendation of the committee it had appointed.

The district court granted summary judgment in favor of the board of education holding that

> While removal of such books from a school library may . . . reflect a misguided educational philosophy, it does not constitute a sharp and direct infringement of any first amendment right.

On appeal to a three-judge panel of the United States Court of Appeals for the Second Circuit, the judgment of the district court was reversed by a two-to-one majority and the case remanded for trial.

On certiorari to the Supreme Court, the decision of the Second Circuit was affirmed by a vote of 5 to 4, with Justice Brennan writing the plurality opinion, in which Justices Marshall and Stevens joined and in which Justice Blackmun joined with the judgment and concurred in part in a separate opinion. Justice White concurred in the judgment, thereby constituting the majority, while Chief Justice Burger and Justices Powell, Rehnquist, and O'Connor dissented in four separate opinions, with Justices Powell, Rehnquist, and O'Connor joining in Chief Justice Burger's dissent and the Chief Justice and Justice Powell joining in Justice Rehnquist's dissent.

Although Justice White clearly opposed the grant of certiorari, the issue presented by *Pico* was preeminently ripe for consideration by the Supreme Court. Starting in 1971 and continuing throughout the decade of the 1970s, courts were encountering with increasing frequency cases in which school boards were accused of, and even admitted to, removing books from their school libraries—not because of obsolescence, lack of shelf space, or lack of relevance, but rather because the books were deemed inconsistent or contrary to the "value inculcation" objectives of the curriculum. As in the *Pico* case, these cases consistently involved the removal of a library work previously identified as worthy of acquisition under accepted book selection criteria. Likewise, they involved books that were elective reading and not part of the required curriculum. Moreover, they were invariably removed without regard for established procedures for "culling" or "winnowing" works no longer deemed appropriate for retention.

The earliest of the school library book suppression opinions was the Second Circuit's 1972 decision in *Presidents Council District 25* v. *Community School Board No. 25*. There, the court upheld the removal of *Down These Mean Streets* by Piri Thomas from the library over the objection of parents, teachers, the local PTA, librarians, and students, as well as the principal of a junior high school in the district. The court declined "to review either the wisdom or the efficacy of the determination of the Board" on the ground that it was precluded by the Supreme Court's decision in *Epperson* v. *Arkansas* from intervening "in the resolution of conflicts which arise in the daily operation of school systems and which do not directly and sharply implicate basic constitutional values."

In *Presidents Council*, the court did not perceive the elimination of the book as involving an effort to aid or oppose religion as did the state statute prohibiting texts teaching evolution, which *Epperson* condemned. Nor did the court perceive the elimination of the book from the library as analogous to the ban on nondisruptive silent speech, which the Supreme Court condemned in *Tinker* v. *Des Moines Independent Community School District.*

In 1976, the Court of Appeals for the Sixth Circuit was confronted, in *Minarcini* v. *Strongsville City School District,* with a challenge to the school district's removal of Joseph Heller's *Catch 22* and Kurt Vonnegut's *Cat's Cradle* and *God Bless You, Mr. Rosewater* from its school library. The court found that the "Board removed the books because it found them objectionable in content and because it felt it had the power, unfettered by the First Amendment, to censor the school library for subject matter which the Board members found distasteful."

In contrast to the Second Circuit, the Sixth Circuit held that "[t]he removal of books from a school library is a much more serious burden upon freedom of classroom discussion than the action found unconstitutional in *Tinker* v. *Des Moines Independent Community School District.*" It based this holding first, on its perception that "[a] library is a mighty resource in the free marketplace of ideas, and second, on its understanding that the First Amendment protects the "right to know" because, as Justice Blackmun stated in *Virginia State Board of Pharmacy* v. *Virginia Citizens Consumers Council, Inc.,* "where a speaker exists . . . the protection afforded is to the communication, to its source and to its recipients both."

Relying on the *Minarcini* rationale, in 1978, the Massachusetts federal district court required a Chelsea school committee to return to the high school library an anthology entitled *Male and Female under 18,* which included a poem the committee found "objectionable," "obnoxious," "filthy," "vile and offensive garbage" (*Right to Read Defense Committee* v. *School Committee of the City of Chelsea*). The Chelsea court found that the poem was "tough but not obscene" and "no substantial governmental interest was served by cutting off students' access to *Male and Female* in the library." As in *Minarcini,* the court distinguished between the school board's power to control curriculum content and its power to control library collections. It also distinguished between the school board's power to select books for the library and its power to remove books once selected.

Adopting the *Chelsea* analysis, the Federal District Court for New Hampshire, in *Salvail* v. *Nashua Board of Education,* required the

Nashua Board of Education to return to its high school library copies of *Ms.* magazine, which had been removed because they allegedly "contained advertisements for 'vibrators, contraceptives, materials dealing with lesbianism and witchcraft and gay material' as well as advertisements for trips to Cuba, records by communist folk singers, and a procommunist newspaper." The Nashua court found that the board had failed "to demonstrate a substantial and legitimate government interest sufficient to warrant the removal of *Ms.* magazine from the Nashua High School Library."

The 1980s opened with two circuits presented with three cases challenging the removal of materials from high school libraries. In two of these cases the challenge was rejected. The third case was *Pico.*

The Seventh Circuit rejected the challenge in *Zykan* v. *Warsaw Community School Corporation.* There, the school board ordered the removal of several books from the high school library, including *Growing Up Female in America, Go Ask Alice, The Bell Jar,* and *The Stepford Wives.*

The uncontroverted record in *Zykan* showed that the school board turned the "offending" books over to complaining citizens who caused them to be publicly burned. While the court condemned this ceremony as "contemptible," it nevertheless concluded that the complaint failed to state a cause of action. The court held that

> [T]wo factors tend to limit the relevance of "academic freedom" at the secondary school level. First, the student's right to and need for such freedom is bounded by the level of his or her intellectual development. . . . Second, the importance of secondary schools in the development of intellectual faculties is only one part of a broad formative role encompassing the encouragement and nurturing of those fundamental social, political, and moral values that will permit a student to take his place in the community.

By the operation of these factors, the court concluded that

> complaints filed by secondary school students to contest the educational decisions of local authorities are sometimes cognizable but generally must cross a relatively high threshold before

entering upon the field of a constitutional claim suitable for federal court litigation.

While the Seventh Circuit was deciding *Zykan,* the Second Circuit was presented with two opportunities to reconsider its 1972 *Presidents Council* opinion. The first was the *Pico* case and the second was *Bicknell* v. *Vergennes Union High School Board of Directors.* Decided the same day, by the same panel, both *Pico* and *Bicknell* involved the removal of books of considerable literary reputation from the school library. The dismissal of the complaint in *Bicknell* was affirmed, and the dismissal of the complaint in *Pico* was reversed, both by two-to-one majorities. In each case, one judge saw both cases as an unconstitutional effort to purge the school library of ideas deemed inconsistent with the value inculcation objectives of the curriculum. Also, in each case, one judge saw both cases as an appropriate and constitutionally proper exercise of the value inculcation function traditionally assigned secondary education. The deciding judge in each case distinguished between *Bicknell* and *Pico* on the basis of the board's motive for removal. In *Bicknell* he found the motive to be the books' "vulgar and indecent language," which justified removal, whereas in *Pico* he found the motive to be the books' "ideas" or content, apart from vulgar or indecent language, which did not justify removal.

While all of these cases, including *Pico,* arose in the context of First Amendment challenges to the removal of books from school libraries, they all turned on differences in judicial perceptions of the proper role of school officials in the educational process. As a consequence, the primary effect of the Supreme Court's consideration in *Pico* was to identify what must be characterized as a fundamental philosophical dispute over the nature and function of elementary and secondary education in America. This dispute, revealed most graphically in the *Pico* opinions, divided the Court into two substantially equal and determined factions.

One faction, led by Chief Justice Burger, clearly perceived elementary and secondary education to be "indoctrinative" or "prescriptive" in purpose. The other faction, led by Justice Brennan, clearly perceived such education to involve an "analytic" objective that cannot constitutionally be subordinated to or frustrated by the indoctrinative function.

Under the indoctrinative or prescriptive concept of education, information and accepted truths are furnished to a theoretically passive, absorbent student. The function of teacher, school, and educational materials is to convey these truths, rather than to create new wisdom. On the other hand, the analytic educational concept contemplates the examination of data and values in a way that involves the teacher, school, and students in a search for truth.

The self-evident source of Justice Brennan's concern with Chief Justice Burger's perception of schools as "vehicles for 'inculcating fundamental values necessary to the maintenance of a democratic political system'" is that, so used, students will become nothing more than "closed circuit recipients of only that which the State chooses to communicate."

Justice Brennan's concern with laws, official conduct, and policies, which "cast a pall of orthodoxy over the classroom," has been a consistent, recurrent, and intensifying theme in opinions he has written in First Amendment cases since he first expressed it in *Keyishian* v. *Board of Regents*. There, he contended that "the classroom is peculiarly the 'marketplace of ideas,'" and that "the Nation's future depends upon leaders trained through wide exposure to that robust exchange of ideas which discovers truth 'out of a multitude of tongues, [rather] than through any kind of authoritative selection.'"

Justice Brennan, in his dissent in *Paris Adult Theatre I* v. *Slaton*, revealed, perhaps most clearly, the source and nature of his fear of the "value inculcation" model of education. There he quoted the following language from the Court's 1923 decision in *Meyer* v. *Nebraska:*

In order to submerge the individual and develop ideal citizens, Sparta assembled the males at seven into barracks and entrusted their subsequent education and training to official guardians. Although such measures have been deliberately approved by men of great genius, their ideas touching the relations between individual and State were wholly different from those upon which our institutions rest.

Justice Brennan's insistence that schools function as "marketplaces" of ideas as well as a means of "promoting respect for authority and traditional values be they social, moral, or political" reveals

305

his doubt about the ability of a political majority to resist imposing its orthodoxy at the expense of individual inquiry and intellectual freedom.

As Justice Brennan's First Amendment opinions consistently reflected his abiding concern for individual freedom of inquiry, Justice Burger's First Amendment opinions, in *Pico* and other cases, reflected his equally abiding concern for the promotion and protection of the "social interest in order and morality."

Having concluded that schools may legitimately be used for inculcating "fundamental values," Chief Justice Burger had no hesitation in granting school authorities "broad discretion to fulfill that obligation," including the right to make "content based decisions about the appropriateness of retaining materials in the school library and curriculum." Justice Burger's concern with the conduct of school authorities was not that they might impose orthodoxy in the classroom but rather that they might impose an orthodoxy that does not accurately reflect community values. This risk, however, Chief Justice Burger dismissed summarily on the basis of the following syllogism: "[L]ocal control of education involves democracy in a microcosm" because "in most public schools in the United States the parents have a large voice in the school," and, therefore, "through participation in the election of school board members, parents influence, if not control, the direction of their children's education." And because "a school board is not a giant bureaucracy far removed from accountability for its actions; it is truly 'of the people and by the people,'" it follows that "a school board reflects its constituency in a very real sense and thus could not long exercise unchecked discretion in its choice to acquire or remove books." Therefore, "if parents disagree with the educational decisions of the school board, they can take steps to remove the board members from office."

The empirical basis for this model of parent-teacher-student-school board relationships is, however, not readily identifiable. As of this writing, less than 20 percent of the voters are parents of elementary and secondary school children. The six-year average term of a school board member nationwide makes change in board composition and orientation a process requiring years. In most communities the school system, governed by the school board, is larger in terms of bureaucracy, budget, and manpower than any other government activity.

Total reliance on participative political solutions to controversies involving value inculcation is difficult to reconcile with the highly charged circumstances that almost invariably surround the removal of library materials. In *Zykan*, the removal was demanded not by parents but by an organization of senior citizens, which then burned the books. In *Chelsea*, the offending book was removed on the complaint of a single parent and over the objection of many. The celebrated Kanawha County, West Virginia, textbook controversy prompted death threats, school boycotts, attacks on school buses, and bombing of schools. Even in *Pico*, the books were banned from the library, not on the basis of a complaint from a local parent but on the basis of an "objectionable book list" prepared by an organization called Concerned Citizens and Taxpayers for Decent School Books of Baton Rouge, Louisiana, and distributed to three members of the Island Trees School Board at a meeting of a "conservative" organization in Watkins Glen, New York.

Chief Justice Burger's solution to the failure of a school board to reflect correctly the community values to be inculcated by the secondary school appears philosophically consistent with his solution for those whose values are not represented in the curricular orthodoxy. "They," said Chief Justice Burger, "have alternative sources to the same end. Books may be acquired from book stores, public libraries, or other alternative sources unconnected with the unique environment of the local public schools."

Justice Rehnquist, in his *Pico* dissent, joined by the Chief Justice, expressed the same perception in these words:

> When it acts as an educator, at least at the elementary and secondary school level, the government is engaged in inculcating social values and knowledge in relatively impressionable young people. . . . In short, actions by the government as educator do not raise the same First Amendment concerns as actions by the government as sovereign.

The willingness of no fewer than four justices of the Supreme Court to accept and endorse this view of the First Amendment's application to secondary education was a significant indication of the philosophical change that had occurred on the Court since 1943, when it held, in *West Virginia State Board of Education v. Barnette*, that "the Fourteenth Amendment, as now applied to the States, protects the citizens against the State itself and all of its creatures—Boards of Education not excepted."

But even more to the point is Justice Jackson's observation in *Barnette* that

> Probably no deeper division of our people could proceed from any provocation than from finding it necessary to choose what doctrine and whose program public educational officials may compel youth to unite in embracing. . . . the First Amendment to our Constitution was designed to avoid these ends by avoiding these beginnings.

The concept that secondary school can, consistent with the First Amendment, be reduced to a purely indoctrinative function serving the will of any transient political majority that might gain control of the system appears as a repudiation of the very purpose for which this amendment was adopted. That purpose was not to protect the rights of the majority but, rather, to protect the rights of the minority from the majority. As Justice Jackson put it in *Thomas v. Collins:*

> This liberty was not protected because the forefathers expected its use would always be agreeable to those in authority or that its exercise always would be wise, temperate, or useful to society. As I read their intentions, this liberty was protected because they knew of no other way by which free men could conduct representative democracy.

The concept that the secondary school can constitutionally be restricted to a value inculcating mechanism is affirmatively counterproductive to the society and the people in at least three fundamental respects: first, the concept absolutely guarantees that secondary schools will become political and ideological battlegrounds. It assures the "winner" of the competition for control of the school system, for the time he can remain in control, the right not only to control curriculum content but also to purge the school library of competing ideas. This is an opportunity no demagogue or ideologue can or will resist; and the Kanawha County chaos will be the norm, not the exception.

Second, the concept is in direct opposition to the objective of educational integration recognized by the Supreme Court as a constitutional mandate since *Brown* v. *Board of Education.* The success of such integration is a function of, and is measured by, not merely the numerical mix of races, religions, and nationalities in a school, but also in the capacity of the school to accommodate a variety of cultural, social, economic, and political perspectives and values. Educational parochialism is a fountainhead of bigotry; and such parochialism is promoted, not deterred, by an indoctrinative mechanism that brooks no opposing viewpoints and values. Indeed, the very utility of the school as an "assimilative force" in our society is frustrated if the values that it inculcates are mere functions of the accident of geography, school district boundary, or school board composition at any point in time.

Finally, and perhaps most inconsistent philosophically with the "values on which our society rests," is the concept that the secondary public school, unlike the institution of higher learning, can be restricted to a narrow indoctrinative function. This constitutes nothing more nor less than constitutionally protected "educational elitism." The distinction that Justice Rehnquist made in *Pico* between the application of the First Amendment to secondary schools and its application to institutions of higher education is implicitly based on the factually unsupportable conclusions of the Seventh Circuit in *Zykan* that "high school students lack . . . intellectual skills necessary for taking full advantage of the marketplace of ideas . . .," and that the student's need for academic freedom "is bounded by the level of his or her intellectual development."

This theory that access to the "marketplace of ideas" is reserved only to those who have the financial, physical, or mental capacity or the personal or professional interest to enter what the *Zykan* court described as "the rarefied atmosphere of the college or university" seems fundamentally at variance with the great tradition of American public education. Of particular concern is the notion that the "need" for access to the marketplace of ideas is a function of intellectual development, when most educators recognize such access as "indispensable" to intellectual development.

The plurality opinion in *Pico* rejects the concept that there are no limits to the measures or means that secondary school authorities may employ to inculcate values in their students. It does so by recognizing a constitutional "right to receive information." Although such right is condemned by Justices Burger, Rehnquist, and Powell as having simply "no application to the one public institution which, by its very nature, is a place for the selective conveyance of ideas," even they do not deny that the "right to receive information" has long been recognized by the Court as an indispensable and constitutionally protected corollary to the rights of free speech and press. As James Madison expressed it, "A popular Government, without popular information, or the means of acquiring it, is but a Prologue to a Farce or a Tragedy, or perhaps both."

Specific recognition of the "right to receive information" is of paramount importance to what has now become a "knowledge society." Knowledge is power and access to all our society has to offer. The existence of the "right to receive information" does not negate the indoctrinative function of secondary schools. It merely requires that such function be performed by persuasion and example, by focus and emphasis, and by selection and presentation, rather than by suppression and excision.

The judicial recognition in *Pico* of a "right to receive information" and of the special role played by the school library in implementing this right, however limited in its support among the justices, offers a significant line of legal defense against censorship. The judicial debate over the nature and role of public education and over the applicability of the First Amendment to public schools has continued. The hope that the largely positive outcome of the *Pico* case represented for the cause of intellectual freedom, however, could not have been more timely and still has strength today. Historic institutions, values, and traditions are being buffeted by winds of change; but, as President Kennedy observed, "freedom and security are but opposite sides of the same coin—and the free expression of ideas is not more expendable but far more essential in a period of challenge and crisis."

2

School Library Censorship
and the Courts:
After Hazelwood

Robert S. Peck

arents often agonize over what they will allow their children to
do. Now that the kids are eight and ten, how late should they be
allowed to stay up? Are they watching too much television? Are
there certain magazines or books that they should not be allowed to
read? These are difficult questions for which there are no right answers that serve all families. Still, parents hold a unique position of
authority. Their decisions, at least in the home and to the extent they
can exercise control, are unappealable. The only reason a parent
need give is "because I say so."

Although the same temptations to control youthful expression
and access to material are present in the classroom, the same finality
does not necessarily apply to decisions made by educational authorities, particularly when the suitability of books for children is
involved. School officials must comply with the right of free expression, guaranteed by the First Amendment. Just how the First Amend-

---

Robert S. Peck, an attorney, is the director of legal affairs for the Association
of Trial Lawyers of America and has authored several books in the field of
constitutional law. He is a vice president of the Freedom to Read Foundation Board of Trustees and served as president of the Board, 1988–90.

ment applies to school books and what violates that constitutional standard remains ill-defined under current judicial precedents.

Courts have had particular difficulty in ruling on these issues. The dilemma the courts face in schoolbook cases arises from two seemingly unrelated legal principles: freedom of expression and judicial restraint. The courts have interpreted the First Amendment's free-speech guarantee to disable a public school official from claiming parentlike authority to make arbitrary and unappealable decisions about the books available to students. In an important 1982 U.S. Supreme Court case, *Island Trees Union Free School District No. 26 v. Pico,*[1] several students brought a lawsuit seeking the return of nine books that had been removed by the board of education from the school library's shelves. The school officials justified the books' removal on the grounds that the banished publications were "anti-American, anti-Christian, anti-Semitic, and just plain filthy."[2] In upholding the students' right to sue in this case, a clear majority of the justices agreed that school boards do not have unfettered authority to select library books, and First Amendment rights are implicated when books are removed arbitrarily. An overwhelming majority of the Court also condemned politically motivated book removals.

The Court's decision, however, was a fractured one, with seven of the nine justices writing separate opinions. Although the Court held that the First Amendment prevents government officials, which includes public school officials, from denying access to ideas with which they disagree, the justices strongly suggested that decisions based on educational suitability would be upheld, particularly where a regular system of review using standardized guidelines was followed. The Court's caveat about educational aptness stands as a proxy for the judicial restraint principle. It is a long-standing judicial practice to avoid interfering in areas where the courts have little expertise or license to act. In the field of education, this principle manifests itself through judicial recognition that "the education of the Nation's youth is primarily the responsibility of parents, teachers, and state and local school officials, and not of federal judges."[3] In the 1988 *Hazelwood School District v. Kuhlmeier* decision, the Supreme Court added:

> It is only when the decision to censor a school-sponsored publication, theatrical production, or other vehicle of student expres-

sion has no valid educational purpose that the First Amendment is so "directly and sharply implicate[d]," as to require judicial intervention to protect students' constitutional rights.[4]

In *Hazelwood*, the Court found no constitutional bar to a principal's conduct when he removed two pages of a student newspaper produced as part of a high school journalism class. The Court held that teachers, principals, and school boards may legitimately make decisions that might otherwise smack of unconstitutionality, in order to further the school's educational mission. The Court declared that school-sponsored expressive activities can be subjected to content control as long as the censorious conduct is "reasonably related to legitimate pedagogical concerns."[5]

Many critics have branded the *Hazelwood* decision a rogue elephant upsetting the field of established First Amendment precedents because it appears to place educationally motivated censorship beyond the ambit of First Amendment inquiry. The Court, however, has always been enamored of the notion that legitimate educational purposes can justify some infringement of free expression. In a landmark 1969 decision, *Tinker* v. *Des Moines Independent Community School District*,[6] the Court held that neither "students [n]or teachers shed their constitutional rights to freedom of speech or expression at the schoolhouse gate."[7] Yet, in the same case, the Court also recognized school officials could suppress speech when necessary to avoid material and substantial interference with schoolwork or discipline or to protect the rights of others. Still, the Court cautioned that "in our system, undifferentiated fear or apprehension of disturbance is not enough to overcome the right to freedom of expression . . . Any word spoken, in class, in the lunch room, or on the campus that deviates from the views of another person may start an argument or cause a disturbance. But our Constitution says we must take this risk."[8]

When the issue is the removal of school library books, justifications based on educational suitability and interference with the learning environment require courts to answer a number of related questions: When is a decision to remove books actually based on legitimate educational reasons, and when is it based on constitutionally impermissible ones? How can the litigants prove what was in the mind of the alleged censor in order to demonstrate his or her true motivation? When someone dislikes the viewpoint a book advocates, cannot a rationale based on plausible educational objections insulate an unconstitutionally motivated book banning from judicial inquiry?

These are questions likely to be confronted by the courts over a period of time. As yet, they remain unsettled. Still, one pattern is already discernable. The most plausible "educational reason," in the eyes of the courts, for removing a book is that it is vulgar or indecent. Vulgarity or indecency, of course, are not constitutionally justifiable reasons for banning a work from a public library. Only a higher standard, obscenity, can provide a legitimate rationale. "The special characteristics of the school environment," however, allow the age of the likely audience to be a constitutionally permissible deciding factor, according to recent court decisions. In virtually every instance where the censorship act has been upheld, it has been because of the sexual content of the work. Thus, in *Seyfried* v. *Walton* (1981),[9] the U.S. Court of Appeals for the Third Circuit sided with a school superintendent who canceled the play *Pippin*, because even an edited version of it had too much sexual content.

The sexual-content test applies even when schools attempt to regulate the distribution of underground newspapers, which in no way may be regarded as school-sponsored publications and thus are not subject to measurement against the school's purported educational mission. In a post-*Hazelwood* decision, the U.S. Court of Appeals for the Ninth Circuit considered the issue of school regulations aimed at underground newspapers. Under a policy adopted by the Renton, Washington, school district, unofficial publications distributed on school grounds required the prior approval of school officials. At a school barbecue, students and at least one parent distributed copies of an underground newspaper called *Bad Asta*, which criticized certain school policies affecting students, contained poetry by well-known American authors, and reported the results of a mock teacher-evaluation poll. Although the school principal found no part of the publication objectionable, he reprimanded the students, placing the disciplinary action in the students' permanent files, for violating the prior-approval policy. The students and their parents sued the school to challenge the constitutionality of the policy.

Generally, preapproval requirements are viewed as prior restraints on publication, a category that carries a "heavy presumption" of unconstitutionality.[10] On the basis of its review of the *Bad Asta* case, the Ninth Circuit concluded that "a policy which subjects all non-school-sponsored communications to predistribution review for content censorship violates the first amendment."[11] The court, however, limited its holding "to school distribution policies which are content based, and does not pertain to regulations of time, place, and manner of distribution."[12] The court also did not consider its ruling to affect a school's authority to punish students for unacceptable or disruptive behavior after publication.

One year earlier, the U.S. Court of Appeals for the Eighth Circuit reached a contrary conclusion, permitting predistribution review of underground newspapers.[13] The challenged policy guidelines enabled school officials to ban on-campus distribution of material that was "obscene to minors," "libelous," "pervasively indecent or vulgar," or likely to cause "a material and substantial disruption of the proper and orderly operation of the school or school activities." In addition, the guidelines prohibited advertising of "any product or service not permitted to minors by law" and material that "invades the privacy of another person or endangers the health or safety of another person." Only the last ground was found to violate constitutional proscriptions, because Minnesota, where the lawsuit originated, does not recognize civil liability for invasion of privacy. All other grounds for prohibition of a publication had previously been approved in Supreme Court decisions.

An additional wrinkle on the underground newspaper issue was addressed by the U.S. Court of Appeals for the Second Circuit in *Thomas* v. *Board of Education*.[14] The case involved an off-campus newspaper, *Hard Times,* that was produced by high school students as a satirical and sexually blunt publication. The newspaper was sold for twenty-five cents a copy and only available off school grounds. After a teacher confiscated an issue from a student in class and the principal decided against taking any action against the student publishers, the school board suspended the students for five days, required that they be separated from other students during study hall, and placed a note about the incident in each student's academic files. The students successfully sued to challenge the school board's action.

The Second Circuit acknowledged that "school officials must have some latitude within the school in punishing and prohibiting ordinarily protected speech both out of regard for fellow students who constitute a captive audience, and in recognition of the fact that the school has a substantial educational interest in avoiding the impression that it has authorized a specific expression."[15] Nevertheless, that latitude cannot be properly invoked in this instance, the court said, "because school officials have ventured out of the school yard and into the general community where the freedom accorded expression is at its zenith."[16] When officials attempt to enforce their authority beyond the school's boundaries, the court added, "their actions must be evaluated by the principles that bind government officials in the public arena."[17]

The underground newspaper cases establish that school authorities are vested with substantial authority to prevent the on-campus distribution of publications likely to cause a substantial disruption to the functioning of the school. Obscene, libelous, vulgar, and otherwise disruptive material all qualify as grounds for denial of permission to make use of school grounds for distribution. However, enforcement of such authority must be made pursuant to a written policy that spells out the permissible grounds for denial of access to school grounds. In essence, the policy is valid if it relies on disruptive grounds that have already been approved by the Supreme Court and limits its restrictions to content-neutral time, place, or manner policies. Moreover, when the school adopts a written policy requiring prior approval for on-campus distribution, the policy must also contain a reasonable time limit on the length of the approval process.[18]

When the underground publication is distributed entirely off campus, school authorities are subject to the same First Amendment considerations that apply to government authorities with respect to newspapers generally. Thus, obscene publications that are accorded no First Amendment protections would still be subject to confiscation and punishment by school authorities, even if distributed off campus.

Just as sexual content may render certain underground newspapers subject to regulation, the strongly offending nature of speech that contains a high degree of sexual reference was a critical factor in the Supreme Court's decision in *Bethel School District No. 403* v. *Fraser* (1986).[19] Matthew Fraser, a high school student, was suspended from school for making sexually suggestive remarks in a student-government assembly. Fraser challenged his suspension unsuccessfully. The Supreme Court, in an opinion written by Chief Justice Warren Burger, a dissenter in the *Island Trees* case, held that "[i]t does not follow . . . that simply because the use of an offensive form of expression may not be prohibited to adults making what the speaker considers a political point, that the same latitude must be permitted to children in a public school."[20] Chief Justice Burger went on to declare, "[t]he undoubted freedom to advocate unpopular and controversial views in schools and classrooms must be balanced against the society's countervailing interest in teaching students the boundaries of socially appropriate behavior."[21]

Combining the Supreme Court's approaches in *Fraser* and *Hazelwood*, the Eleventh Circuit upheld a school board's removal of a previously approved class textbook because of the material's perceived vulgarity and sexual explicitness. In *Virgil v. School Board of Columbia County* (1989),[22] the book's banishment to locked storage was occasioned by selections from *Lysistrata*, written around 411 B.C. by Aristophanes, and *The Miller's Tale*, written around 1385 by Geoffrey Chaucer. For judicial purposes, the classical nature of the material was irrelevant. Although the court upheld the school board's censorship action, the judges felt compelled to "seriously question how young persons just below the age of majority can be harmed by these masterpieces of Western literature."[23] Instead, the court focused on the fact that these were materials used within the curriculum and thus bearing the imprimatur of school approval. It then found that the reason for the textbook's removal from the curriculum was the passages' "explicit sexuality and excessively vulgar language,"[24] which it held to be a legitimate pedagogical concern. Ironically, the court found the school board's action reasonable because the textbook, as well as other versions of the disputed selections, remained available in the school library, thereby suggesting that yet a different standard of analysis would be apropos to the removal of a book from a school library. That same approach, differentiating between curricular activity and other activities within the school environment, was adopted by a federal court in New York in the case of *Romano v. Harrington* (1989),[25] where a faculty advisor's responsibility for supervising the content of an extracurricular student newspaper was at issue. These cases, building on the Supreme Court's *Hazelwood* decision, appear to establish that there are different levels of constitutional protection for books and other publications depending on whether the material is removed from a public library, a school library, or a classroom.

Some states, however, do not follow the *Hazelwood* approach. Courts in New Jersey and Oregon have held that their state constitutions give students greater free expression protection than the U.S. Supreme Court has recognized under the First Amendment.[26] Other states have enacted statutory protections for student expression. These states include California, Colorado, Iowa, Kansas, and Massachusetts.

In contrast to the cases where there is evidence of indecency or obscenity, other educational purposes justifying censorship have been more difficult to prove. In *Pratt v. Independent School District No. 831* (1982),[27] the U.S. Court of Appeals for the Eighth Circuit found the removal of a film version of "The Lottery" and a related film trailer from the curriculum unconstitutional. The films had been part of the curriculum for five years but were excised after parents and other citizens complained about the story's violence and its impact on students' religious and family values. The court declared that the film was eliminated because of its "ideological content" in contravention of the First Amendment.

It may seem difficult to conceive how a description of violence or an assault on traditional values may be protected by the First Amendment, whereas mere sexual innuendo may not. The explanation is more cultural than legal. A society that values intellectual freedom can oppose controversial notions but, at the same time, proudly defend the right of anyone to express those insidious ideas. That is the essence of a free society—to allow ideas to compete with each other for majority approval. Yet sex is a different category of expression. That is why the Supreme Court has repeatedly held that obscenity falls outside the bounds of protected free speech. (The Oregon Supreme Court ruled in 1987 that obscenity comes within the free-speech protections of that state's constitution and has done so without bringing about the moral downfall of the state.) Society's sexual taboos explain why violent movies and television programs are often accessible to minors, but those with "adult content" are not. If there is a societal consensus on any free-speech issues, it is that children should not be exposed to sexual content. If this means that children's free expression rights are less than adults', society does not appear to mind.

Previous attempts to prevent youths from having access to literature that describes or depicts violence have been struck down by the courts. In a 1948 case, the Supreme Court invalidated a law that prohibited the distribution to minors of any publication "principally made up of . . . accounts of criminal deeds, or pictures, or stories of deeds of bloodshed, lust or crime."[28] This was intended to protect minors from exposure to what was deemed to be harmful published materials on the theory that the publications could lead to violent criminal activity by its young readers. Even though the justices saw "nothing of any possible value to society in these magazines," the Court held that "they are as much entitled to the protection of free speech as the best of literature."[29] Using similar reasoning and citing *Winters* favorably, a federal appeals court recently invalidated a Missouri law that prohibited the rental or sale of violent videocassettes to minors.[30] The Tennessee Supreme Court reached the same conclusion.[31]

This means that the books most likely to be the successful targets of censors are those with a degree of sexuality that some educational authority considers harmful to minors or disruptive to the educational mission of the school. Those committed to intellectual freedom must be prepared to challenge that rationale, especially when it is actually a subterfuge for ideological objections, for although the Supreme Court has found that government may "adopt more stringent controls on communicative materials available to youths than on those available to adults," the Court has also said that "[s]peech . . . cannot be suppressed solely to protect the young from ideas or images that a legislative body thinks unsuitable for them. In most circumstances, the values protected by the First Amendment are no less applicable when the government seeks to control the flow of information to minors."[32]

Still, sex is not the only target of censors. Religious fundamentalists have been the instigators of an increasing number of censorship incidents. They have been more successful in influencing local school policies than they have been in winning legal victories.

Many of these deeply religious individuals see the books used in schools and the ideas contained in them as assaults on their fundamentalist views, attacks aimed at leading their children away from the parents' religion. Their counterattacks on books are a means of self-defense but are also an indication of their intolerance for other viewpoints.

In 1985, more than 130 textbook censorship incidents took place, spread over forty-four states.[33] The numbers show no sign of diminishing. Three 1987 cases gained a certain notoriety. In Hawkins County, Tennessee, *The Diary of Anne Frank* and *The Wizard of Oz* were among the books accused of being "anti-Christian." *Anne Frank*, the fundamentalists claimed, suggested that all religions were the same in a passage that indicated that any religious belief could serve as a source of strength in trying times. The statement was antithetical to the objecting parents' fundamentalist tenets that held there is only one true religion. *Oz* promoted witchcraft and self-reliance at the expense of trust in God, according to its detractors. Other books were deemed objectionable for promoting feminism and other philosophies that the claimants found heretical. Although the fundamentalists were ultimately unsuccessful in their lawsuit, *Mozert* v. *Hawkins County Board of Education* (1987),[34] controversies such as these have ripple effects that chill the vitality of intellectual freedom. Rather than face further objections from the fundamentalist parents behind the lawsuit, the school involved denied a group of students permission to stage *Anne Frank* as a play. In this incident, no one came out the winner. The religious fundamentalists lost their lawsuit, but the school was cowed into playing it safe and avoiding controversy because of the high cost in emotional energy, time, and dollars in standing up for First Amendment values. Unfortunately, the cause of intellectual freedom is only served when people are willing to fight. Liberty erodes when controversy is avoided rather than confronted.

In Mobile, Alabama, the issue was whether the school was attempting to foist a religion called "secular humanism" on the children. Seeking changes in the curriculum and the removal of some forty-five textbooks, a lawsuit, *Smith* v. *Board of School Commissioners* (1987)[35] was brought by 624 Christian Evangelicals. At the heart of their complaint was a claim that textbook publishers and classroom teachers were denying any role to religion in American society out of a misplaced fear of breaching the constitutional separation of church and state. In its place, their theory stated, secular humanism, an antireligious "religion," was being promoted, and this, in fact, violated the concept of separation. While many could agree with the first part of their claim—that mention of religion had been so removed from the curriculum as to become an educational disservice— their solution, censorship of existing materials, violated free expression, as the U.S. Court of Appeals for the Eleventh Circuit held in the case. The answer was not less speech but more. Like the attraction of the proverbial better mousetrap, the publication of better textbooks—with an appropriately balanced treatment of the role of religion in American society—would naturally supplant the watered-down texts then in use as schools beat a path to the publisher of the improved texts.

The third case, *Edwards* v. *Aguillard* (1987),[36] was the latest chapter in the continuing battle over Darwinian evolution that dates back to the 1925 "monkey trial" of John T. Scopes. Seeking "equal time" for the biblical story of Genesis, a 1981 Louisiana law outlawed the teaching of evolution in the public schools unless "creation science" was also taught. In its decision, the Supreme Court overturned the law as an unconstitutional attempt to inject a particular religious belief into the public schools.

Challenges to our First Amendment freedoms are continuous, often variations on themes that have come before. There are no final victories. Ultimately, it is not the courts but the people who must take a stand to protect their liberty. Despite the protection afforded us by the existence of the First Amendment, our precious freedoms remain only when people are knowledgeable about the challenges to our free expression rights and participate in resolving the issues. Only then will our speech remain uninhibited and robust. Intellectual freedom remains, as Andrew Hamilton said in defense of colonial printer John Peter Zenger in 1735, "the best Cause."

NOTES

1. 457 U.S. 853 (1982).
2. Id., at 857.
3. *Hazelwood School District* v. *Kuhlmeier*, 484 U.S. 260, 273 (1988).
4. Id., at 571.
5. Id.
6. 393 U.S. 503 (1969).

7. Id., at 506.
8. Id., at 508.
9. 668 F.2d 214 (3d Cir. 1981).
10. *Bantam Books, Inc.* v. *Sullivan*, 372 U.S. 58, 70 (1963).
11. *Burch* v. *Barker*, 861 F.2d 1149, 1157 (9th Cir. 1988).
12. Id., at 1158.
13. *Bystrom* v. *Fridley High School*, 822 F.2d 747 (8th Cir. 1987).
14. 607 F.2d 1043 (2d Cir. 1979), cert. denied, 444 U.S. 1081 (1980).
15. Id., at 1049.
16. Id., at 1050.
17. Id.
18. *Rivera* v. *East Otero School Dist. R-1*, 721 F.Supp. 1189 (D. Colo. 1989).
19. 478 U.S. 675 (1986).
20. Id., at 682.
21. Id., at 681.
22. 862 F.2d 1517 (11th Cir. 1989).
23. Id., at 1525.
24. Id., at 1523.
25. 725 F.Supp. 687 (D.N.Y. 1989).
26. *Desilets* v. *Clearview Reg. Bd. of Educ.*, No. C-23-90 (NJ Super. Ct. Law Div. May 7, 1991), aff'd on other grounds, 630 A.2d 333 (AD 1993), aff'd No. A-133-93 (Sept. 22, 1994); *Barcik* v. *Kubiaczyk*, 873 P.2d 456 (Or. Ct. App. 1994).
27. 670 F.2d 771 (8th Cir. 1982).
28. *Winters* v. *New York*, 333 U.S. 507, 508 (1948).
29. Id., at 510.
30. *Video Software Dealers Ass'n* v. *Webster*, 968 F.2d 684, 688 (8th Cir. 1992).
31. *Davis Kidd Booksellers, Inc.* v. *McWherter*, 866 S.W. 2d 520 (Tenn. 1993).
32. *Erznoznik* v. *City of Jacksonville*, 422 U.S. 205, 211 (1975).
33. *Attacks on the Freedom to Learn* (Washington, D.C.: People for the American Way, 1985).
34. 827 F.2d 1058 (6th Cir. 1987), cert. denied, 484 U.S. 1066 (1988).
35. 827 F.2d 684 (11th Cir. 1987).
36. 482 U.S. 578 (1987).

3

The Buckley Amendment: Student Privacy versus Parents' Right to Know

Anne Levinson Penway

The Family Educational and Privacy Rights Act of 1974, 20 U.S.C. Section 1232(g)—commonly referred to as the Buckley Amendment after its sponsor, Senator James Buckley of New York—provides students over eighteen access to their own school records and the parents or guardians of minor students access to the school records maintained on their minor children. It also protects the privacy of those records by prohibiting access by other persons without the knowledge or consent of students or their parents. Schools are required to provide parents, legal guardians, and students eighteen years or older a hearing for the purposes of challenging inaccurate, misleading, or false information contained in their school file. Should a school fail to comply, there is no private right to sue to enforce its terms. Instead, complaints about failure to abide by the terms of the law must be submitted to the Family Policy Compliance Office of the United States Department of Education.

It should be understood that the law does not *prohibit* disclosure of records—it simply imposes the penalty of loss of federal

Anne Levinson Penway is assistant director of the Office for Intellectual Freedom. She also serves as deputy executive director of the Freedom to Read Foundation.

funds on schools that release records in violation of its terms: "Under the Family Educational Rights and Privacy Act (FERPA) and the Regulations thereunder, a school's release of a student's records or personally identifiable information to unauthorized persons will result in withholding of federal funds" (*Webster Groves School District* v. *Pulitzer Publishing Company*, 898 F.2d 1371, 1375 [8th Cir. 1990]).

The important question for school librarians is, Does the Buckley Amendment apply to school library records? The precise definition of "education records," which are required to be disclosed to parents under the Buckley Amendment, has been the subject of much debate, very little case law, and little elaboration via the Code of Federal Regulations, where some additional explanation of the statute's terms may be found (see 32 C.F.R Section 99).

Nevertheless, school librarians may one day find themselves in the position of having to determine whether or not they are bound by law to release otherwise-confidential information about students to their parents or guardians. The language of the law, and the Department of Education's interpretation of it, are broad and inclusive, suggesting that all records containing personally identifiable information about a student are covered. But there are several exceptions in the definition section of the statute applicable to elementary and secondary school students. One of these exceptions covers records of instructional, supervisory, and administrative personnel, which are in the sole possession of the person who made them and which are not accessible or revealed to anyone else except a substitute.

Before even considering arguments about whether or not the Buckley Amendment should apply to school library records, librarians and school administrators should make sure they have a thorough understanding of the philosophy behind the professional, ethical, and often legal requirement that library records be kept confidential. Library circulation and registration records are maintained solely for administrative purposes—the only reason they are kept is for the library to keep track of its materials. They are not created as a means of spying on patrons' reading habits nor of providing a government-sponsored intermediary between parent and child for the purpose of monitoring the child's reading habits. Ideally, parents should be guiding their own children's reading selections and should not rely on librarians to report on their children for them. Library patrons, including minors, will not feel free to exercise their constitutional right to receive information if they believe their selections are being monitored. Furthermore, it is inappropriate to call someone under suspicion, or to prejudge that person's character, because of his or her reading habits. A free society trusts its members to make their own separate decisions about what they choose to read and how they choose to act. Freedom of thought and conscience cannot be maintained in a society that does not allow its citizens to read and explore all points of view freely, without fear of social or governmental reprisal based upon the misguided assumption that what a person chooses to read is an absolute indicator of what that person believes or how that person is likely to behave.

Young people must be taught that they, too, have the right to read, and that they must learn to examine and differentiate between many different points of view and opinions in order to arrive at and defend their own in an intellectually sound and fully informed manner. In a democratic society, self-governing citizens must feel free to fully inform themselves, to become responsible participants in the democratic and social processes of a free nation.

For these sound philosophical reasons, free expression advocates, proponents of children's rights, and the ALA's Office for Intellectual Freedom oppose the application to school library records of the Buckley Amendment's requirement of disclosure to parents. First, one of the major purposes of the Buckley Amendment is to protect student privacy, something librarians are already committed to do. Librarians' professional ethics, and laws in forty-five states and the District of Columbia, protect the confidentiality of library records and either require or allow them to be withheld from anyone other than library personnel absent a court order.

Second, library records are not kept as a record of the scholastic development of a student. Circulation records are usually obliterated automatically when an item is returned, so one could argue that the records are not "maintained" in the manner contemplated by the statute. One of Senator Buckley's concerns in proposing the law, as explained in one of the few cases dealing with its terms, was that a single vindictive remark or inaccuracy could lurk undetected in a student's record, ruining future opportunities without the student's knowledge:

An example of the type of abuse which FERPA was designed to prevent is the insertion of potentially prejudicial anecdotal comments and factual inaccuracies into a student's school records. When parents and students are not allowed to inspect such school records and make corrections, such material can have a devastatingly negative effect on the academic future and job prospects of an innocent, unaware student. A simple inaccuracy or a comment by a spiteful, neurotic teacher can potentially ruin a student's future. (*Bauer* v. *Kincaid*, 759 F.Supp. 575, 590 [W.D. Mo. 1991])

Library records do not contain personal observations and are therefore not the kind of records that could include such little "time bombs," which would need to be corrected, are not permanently maintained, and are not transmitted to anyone who could use them in any way against a student in the future. This, of course, is one of the reasons librarians keep such records confidential in the first place.

Maintaining the confidentiality of library records comports at least with the spirit of the Buckley Amendment with regard to privacy.

This interpretation of the status of school library records under the Buckley Amendment has never been tested directly in court. A 1991 federal court decision (in *Bauer* v. *Kincaid*, supra) defined school records narrowly to include only those "records relating to individual student academic performance, financial aid, or scholastic probation which are kept in individual student files." The court also explained the purpose of the Act: "The underlying purpose of FERPA was not to grant individual students a right to privacy or access to educational records, but to stem the growing policy of many institutions to carelessly release educational information" (*Bauer* v. *Kincaid*, at 590). Again, library records contain no significant educational information and are already maintained as confidential. The decision in *Bauer* is not binding outside the district in which it was rendered, but since it is one of only a very few cases interpreting the statute, it sets a precedent upon which to base an argument for future cases.

The law governing confidentiality of library records of minor patrons—and more broadly, the rights of children versus the rights of their parents—is indefinite and still developing. The ethical stance taken by librarians, however, is more clear: ALA policy and the Office for Intellectual Freedom advocate according the same confidentiality protection to minors as to adult patrons.

Children and young adults will not learn to exercise their own intellectual freedom if they are taught that the guarantees of the Constitution do not apply to them. Protecting their right to read freely and use library resources is critically important if we wish to raise new generations to be active First Amendment advocates and protectors of the Constitution, which provides the basis for government by and for all the people.

4

Public Libraries as Limited Public Fora for Access to Information

Anne Levinson Penway

On March 23, 1992, the United States Court of Appeals for the Third Circuit handed down its decision in *Kreimer* v. *Morristown*.[1] The case, which involved a challenge to the patron behavior rules of the Morristown, New Jersey, Public Library, had been one of passionate debate in public library circles, much of which was, unfortunately, uninformed and misdirected. Indeed, the debate tended to focus on librarians' feelings about so-called problem patrons, including homeless patrons, and their alleged behavior, whereas the litigation focused only on whether the actual written rules adopted by the Morristown library were constitutionally acceptable.

The case arose out of a dispute between the Morristown library and one of its patrons, a homeless man named Richard Kreimer. Kreimer was accused of engaging in unacceptable behavior in the library, in violation of the library's rules for patron conduct. When Kreimer sued, contending that he had been barred from the library in violation of his constitutional right to have access to information, the library filed a motion for summary judgment, asking the court to rule, as a matter of law, that its rules were permissible under the

---

Anne Levinson Penway is assistant director of the Office for Intellectual Freedom and deputy executive director of the Freedom to Read Foundation.

Constitution. Rulings on motions for summary judgment are based on undisputed facts and make no factual rulings—instead, they address how the law applies to the facts at hand. In this case, the "undisputed facts" were the words of the rules themselves. Kreimer's specific behavior was not before the court and was not an element in its decision.

Initially, the federal district court, in a controversial opinion by Judge Lee Sarokin, found that the rules, which permitted ejecting a patron for "foul odor," "staring," and other infractions, were overbroad. The library appealed to the United States Court of Appeals for the Third Circuit.

That court reversed the lower court's decision in part, but adopted the reasoning presented in separate amicus curiae briefs filed by the Freedom to Read Foundation and the New Jersey Library Association. The Third Circuit ruled, for the first time, that public libraries are designated limited public fora for access to information and that First Amendment rights are implicated when library rules and regulations threaten to restrict that access. The court also upheld the right of libraries to make reasonable rules to facilitate access for all library patrons. Finally, the court upheld the specific rules and regulations of the Morristown library, finding that they either were reasonable regulations on nonexpressive activity or content-neutral restrictions on activity that might have an expressive element but interfered with the operation of the library.

While press reports tended to focus on Kreimer's alleged conduct, the court was careful to note that it did not make factual findings concerning that conduct. The ruling dealt only with the facial validity of Morristown's rules and regulations.

Following a careful review of Supreme Court precedents, the Third Circuit held that "our review of the Supreme Court's decisions confirms that the First Amendment does not merely prohibit the government from enacting laws that censor information, but additionally encompasses the positive right of public access to information and ideas. . . . [T]his right . . . includes the right to some level of access to a public library, the quintessential locus of the receipt of information."

Once it had recognized the constitutional right of public access to information and ideas in public libraries, the court took up the question of what kind of public forum analysis applies, "because the extent to which the government may limit access depends on whether the forum is public or non-public." The United States Supreme Court has, in several decisions, defined three types of such fora—public, limited or designated public, and nonpublic. The first type, *public fora*, encompasses places such as public streets, parks, and sidewalks, which have been traditional venues of freedom of expression and the dissemination of information by speakers to the public. *Limited or designated public fora* are places that have been set aside by the government for expressive activity. In these two types of fora, the government may impose only "reasonable time, place and manner" restrictions on speech. *Nonpublic fora* are government buildings and other such areas, which do not have as their primary role acting as a venue for expression. More restrictive rules may be applied in such places.

The Third Circuit held that public libraries are designated or limited public fora.

> It is clear to us that a public library, albeit the quintessential locus for the exercise of the right to receive information and ideas, is sufficiently dissimilar to a public park, sidewalk or street that it cannot reasonably be determined to constitute a traditional public forum. Obviously, a library patron cannot be permitted to engage in most traditional First Amendment activities in any library, such as giving speeches or engaging in any other conduct that would disrupt the quiet and peaceful library environment. We thus rejected the District Court's conclusion that the library constitutes a "quintessential, traditional public forum whose accessibility affects the bedrock of our democratic system. . . ." In our view, . . . the library constitutes a limited public forum, a type of designated public fora.

A significant factor in the court's ruling was the Morristown library's mission statement and the stated purposes of the rules at issue in the case. These were to "allow all patrons of the Joint Free Public Library of Morristown and Morris Township to use its facilities to the maximum extent possible during its regularly scheduled hours." The Third Circuit was persuaded that this language established a governmental intent to open the library to the public for expressive activity, "namely, the communication of the written word." The court also noted that the record in the case indicated that the library exercises its authority to exclude a patron only after his or her violation of the library's rules. The rules themselves make clear that the library is open to the public only for specified purposes: reading, studying, or using library materials. The library has not opened its doors for the exercise of all First Amendment activities (such as demonstrations or soapbox speeches).

The court held that in a limited public forum, constitutional protection is afforded "only to expressive activity of a genre similar to those that government has admitted to the limited forum." Applying that standard, the court found "the library is obligated only to permit the public to exercise rights that are consistent with the nature of the library and consistent with the government's intent in designating the library as a public forum. Other activities need not be tolerated."

Proceeding to an examination of the specific rules at issue, the court held that each of the challenged rules met the required standard of reasonableness and were not vague or overbroad. The court spent the most time analyzing the so-called smell rule, which prohibited patrons whose "bodily hygiene is so offensive as to constitute a nuisance" from remaining in the building. The court found that the "smell" rule was sufficiently narrow and that the library's purpose was served by the requirement that its patrons have non-offensive bodily hygiene. The rule left open alternative channels for communication because all a patron had to do was comply with the rules in order to use the library's facilities. The court specifically stated that it did not read the rule as one that permanently barred a patron from reentering the library once the patron had complied with the requirements, in the absence of what the court termed "pervasive abuse." Interestingly, the Third Circuit noted,

> [W]hile the District Court was probably correct that the rule may disproportionately affect the homeless who have limited access to bathing facilities, this fact is irrelevant to a facial challenge and further would not justify permitting a would-be patron, with hygiene so offensive that it constitutes a nuisance, to force other patrons to leave the library or to inhibit library employees from

performing their duties. Moreover, we do not face the more difficult scenario in which one individual possesses First Amendment rights and others do not. Here, if the First Amendment protects the right to reasonable access to a public library, as we hold it does, this is a right shared equally by all residents of Morristown and Morris Township. . . . Kreimer's right has no lesser, or greater, significance than that of other residents. Accordingly, his right to reasonable access to the library cannot be expanded to such an extent that it denies others the same guarantee.

Responding to the concern that enforcement of the "smell" rule depended on a third person's subjective reaction of being annoyed, the court observed that "the determination of whether a given patron's hygiene constitutes a nuisance involves an objective reasonableness test, not an annoyance test."

Thus, the court held that the Morristown library's rules were reasonable, that the library did not act in an arbitrary or discriminatory manner in enacting them, and that a violation of the rules would disrupt the smooth functioning of the library. It reversed the decision of the lower court and remanded the case for resolution of remaining issues and for entry of a partial summary judgment in favor of the library, upholding the facial constitutionality of its rules.

Although the Third Circuit's decision is binding only in New Jersey, Pennsylvania, Delaware, and the Virgin Islands (the area of the Third Circuit's jurisdiction), it is the only federal appeals court decision that has directly ruled that libraries are designated public fora for access to information and that infringements of that access must be analyzed under First Amendment principles. It therefore will be persuasive precedent for courts addressing similar issues in the future.

In response to the many requests that arose during the period the litigation was moving through the courts, the American Library Association's Intellectual Freedom Committee (ALA-IFC) developed "Guidelines for the Development of Policies and Procedures regarding User Behavior and Library Usage," designed to provide a framework of important considerations for libraries that were developing or revising patron behavior policies.[2]

The concept of libraries as limited public fora also has arisen in the context of library meeting room use. The United States Court of Appeals for the Fifth Circuit ruled in 1989 that the Oxford, Mississippi, Public Library had established its meeting rooms as a limited public forum in that it allowed a wide variety of groups to meet there whether or not their meetings were library related or library sponsored. The local chapter of a conservative religious women's organization, Concerned Women for America, had requested the use of the room for a meeting that would include prayer. The library rejected the request, citing its policy of excluding religious uses of the meeting room, a policy that was probably developed in order to avoid the accusation that the library was violating the Establishment Clause of the First Amendment by sponsoring religious practices.

The group sued, claiming they had been unconstitutionally excluded because of the content of their speech—and the Fifth Circuit court agreed. Holding that the library had allowed groups such as the local swim club and military recruiters to use the room, groups that stretched the definition of those permitted in the library's own policy, the court found that the library had established a limited public forum in its meeting room and therefore could not discriminate against groups because of the content of the speech in which they wished to engage, including religious speech.[3]

Subsequently, the ALA-IFC revised the Interpretations of the *Library Bill of Rights*, "Exhibit Spaces" and "Meeting Rooms," to reflect the court's reasoning, splitting the Interpretation into one dealing specifically with meeting rooms and another dealing with exhibit spaces and bulletin boards. All three areas present issues that are appropriately considered using limited public forum analysis.[4]

Supporters of intellectual freedom viewed the decisions in *Kreimer* v. *Morristown* and in *Concerned Women for America* v. *Lafayette County* (the Oxford, Mississippi, case) as positive for libraries in general—they helped carve out First Amendment protection for libraries to make ideas and information from all points of view available and accessible. They place publicly supported libraries firmly within a well-established body of First Amendment law that will, in the future, provide more clarity and guidance in resolving issues of access, collection development, and the equitable provision of library services to all library patrons.

NOTES

1. 958 F.2d 1242 (1992).
2. See part II, section 7.
3. *Concerned Women for America* v. *Lafayette County*, 883 F.2d 32 (5th Cir. 1989).
4. See part I, sections 2.9 and 2.13.

PART VI

Working for
Intellectual Freedom

1

What ALA Can Do to Help Librarians Combat Censorship

The American Library Association maintains a broad program for the promotion and defense of intellectual freedom, composed of the Intellectual Freedom Committee; the Office for Intellectual Freedom; the Intellectual Freedom Round Table; the Intellectual Freedom Action Network; the Freedom to Read Foundation; and the LeRoy C. Merritt Humanitarian Fund.

Establishment of Policy

According to its revised statement of responsibility, approved by the Council in 1970, the purpose of the Intellectual Freedom Committee, a committee of the Council, is "to recommend such steps as may be necessary to safeguard the rights of library users, libraries, and librarians, in accordance with the First Amendment to the United States Constitution and the *Library Bill of Rights* as adopted by the ALA Council; to work closely with the Office for Intellectual Freedom and with other units and officers of the Association in matters touching intellectual freedom and censorship."[1]

The first part of this responsibility is discharged in large measure through the recommendation of policies concerning intellectual freedom to the ALA Council. The Council-approved policy statements (Interpretations of the *Library Bill of Rights,* resolutions, etc.) on such matters as free access to libraries for minors, labeling of library materials, censorship of library materials because of alleged racism or sexism, and the like, not only provide the frontline librarian with concrete guidelines for establishing policy, but also establish a professional standard the Association is committed to defend. It is on the basis of such policy statements that the Association can come to the aid of a librarian whose professional conduct in defense of the principles of intellectual freedom is challenged.

Educational and Professional Support

The basic program of the Intellectual Freedom Committee is educational in nature. The most effective safeguards for the rights of library users and librarians are an informed public and a library profession aware of repressive activities and how to combat them. Toward this end, the administrative arm of the Intellectual Freedom Committee, the Office for Intellectual Freedom, implements ALA policies on intellectual freedom and educates librarians about the importance of the concept. The Office for Intellectual Freedom maintains a wide-ranging program of educational and informational publications, projects, and services.

The *Newsletter on Intellectual Freedom,* the official bimonthly publication of the Intellectual Freedom Committee, was initiated in 1952 and has been edited and produced by the OIF staff since 1970. The *Newsletter* is addressed to both librarians and members of the general public concerned about intellectual freedom. Its main purpose is to provide a comprehensive national picture of censorship efforts, court cases, legislation, and current readings on the subject. Through original and reprinted articles, the *Newsletter* offers a forum for expressing varying views about intellectual freedom, while providing a means for reporting activities of the Intellectual Freedom Committee, the Office for Intellectual Freedom, and the Freedom to Read Foundation. In 1982, noted civil liberties authority Nat Hentoff named the *Newsletter* "the best small publication in America." It is available by subscription from the Office for Intellectual Freedom.

The *Intellectual Freedom Action News* is a different publication: a brief, informal monthly newsletter designed to provide updates on late-breaking censorship controversies or legislation that could affect intellectual freedom in libraries and to alert members and supporters to areas where they may find additional information or localities where their assistance is needed. The *Action News* serves as the newsletter (both print and electronic) for the Intellectual Freedom Action Network, a grassroots, ad hoc group of volunteers who have identified themselves as willing to come forward in support of the freedom to read in censorship controversies in their communities (see Membership Involvement, below). It is also circulated to state chapter and divisional intellectual freedom committees, ALA chapter councilors, and others who indicate interest. The *Action News* provides information that may assist network members in the promotion and defense of intellectual freedom, and it gives suggestions for new programs and project ideas.

The Office for Intellectual Freedom also produces and distributes documents, articles, and ALA policies concerning intellectual freedom to both librarians and the general public. Monographs, resource guides, training materials, and manuals (in addition to the *Intellectual Freedom Manual*) include the annually produced *Banned Books Week Resource Kit; Confidentiality in Libraries: An Intellectual Freedom Modular Education Program;* and *Censorship and Selection: Issues and Answers for Schools* (rev. ed., by Henry Reichman). During nationwide controversies concerning individual titles, press clippings, editorials, and public statements detailing the ways various libraries around the country handled requests to remove specific materials are compiled and sent out to others handling similar problems.

The Office also seeks to make the library profession's support and concern for intellectual freedom known to the general public through the mass media and other fora. Both the Intellectual Freedom Committee and the Office for Intellectual Freedom cooperate with other national organizations, such as the Association of American Publishers, the American Booksellers Association, the American Booksellers Foundation for Free Expression, People for the American Way, Americans United for Separation of Church and State, the National Coalition against Censorship, and state and regional First Amendment organizations in activities that support free expression.

One of the most often used and least heard about functions of the Office is its provision of advice and consultation (case support) to individuals in the throes of potential or actual censorship controversies. Rarely does a day go by without a request by phone or letter asking for advice about a specific book, video, or audio recording that has drawn the censorious attention of an individual or group. When asked for assistance, the Office provides reviews and information about the author of the challenged material, applicable ALA policies, advice about the implementation of reconsideration policies, and other counseling specific to the situation at hand. If needed, the Office will provide a written position statement defending the principles of intellectual freedom in materials selection. Or, if requested, the Office can provide the names of persons available to offer testimony or support before library boards, supplied from the ranks of the Intellectual Freedom Action Network and state library association intellectual freedom committees. The options chosen are always the prerogative of the individual requesting assistance. If a censorship problem arises, librarians should call the Office for Intellectual Freedom (50 East Huron Street, Chicago, IL 60611) at (312) 280-4223 or (800) 545-2433, extension 4223.

In 1990, the Office for Intellectual Freedom established a censorship database to record and report statistics on challenges to library materials across the country. The database is a useful tool for identifying trends in types of censorship cases and for documenting responses and solutions to these cases. All librarians are encouraged to document and report challenges—and their outcome—to the Office for Intellectual Freedom. Information about the particular institution, its specific location, and the parties involved are kept confidential until—and only if—the information is published elsewhere.[2]

The Office for Intellectual Freedom welcomes reports in the form of newspaper clippings, magazine articles, cards, and letters in addition to the standard reporting form shown in figure 5.[3]

Combating Repressive Legislation

Repressive legislation on such matters as obscenity and material deemed harmful to minors can severely restrict the activities of the librarian who strives to provide service in accordance with the principles of the *Library Bill of Rights*. When requested, therefore, the ALA, through the Intellectual Freedom Committee and the Office for Intellectual Freedom, as well as the Freedom to Read Founda-

---

ALA OFFICE FOR INTELLECTUAL FREEDOM—CENSORSHIP DATABASE FORM

OIF USE ONLY
OIF Record No.:   -   Date of Report: Filed by:

I. OBJECT OF CHALLENGE

Title: **Copyright/Issue Date**

Author/Performer(s):
(last, first name)
Publisher/Producer:

Print: ___Book ___Textbk. ___Mag. ___Newsppr. ___Pamph. ___Play ___Student Publn.

Non-Print: ___Artwork ___Film ___Photo ___Sound Recording ___Video

Or: ___Collection ___Exhibit ___Performance ___Speech ___Other:

Grounds for Challenge: (check all applicable)

1. Cultural	**2. Sexual**	**3. Values**	**4. Social Issues**
___Anti-Ethnic	___Homosexuality	___Anti-Family	___Abortion
___Insensitivity	___Nudity	___Offensive Language	___Drugs
___Racism	___Sex Education	___Political Viewpoint	___Occult/Satanism
___Sexism	___Sexually Explicit	___Religious Viewpoint	___Suicide
5. OTHER:		___Unsuited to Age Group	___Violence

II. INITIATOR OF CHALLENGE

Individual: ___Administrator ___Bd. Member ___Clergy ___Parent ___Teacher ___Patron

Group: ___Government ___Pressure Group ___Religious Orgn. ___Other

Organizations Supporting Challenge:

III. INSTITUTION BEING CHALLENGED

Name: Phone:

Address:

City: State: Zip:

School-Related: ___School or ___School Library: Grade Level ___to ___

Other Library: ___Academic ___Public ___Prison ___Special

Or: ___Community Group ___Museum/Gallery ___Publisher

___Student Group ___Theatre ___Other:

Person Reporting (optional):   Title:

Address/Phone (if different from above):

PLEASE NOTE: THIS INFORMATION IS FOR STASTISTICAL USE ONLY, AND NAMES OF
INDIVIDUALS AND INSTITUTIONS WILL BE KEPT CONFIDENTIAL.
Feel free to attach news clippings or other supporting material.
Return to: Office for Intellectual Freedom, 50 East Huron Street, Chicago, IL 60611
Feel free to copy form

FIGURE 5
ALA Office for Intellectual Freedom Censorship Database Form

tion, supplies testimony, either singly or jointly, informing lawmakers of the potential effects of the legislation on the principles of intellectual freedom as applied to library service. Pending legislation in the United States Congress is frequently brought to the attention of these groups by the ALA Washington Office. With the assistance of legal counsel, the Office for Intellectual Freedom will provide an analysis of the proposed state or local statute affecting intellectual freedom brought to its attention.

Financial and Legal Assistance

The Freedom to Read Foundation was incorporated as a separate organization in 1969 by the American Library Association to act as its legal defense arm for intellectual freedom in libraries. The purposes of the Foundation are as follows:

Promoting and protecting the freedom of speech and of the press;

Protecting the public's right of access to information and materials stored in the nation's libraries;

Safeguarding libraries' right to include in their collections, and to make available to the public, any creative work that they may legally acquire; and

Supporting libraries and librarians in their defense of First Amendment rights by supplying them with legal counsel or the means to secure it.

The Foundation's work has been divided into two primary activities:

The allocation and disbursement of grants to individuals and groups primarily for the purpose of aiding them in litigation; and

Direct participation in litigation dealing with freedom of speech and of the press.

The Foundation is devoted to the principle that the solution to offensive speech is more speech, and the suppression of speech on the grounds that it gives offense to some infringes on the rights of all to a free, open, and robust marketplace of ideas. The Foundation combats through litigation statutes or government actions that limit, or could have the effect of limiting, the availability and accessibility of constitutionally protected information in libraries. Librarians affected by repressive statutes or official actions should notify the Freedom to Read Foundation. Librarians whose professional positions and personal well-being are endangered because of their defense of intellectual freedom, and library boards, librarians, and library employees threatened with legal action on such grounds, also should inform the Foundation.

Librarians requiring immediate financial aid should contact the LeRoy C. Merritt Humanitarian Fund. The Merritt Fund was established in recognition of the need for support at the moment an individual is in jeopardy or is fired in the cause of intellectual freedom or as a result of discrimination. Both the Foundation and the Merritt Fund are administered through the Office for Intellectual Freedom.

Membership Involvement

ALA encourages its members to become actively involved in the defense of intellectual freedom. The Intellectual Freedom Round Table, established in 1974, is a membership organization within the American Library Association. Participation in the Round Table allows members of the Association close contact with ALA's overall intellectual freedom program.

The Round Table is what its members make of it; all officers are elected by the members. The Round Table sponsors the main intellectual freedom program at ALA's annual conference and cosponsors other programs on various intellectual freedom–related subjects, circulates its own newsletter, and coordinates exchanges of experience among state library association intellectual freedom committees. The Round Table and individual Round Table members are available to assist the IFC, the OIF, and the Freedom to Read Foundation in various joint activities.

The Round Table administers the annual John Phillip Immroth Memorial and State and Regional Achievement Awards, and the biennial Eli M. Oboler Memorial Award. The Immroth award recognizes extraordinary personal courage in the defense of intellectual freedom and may be presented to an individual or group of individuals. The State and Regional Achievement Award is an annual award to the state intellectual freedom committee that has implemented the most successful and creative state project during the preceding year. The Oboler award, first presented in 1988, recognizes the best work in the area of intellectual freedom published in the two calendar years prior to the presentation of the award.

In response to IFRT members' requests for a more active voice in intellectual freedom issues, the Office for Intellectual Freedom established, in the fall of 1994, the Intellectual Freedom Action Network. The purpose of the network is twofold: First, participants are asked to submit to OIF information on groups that are attempting to censor materials in libraries. Although many of these groups are nationally based, they may also have local chapters. Local groups without a national affiliation are also very powerful in communities. Second, members of the network are asked to lend support when a controversy erupts in their community. Such support can take the form of a letter to the editor, attending a school or library board meeting—or even calling a colleague who is being challenged so that he or she knows there's somebody out there who cares.

The OIF keeps the Intellectual Freedom Action Network up-to-date by maintaining a "listserv" of members, who receive information on controversies for which assistance would be appreciated via electronic mail. The same information, additional background, and lists of resources are provided via the *Intellectual Freedom Action News* in both electronic and hard copy format. Network members have been helpful in several local and statewide controversies involving book challenges, proposed changes in library policy and operation that would limit access to library materials, and state legislation that would restrict the availability of constitutionally protected expression.

The Network was formed as a "rapid response" force to counter the successful and widespread efforts of national censorship pressure groups to organize and mobilize local chapters working on the local level to restrict the availability of expressive materials with which they disagree or find offense. Librarians who were being attacked by such groups were encountering an organizational level to which they could not, alone, respond. The Action Network works to address the need for support and eliminate the sense of isolation that so often plagues librarians who find themselves in the eye of the censorship storm.

All librarians and supporters of intellectual freedom should join the Action Network by calling OIF at (800) 545-2433, extension 4221.

Many other avenues of activism in support of intellectual freedom are open to ALA members on state and local levels. The *Library Bill of Rights* calls on libraries to "cooperate with all persons and groups concerned with resisting abridgment of free expression and free access to ideas." Such groups and individuals exist in virtually every community, and very often it is the formal and informal ties established by individual ALA members that enable ALA to cooperate with them.

Of special importance, of course, are the state library association intellectual freedom committees. The extent and nature of the activities of these committees vary from state to state. Some groups are more active than others. In some states, the committees have worked with other organizations to build impressive state coalitions in defense of intellectual and academic freedom. Elsewhere they have concentrated on compiling and developing state intellectual freedom manuals and continuing education materials. The relationship of the ALA Intellectual Freedom Committee and the Office with the state committees is one of mutual cooperation and assistance. The Office supports the work at the state level with information, coordination, and ideas. On their part, the state committees can be the Office's "eyes and ears" at the local level. In addition, of course, when incidents or other controversies arise, it is frequently the state library association intellectual freedom committee that "mobilizes the troops" and, in cooperation with ALA, provides embattled librarians with "on-the-spot" assistance.

Becoming involved and working together with colleagues and friends, librarians can fulfill their mission to confront censorship and protect access to the broadest range of information.

NOTES

1. American Library Association, 1994/1995 *Handbook of Organization,* 8.
2. For statistical purposes, and to inform the public of the prevalence of censorship problems in our society, the Office might release only the

name of the challenged material and the state in which the challenge occurred.

3. The form is subject to periodic revisions that may be required to facilitate data entry and correspond to changes in technology or software. Contact the Office for Intellectual Freedom for current copies of the form.

2

Your State
Intellectual Freedom Committee

Over several decades, ALA and the library community as a whole have built an impressive network of support for intellectual freedom. But the foundation of this network remains the too often unacknowledged efforts of volunteer librarians, library trustees, and library users at the state and local levels. Such people have contributed and continue to contribute to the cause of intellectual freedom in many ways and through many organizational forms. The most basic and common outlet for intellectual activism, however, is the state library association intellectual freedom committee.

These committees exist under differing conditions and take on varied organizational forms. But one thing is the same everywhere: it is impossible to separate intellectual freedom concerns from other concerns of library associations. State intellectual freedom committees must work closely not only with ALA's Office for Intellectual Freedom and other intellectual freedom and civil liberties groups, but with the entire state library association. The committees should maintain close and regular contact with the officers and executive bodies of their associations. Where the state library association also has a legislation committee or a public relations committee, liaisons should be established, the committee chairs should meet on a regular basis, and where possible the full committees should meet jointly each year.

The articles that follow offer materials to help orient members of state intellectual freedom committees and other individuals working for intellectual freedom in libraries on the state and local levels. They were prepared with the participation of past and present members of the ALA Intellectual Freedom Committee. These pages are not, however, the definitive organizational guide to intellectual freedom activism. Conditions and problems vary from locality to locality. In the final analysis, it will be the enthusiasm and imagination of committee members themselves that both define and determine the success or failure of the committee's work.

Much of what has been said in previous chapters about how individual libraries can prepare to face challenges to intellectual freedom is equally relevant to similar efforts by state associations and other groups. And the additional suggestions made in this section on working with the media, lobbying, coalition work, and responding to major censorship incidents can certainly be applied by many individual libraries. Again, promotion of intellectual freedom and promotion of libraries are inseparable.

3

Building Intellectual Freedom Coalitions

L ibrarians who work for intellectual freedom know that there is broad support for the concept among diverse constituencies. When would-be censors seek to deny access to library materials, a remarkable array of individuals and organizations can and do come to the library's defense. Many of these people are already active in defense of intellectual freedom elsewhere in society.

Article IV of the *Library Bill of Rights* states that "Libraries should cooperate with all persons and groups concerned with resisting abridgment of free expression and free access to ideas." To facilitate such cooperation, libraries, individual librarians, and state intellectual freedom committees have joined with booksellers, publishers, artists, civil libertarians, journalists, authors, musicians, and other groups and individuals with First Amendment concerns in local, state, and regional coalitions in defense of intellectual freedom.

Such coalitions are helpful for several reasons. It is, of course, simply common sense to know, so to speak, who your friends are and how to keep in touch. Beyond this, however, uniting with others in coalition permits greater coordination of effort and allows supporters of intellectual freedom to reach broader audiences. Coalitions can also benefit from an expanded financial base and from the collective prestige, resources, and contacts of the constituent groups. By uniting together, concerned organizations can pool resources to avoid duplications of effort and to concentrate limited funds and personnel where they are most needed. For example, groups concerned with intellectual freedom may collectively monitor legislative activity, or they may form a joint speakers' bureau.

The task of organizing a statewide coalition for intellectual freedom may at first seem intimidating, but coalitions differ greatly from each other. Some are highly structured, full-time organizations themselves. Others are closer to an informal network of communication and support. The same coalition that may, at times of crisis, function like a well-oiled machine, may at other moments be minimally active. In short, a coalition is what its members make it. There is no coalition ideal model. The level of organization and commitment should be appropriate to the needs of those involved and no more. If a state committee's needs can be met through a structure that simply facilitates regular contact and little more, this is also fine.

Everywhere there is a need for greater cooperation and more joint efforts by various supporters of intellectual freedom. The following suggestions will be useful to state intellectual freedom committees seeking to organize a coalition in their states.

The first step in organizing a coalition is to identify those organizations in the state or region whose goals and objectives are consistent with ALA's intellectual freedom principles. Consider inviting local and regional chapters of the American Civil Liberties Union; booksellers and publishers groups; arts groups; religious organizations; civic groups; educational organizations, including the PTA, the National Education Association, the American Federation of Teachers, the National Council of Teachers of English, and groups of school administrators; lawyers' organizations; and societies of authors and journalists. Individuals should also be sought out and encouraged to participate because they may be in the best position to do the kind of day-to-day coordination that will be necessary to keep the coalition functioning.

Develop a succinct letter of introduction to be sent to those invited to the organizational meeting. Spell out clearly your own committee's conception of the proposed coalition, but make it clear that the final goals and objectives, as well as the structure of the group, are to be determined democratically.

At the first meeting, the coalition should draft a statement of its principles and, if desired, a constitution and bylaws. These can be more or less formal, depending on the desires of the constituent groups. Committees with concrete goals and specific projects should be organized immediately so that the coalition does not become bogged down in sterile debate or bureaucratic busywork. Choose responsible officers who have the time and commitment to keep things going.

Some projects for the coalition to take up include design of a public relations brochure, publication of a newsletter, legislative monitoring, organization of an information network to mobilize support during times of crisis, and organization of statewide conferences on intellectual freedom.

A strong state coalition in support of intellectual freedom should not and cannot replace the state library association intellectual freedom committee. But active participation in such coalitions will strengthen the committee's ability to function effectively and help the state association as a whole in its promotion not only of intellectual freedom but also of library services.

4

Lobbying for Intellectual Freedom

Carol C. Henderson

Lobbying is the process through which citizens seek to persuade elected officials to a cause or a particular course of action. In a democracy, lobbying is a legitimate and productive aspect of citizen participation and helps keep democracy healthy and responsive. Lobbying for library interests must be ongoing and is usually most effective when it involves the joint efforts of professional lobbyists and individual librarians and library supporters. In lobbying for intellectual freedom, supporters will find advice and guidelines for library advocacy and library lobbying from ALA, its Washington Office, and its state chapters.[1]

When lobbying on intellectual freedom issues raised by state or federal legislation, keep in mind that First Amendment and censorship issues tend to generate controversy and strong emotions. Lobbying in this arena requires special sensitivity and care in working with elected officials to develop policies supportive of intellectual freedom.

Carol C. Henderson is executive director of the American Library Association Washington Office.

Library Lobbying Builds on Strengths

The library community enjoys a number of advantages in working productively with legislators at local, state, and national levels:

Legislators respond to relevant factual and anecdotal information, succinctly presented; librarians are accustomed to marshaling information.

Legislators respond to numbers and to their own voting constituents; libraries and their supporters exist in every legislative district.

Libraries enjoy a "goodwill" factor; most legislators think well of libraries as self-help institutions and collectively as an existing and respected information infrastructure.

Librarians' and library supporters' dedication to the public good is generally unquestioned; their support of or opposition to a measure is accepted as soundly motivated and not for personal advantage.

Libraries enjoy bipartisan support, and library legislative champions come from both sides of the aisle; library associations such as ALA have worked well with representatives of both major political parties.

Librarians have many friends and allies, who are more numerous than themselves and weigh more heavily in the political scales. Many of these supporters are knowledgeable, well-connected politically, take an active interest in legislative issues, cultivate legislator contacts, and respond to action alerts.

Keep informed and know the issues. The first step in keeping informed on legislative issues is to follow regularly the printed and electronic sources of information from the ALA Office for Intellectual Freedom and the ALA Washington Office. The opportunity for timely and effective action is much greater through use of electronic technologies. The ALA *Washington Newsletter* is issued monthly; but ALAWON, the ALA Washington Office Newsline (available to any individual or organization with e-mail capability), may be issued as often as once a day during periods of intense activity.

Other sources for news and action alerts regarding state-level activity include state library associations and school library media associations, as well as their legislation and intellectual freedom committees.

Organize library and intellectual freedom supporters.   Work closely with the state library association legislation committee and any lobbyists associated with the state library association. The state association is likely to have a Federal Relations Coordinator, a link between the ALA Washington Office and the state's library legislative network. The state association may have a well-organized legislative network in place, with an active telephone tree or other communications structure to alert supporters when action is needed, or to activate the best contacts with particular legislators.

Intellectual freedom committees in the state should coordinate with and make use of these existing networks, which often include library trustees and friends of libraries in strategic positions of influence. At the same time, be sure there is a core group of individuals knowledgeable about intellectual freedom issues and willing and able to speak on short notice at hearings or to participate in key meetings.

Build coalitions.   The very nature and diversity of librarians' work both in libraries and in the communities, campuses, or organizations they serve make them highly capable coalition builders. Librarians can work with groups representing educators and educational institutions, for example, or with groups representing children or parents, or with scholars and news reporters, or with publishers and chambers of commerce, or with citizen and public interest groups. At the national level, the ALA Washington Office has found that librarians are represented in almost every one of the numerous coalitions working the "information superhighway" issues. Library interests relating to the public's access to needed information cross over levels of education, industry concerns, and the many content-related issues of public interest groups.

Thus, a wide variety of groups either shares library objectives or can be persuaded to do so. These groups may work with the library field on all issues of concern or only on one measure. Some organizations or industry groups may join librarians on one bill and be on the other side of the table on the next piece of legislation.

For the most part, American politics is coalition politics rather than confrontation politics. Candidates and elected officials strive to satisfy as many elements of their constituency as possible. It is helpful to demonstrate to legislators that many nonlibrary organizations support library efforts. If a library group takes a position on a bill, that position is strengthened if the statement is signed by many other organizations.

These coalition relationships must be seeded and nurtured. Library advocates should make contact and keep in touch with the leadership and the legislative activists of organizations with similar objectives. Coalition building and nurturing should be organized to develop clear lines of communication and action, to avoid duplication of effort, and to avoid conflicting messages. Keep a current file of coalition contacts so that they can be called upon to help when the need arises.

Use the media. Public opinion should not be overlooked. In addition to letters to legislators, timely, concise, and cogent letters to the editor, as well as op-ed pieces, should be sent to newspapers and other publications. The public relations programs of individual libraries can be called on to good effect on legislative and regulatory issues. If an editorial or columnist calls for lower government expenditures, a letter should point out the effects of a cutback on library users. If a pending bill is endorsed or opposed, a letter should present the library position.

Try to develop a good working relationship with the publications and media outlets of greatest influence in the area. Don't wait until a time of desperate need. ALA's recent "Library Advocacy Now!" materials and training packages provide excellent tips and advice on getting the library message across to both opinion molders and decision makers.

Know the legislative process. Learn how the state legislature works, when it is in session, what the committees are, where relevant legislation will be referred, and what steps a bill must go through to be enacted. Know who has power in the legislature and who has influence on those with power. What are the priorities of the party in power? What other issues are on the agenda of the committee that has jurisdiction over library or intellectual freedom issues? Know the committee assignments of the state's congressional delegation.

Know the legislators, and know who knows them. In general, only a few legislators will take a strong and detailed interest in library legislation—some because they have a personal interest, or because of a concerned relative or friend, or because they are on a committee or subcommittee handling bills of this type.

Long before a library measure is being promoted, or before a crisis erupts, it's important to identify sympathetic individuals in the political structure. Keep a current file on library and intellectual freedom supporters in the legislature, a current file of knowledgeable library and intellectual freedom advocates to contact them, and keep in touch with sympathetic legislators on a regular basis.

These friendly legislators and their staffs can become a source of information and advice regarding effective strategy and timing, positions to be taken in hearings, the nature of the testimony that will be most effective, the kinds of witnesses to be secured, and the sources of opposition to a particular measure.

Personal contacts with legislators work best. It is implicit in all that has been said thus far that considerable contact between library supporters and legislators is essential during this process. All persons who are active in legislative affairs will be seeing legislators frequently and in time will know many of them well as individuals. The most useful visits are in the home district rather than at the state capital or in Washington. Become familiar with their home offices and staff. All members of Congress maintain at least one office in the home district, and the staff there will know when the legislator will be at that office and available to citizens.

To meet with a legislator, make an appointment, then leave little to chance. Plan what to say, be well versed on the issue or bill being discussed, and provide a "leave-behind," a one- or two-page memorandum or fact sheet covering the relevant points. A fact sheet on the local library and its services and users would also be valuable. During the meeting, the librarian should give the legislator ample opportunity for questions, ask which staff member to keep in touch with when the legislator is unavailable, and request to be kept informed on progress on the measure under discussion. Similarly, it's important to keep legislators informed of the library's activities, invite them to functions or special activities (particularly those with media presence), or ask them to join a board or advisory group if appropriate.

A small group visit to a legislator is particularly effective, especially if the group includes a trustee or friend of the library and representatives of community groups or of library user constituencies. A good way to gain experience in this type of lobbying is to participate in the annual Library Legislative Day of organized lobbying in the spring in Washington, D.C., organized by the ALA Washington Office and the D.C. Library Association. Library delegations from each state visit congressional offices in team visits, preceded by briefings and followed by a reception. Many state library associations also sponsor state legislative days or special events in the state capital.

Library supporters have discovered during their visits to Washington that often twenty minutes with the key legislative assistant for the representative or senator may be more productive than five minutes with the legislator himself or herself. At the federal level, personal or committee staff draft bills, develop floor statements, brief the legislators, and convey constituent opinion to their bosses. Don't neglect legislative staff.

Meetings with legislators need not be frequent. Usually one meeting before a legislative session begins, preferably in the district, and perhaps one more during the legislative session when an important measure is at a decisive point, will be sufficient. Of course, new legislators should be visited early to ascertain their viewpoints, their interests, and their potential positions regarding library issues.

Follow up with letters. Personal contacts with legislators should precede letters and other less personal communications whenever possible. Letters, faxes, phone calls, and e-mail messages will be much more effective if the sender is a voting constituent known to the office, or the sender can refer to a recent visit or personal contact. Ideally, each legislator should have a flow of contacts with one or more library supporters from the home district or state, a number of letters each year, and at least one visit during each legislative session.

The ALA Washington Office has issued two sets of helpful tips—"Ways to Communicate with Legislators" (fig. 6) and "How to Write a Letter to Your Legislator" (fig. 7). These suggestions apply just as well to state and local lawmakers. The main message is that

ALA Washington Office Fact Sheet

Ways to Communicate with Legislators

PERSONAL VISITS

 Face to face discussion is the most effective means of communication, and it is essential to the establishment of a solid working relationship if you do not already know each other. A meeting is more easily arranged early in a session, before pressures build up.

Constituents are always welcome in Washington. All legislators also have one or more local district offices which Representatives visit periodically during Congressional recesses and between sessions. Visits there will often be more convenient for you than Washington visits. Regardless of where you visit your legislator, be sure you have a firm appointment. Use the district office to make local or capitol appointments. Get to know district staffs. Close working relationships with staff will benefit you in many ways.

Take along others — library director, trustee, Friend, representative of a community organization, citizen and/or student activist, academic-library supporter. Keep the delegation small enough for an easy exchange of viewpoints with the legislator. Leave your card and any written information you may have prepared. Follow up with a letter of appreciation for the time given to you, and include any additional information suggested by the visit.

Five Basic Rules for Effective Communication

1. **Be Brief.** A legislator's time is limited. So is yours.

2. **Be Appreciative.** Acknowledge past support, and convey thanks for current action.

3. **Be Specific.** Refer to local library and district needs.

4. **Be Informative.** Give reasons why a measure should be supported.

5. **Be Courteous.** Be positive and polite. Ask for a specific action or support. Do not demand or threaten.

American Library Association, Washington Office

110 Maryland Avenue, NE • Washington, DC 20002-5675

Tel: (202)547-4440   FAX: (202)547-7363   Internet: alawash@alawash.org

FIGURE 6
ALA Washington Office Tip Sheet

frequently a handful of thoughtful, factually persuasive letters have changed a member's mind or caused him or her to review an issue. Letters should be timely and constructive as well as accurate, brief, and clear.

TELEPHONE CALLS

 Once you have made the acquaintance of your representative, telephone calls are appropriate and easy. Make them sparingly to the legislator, whose time is heavily occupied. Regular contact with staff is possible and often effective.

Telephone to ask support before a hearing or a floor vote; to ask for help with legislative colleagues; to convey urgent local concern. Judge how far to pursue by the reaction. Remember that it is more difficult for a legislator to temporize in a conversation than by letter.

LETTERS, LETTERS, LETTERS

 These are the chief fuel which powers any legislative vehicle. They are read. They elicit responses. They represent votes. Each letter writer is deemed to represent several like-minded if less highly motivated constituents.

Letters may be formal or informal, typewritten or handwritten. You should compose them giving your reasons for a position and giving the legislator reasons to support that position. If you are asking support for a particular bill, cite it by number and author, and give its title or subject matter.

ELECTRONIC MAIL, FAX, TELEGRAMS, MAILGRAMS

 These are fast, easy ways to communicate with legislators when the need for action is critical just prior to a committee or floor vote. E-mail has become increasingly acceptable and should follow the same general rules as regular "snail mail" correspondence. Many congressional offices will not respond unless you provide your mailing address in the e-mail message since many offices only reply by written correspondence.

E-MAIL

Generally one follows closely the general good form for regular letter writing. Some offices will not respond to your e-mail, unless you provide your mailing address in th e-mail message as they only reply by "snail mail". Not all Congressional offices have e-mail. Check on available e-mail addresses at:

a) http://thomas.loc.gov

b) http://www.house.gov/

or c) gopher://ftp.senate.gov/

American Library Association, Washington Office
110 Maryland Avenue, NE • Washington, DC 20002-5675
Tel: (202)547-4440   FAX: (202)547-7363   Internet: alawash@alawash.org

---

FIGURE 6. Tip Sheet—Continued

Be persuasive, professional, and persistent. Legislative strategies and tactics require adjustment to changing conditions. Don't neglect the minority party; they may be in power next year. Adjust to the style of a key legislator; facts and figures may work with one

ALA Washington Office Information Sheet
How to Write a Letter to Your Legislator

The most frequently used, correct forms for address are:

To your Senator:

> The Honorable _____ (full name)
> United States Senate
> Washington, DC 20510

To your Representative:

> The Honorable _____ (full name)
> U.S. House of Representatives
> Washington, DC. 20515

Other information:

"Sincerely yours" is in good taste as a complimentary close. Remember to sign your given name and surname. If you use a title in your signature, be sure to enclose it in parentheses.

Forms similar to the above, addressed to your state capital, are appropriate for your state representatives and senators.

Where possible use your official letterhead. If this is not in order, and you write as an individual, use plain white bond paper, and give your official title following your signature as a means of identification and to indicate you competency to speak on the subject.

E-MAIL

Generally one follows closely the general good form for regular letter writing. Some offices will not respond to your e-mail, unless you provide your mailing address in th e-mail message as they only reply by "snail mail". Not all Congressional offices have e-mail. Check on avilable e-mail addresses at:

a) http://thomas.loc.gov

b) http://www.house.gov/

or c) gopher://ftp.senate.gov/

TIPS FOR SUCCESS:

1. Your legislators like to hear from home and want to be kept informed of conditions in the district. Base your letter on your own pertinent experiences and observations.

2. If writing about a specific bill, describe it by number or by its popular name. Legislators have thousands of bills before them in the course of a year, and cannot always take time to figure out to which one you are referring.

3. Legislators appreciate intelligent, well-thought-out letters which present a definite position, even if they do not agree.

4. Even more important and valuable to them is a concrete statement of the reasons for your position - particularly if you are writing about a field in which you have specialized knowledge. Representatives have to vote on many matters with which they have had little or no firsthand experience. Some of the most valuable information they receive comes from facts presented in letters from people who have knowledge in the field.

5. Short letters are almost always best. Members of Congress receive many, many letters each day, and a long one may not get as prompt a reading as a brief statement.

6. Letters should be timed to arrive while the issue is alive. Members of the committee considering the bill will appreciate having your views while the bill is ripe for study and action.

7. Follow through with a thank-you letter, whenever possible.

American Library Association, Washington Office
110 Maryland Avenue, NE • Washington, DC 20002-5675
Tel: (202)547-4440   FAX: (202)547-7363   Internet: alawash@alawash.org

---

FIGURE 7
Information Sheet from ALA Washington Office

chair of a committee, whereas the sponsor in the other chamber may need homey library stories to recount to colleagues or in floor statements. Politics is called the art of the possible, and democratic politics is often the art of compromise. Progress must often come one step at a time. Library groups should not think in terms of "winning" or "losing" but of how to move forward, even if it involves three steps to the side first.

It's important to stay professional in demeanor with enemies as well as friends. Stay alert to the moral and philosophical attitudes of candidates and officeholders. Recognize that those on opposing sides may have legitimate concerns; sometimes those concerns can be addressed through other means without harmful effects on libraries or the First Amendment. Don't make the mistake of being as emotional as those who would censor. Make library concerns known early, and where possible get commitments in support of intellectual freedom before controversy erupts.

Each step in the process of achieving rapport with legislators is simple in itself. The power of these efforts is in their cumulative impact and their multiplication when performed by many others. Each participant in the process and each step in the process is significant. There may be many decision points and calls for action on the way to enactment. There may also be a few times when the process falls short and must be started all over again. Once ALA's Washington Office was established, it took ten years before the first federal library legislation was enacted. Persistence pays off, so keep at it!

NOTE

1. Employees of public libraries classified as 501(c)(3) organizations for tax purposes should review regulations governing the amount of time and funding that can be spent on lobbying. Employees of federal libraries also should become familiar with regulations restricting lobbying activities.

   These regulations do not apply to persons acting as private citizens rather than in their official capacity as public or federal librarians.

5

Dealing with Censors

When libraries follow the policies and procedures outlined in this manual, the overwhelming majority of complaints will be resolved without undue controversy, very often to the mutual satisfaction of the library and the complainant. Sometimes, however, despite the protections offered by a good materials selection policy and review procedure, a major censorship incident still develops. In such cases, beleaguered librarians, library trustees, or concerned library users may contact the state intellectual freedom committee directly for assistance, or they may be referred to the committee by ALA's Office for Intellectual Freedom. Sometimes the state committee will learn of an incident independently and approach those affected with an offer of assistance. It is entirely up to the affected library to decide whether to work mainly through members of the state committee, directly with OIF, or through some convenient combination of members. The library may even choose to reject all outside assistance. In any event, the state committee should maintain close and regular contact with OIF and report all relevant information. Communications failures within the ranks of the anticensorship forces are unnecessary and can be destructive.

When a censorship incident threatens to mushroom into a crisis, everyone involved should observe two basic rules. The first is *not to panic!* No matter how belligerent and seemingly unreasonable the complainants may become, no matter how much some local politicians, the media, or assorted independent careerists may distort the issues, the library and its librarians should strive first and foremost to maintain a calm and professional attitude. The library and the state committee should insist that established policies and procedures be upheld. Make a careful and reasoned response to all allegations. Keep the discussion focused on the major intellectual freedom issues. At all times, refrain from making personal attacks on opponents, no matter how tempting.

The second basic rule is that the person directly involved must *always retain the final word!* To the state intellectual freedom committee, a local incident may appear to be a golden opportunity to educate the public and promote the principles of intellectual freedom. To the beleaguered librarian, however, it may seem like a nightmare— to be resolved in a manner consistent with professional principles, to be sure, but as quickly and quietly as possible. In such instances, OIF, the Freedom to Read Foundation, the state committees, and the Intellectual Freedom Action Network all exist to assist and support the people directly involved. The nature and extent of that assistance and support are ultimately determined by those people. If, for example, a beleaguered librarian wants to avoid statewide or national publicity, nothing should be done to attract such attention.

Although it may be tempting to immediately "pull out all the stops" in meeting a censorship challenge, to do so may be detrimental. Too many false alarms make it difficult to mobilize broad support when it is truly needed. Outside involvement may also force people and institutions into dogmatic positions from which they find it difficult to compromise or retreat. It is never useful to place people needlessly in positions in which they will "lose face" by having to back down.

Each censorship incident has its own peculiar history. The library and its defenders must generally plot their strategy and tactics on a case-by-case basis. The following principles, however, are generally applicable:

> If the issue involves a local library, be sure that all staff members are kept fully abreast of the situation as it develops.
> Make sure that all members of the library's governing body are kept informed about the incident. Use this opportunity to

educate or reinforce their beliefs about the principles of intellectual freedom in libraries.

Confer with the president or the entire executive board of the state library association and keep these supporters advised about the progress of the situation.

The library's ongoing program of public education about the principles of intellectual freedom should be intensified. All library staff, governing board members, media representatives, and concerned library users should receive a copy of the *Library Bill of Rights* and those of its Interpretations that are relevant to the issue at hand.

If national, state, or even local media become involved, all media statements should be centrally coordinated.[1] The state library association and its intellectual freedom committee should be certain that all public statements have been cleared in principle with the affected library or librarians. In dealing with the media, it is important to stress the principles involved in the incident, to point out the implications of censorship for First Amendment freedoms, and to emphasize the library's responsibility to provide access to information for all members of the community it serves.

If radio or television talk shows or interviews are scheduled, library supporters should be alerted so that individuals may attend or even participate. The pro-censorship forces should not be permitted to "stack" the audience or otherwise dominate media coverage, thereby giving the false impression that they represent the majority.

Lines of communication to the complainants should always remain open, no matter how strained the situation becomes. The freedom to read is not negotiable, but an acceptable and principled solution to a crisis is better attained through dialogue than confrontation.

If legal action is threatened, the library's legal counsel should be advised at once. If the library does not have legal counsel, assistance can be obtained with the advice of the Freedom to Read Foundation. Attorneys for the Foundation are available to consult with local counsel.

When the incident is settled, a responsible representative of the library and, if appropriate, the state committee should write to or thank personally the media representatives, organizations, legislators, officials, board members, and other individuals who came forward in support of intellectual freedom. If the issue is unresolved, these supporters should be kept advised of the situation.

After the challenge is resolved, key members of the library staff, the governing body, members of the state committee, and others intimately involved with the incident should meet to summarize how the issue was handled and consider how the procedure may be improved in the future.

Coping with Stress

In these pages, the importance of maintaining a calm approach and professional response in the face of challenges has been repeatedly emphasized, yet this is easier said than done. A besieged librarian, surrounded by angry protestors who may consider the librarian a "pornographer" or worse, may well find a professional demeanor difficult to maintain. Members of state intellectual freedom committees may find the calm handling of crises, while still meeting all their professional responsibilities, elusive when they try to respond to repeated media inquiries from sources ranging from national television networks to the local small town weekly newspaper. Working for intellectual freedom can be extremely stressful. Coping with stress is itself an important part of defending libraries and librarians against censorship.

Members of state intellectual freedom committees need not be psychologists; in providing assistance to librarians involved in censorship incidents and in coping with the strains of activism oneself, however, personal concern, common sense, and knowledge of some basic facts about stress are useful. Stress may result from either positive or negative stimuli. It may take physical, emotional, psychological, or social forms, and it may be mild or severe, chronic or acute. Stress is never the product solely of external stress factors; it arises from the reaction of individual personality characteristics to environmental factors.

Most people can recognize when they are experiencing stress but cannot so easily identify its cause. A person in the midst of a stressful struggle against censorship may not immediately recognize that it is the demands of this involvement that lie at the root of the stress being felt. People involved in working for intellectual freedom should be aware that increased stress can be one perfectly normal and controllable by-product of their work.

Constructive strategies for coping with stress are geared toward confronting the problem and dissipating its effects. We may not always be able to control the stress factors in our lives, but we can control how they affect us. Here are a few proven, common-sense ideas for managing stress:

> Maintain good health habits, especially during times of crisis. Eat a well-balanced diet, get plenty of sleep, and exercise regularly.
> Take time to get organized. Determine priorities and concentrate on them. Set reasonable demands for yourself and learn to delegate or postpone responsibilities when necessary.
> Get better acquainted with yourself. Acknowledge your successes. Recognize that mistakes do not make you a failure.
> Decompress. Allot time to yourself each day. Experiment with relaxation techniques and give them a chance to work.
> Be creative and vary your routine.[2]

Most of all, keep in mind two very important facts. First, what you are doing is right. Intellectual freedom is worth defending. The problems that arise and the mistakes you may make are secondary. Second, you are never alone. There is support out there for intellectual freedom. Not only do the great majority of Americans back the efforts of libraries to defend intellectual freedom, the library profession stands behind its commitment to intellectual freedom with a full program of support. Librarians and those working for intellectual freedom should never forget that ALA's program of assistance is always available to them.

NOTES

1. See part III, section 5.1, "Public Relations: Crisis Communications," on developing a communications plan.
2. "Coping with Stress" adapted with permission from the Salt Lake City Public Library's Orientation Program, prepared (1980) by the Staff Development Advisory Committee in conjunction with Jed L. Erickson, ALSW, director, Salt Lake Mental Health Crisis Intervention, University Hospital, University of Utah.

Selected Bibliography

Beahm, George, ed. *War of Words: The Censorship Debate*. Kansas City, Mo.: Andrews & McMeel, 1993.

Bielefield, Arlene, and Lawrence Cheeseman. *Maintaining the Privacy of Library Records*. New York: Neal Schuman, 1994.

Boston, Rob. *Why the Religious Right Is Wrong about Separation of Church and State*. Buffalo, N.Y.: Prometheus Books, 1993.

DelFattore, Joan. *What Johnny Shouldn't Read*. New Haven, Conn.: Yale Univ. Pr., 1992.

DeMac, Donna. *Liberty Denied: The Current Rise of Censorship in America*. 2nd ed. New Brunswick, N.J.: Rutgers Univ. Pr., 1992.

Fish, Stanley. *There's No Such Thing as Free Speech . . . And It's a Good Thing, Too*. New York: Oxford Univ. Pr., 1993.

Forestel, Herbert N. *Banned in the USA: A Reference Guide to Book Censorship in Libraries and Public Schools*. Westport, Conn.: Greenwood, 1994.

Goldman, Roger, with David Gallen. *Justice William J. Brennan, Jr.: Freedom First*. New York: Carroll & Graf, 1994.

Haiman, Franklin S. *Speech Acts and the First Amendment*. Carbondale: Southern Ill. Univ. Pr., 1994.

Heins, Marjorie. *Sex, Sin and Blasphemy: A Guide to America's Censorship Wars*. New York: New Press, 1993.

Selected Bibliography

Hentoff, Nat. *Free Speech for Me but Not for Thee: How the American Left and Right Relentlessly Censor Each Other.* New York: Harper-Collins, 1993.

Johnson, Claudia. *Stifled Laughter: One Woman's Story about Fighting Censorship.* Golden, Colo.: Fulcrum, 1993.

Karolides, Nicholas J., Lee Burress, and John M. Kean, eds. *Censored Books: Critical Viewpoints.* Metuchen, N.J.: Scarecrow, 1993.

Korwar, Arati R. *War of Words: Speech Codes at Public Colleges and Universities.* Nashville, Tenn.: Freedom Forum First Amendment Center, 1994.

Marsh, Dave. *Fifty Ways to Fight Censorship.* New York: Thunders Mouth Pr., 1991.

McDonald, Frances Beck. *Censorship and Intellectual Freedom: A Survey of School Librarians' Attitudes and Moral Reasoning.* Metuchen, N.J.: Scarecrow, 1993.

Noble, William. *Book Banning in America: Who Bans Books and Why.* Middlebury, Vt.: Paul S. Eriksson, 1990.

Pally, Marcia. *Sex and Sensibility: Reflections on Forbidden Mirrors and the Will to Censor.* Hopewell, N.J.: Ecco Pr., 1994.

Rauch, Jonathan. *Kindly Inquisitors: The New Attacks on Free Thought.* Chicago: Univ. of Chicago Pr., 1993.

Reichman, Henry. *Censorship and Selection: Issues and Answers for Schools.* Rev. ed. Chicago: American Library Assn., American Assn. of School Administrators, 1993.

Smith, Robert Ellis. *Our Vanishing Privacy.* Providence, R.I.: Privacy Journal, 1993.

Walker, Samuel. *Hate Speech.* Lincoln: Univ. of Nebraska Pr., 1994.

Weigand, Shirley. *Library Records: A Retention and Confidentiality Guide.* Westport, Conn.: Greenwood, 1994.

Index

Index

379

Index

Index